The Taste of Blood

University of Pennsylvania Press
CONTEMPORARY ETHNOGRAPHY SERIES
Dan Rose and Paul Stoller, General Editors

A complete listing of the books in this series appears at the back of this volume

The Taste of Blood

Spirit Possession in Brazilian Candomblé

Jim Wafer

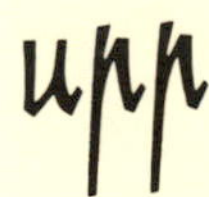

University of Pennsylvania Press
Philadelphia

Printed in the United States of America

Library of Congress Cataloging-in-Publication Data

Wafer, James William, 1948–
The taste of blood : spirit possession in Brazilian Candomblé / Jim Wafer.
p. cm. — (Contemporary ethnography series)
Includes bibliographical references and index.
ISBN 0-8122-3061-2. — ISBN 0-8122-1341-6 (pbk.)
1. Candomblé (Cult)—Brazil. I. Title. II. Series.
BL2592.C35W33 1991 299'.67—dc20 90-28641 CIP

Contents

Participants vii
Pre-text xi

Part 1: Exu

1 The Lips of Pomba-Gira 3
2 Padilha's Vow 11
3 Corquisa 23

Part 2: Caboclo

4 Order and Progress 53
5 Of Keys 88
6 Villages 108

Part 3: Orixá

7 Child Spirits 121
8 The Throne 155
9 Tempo 166

Epilogue: Egum 179
Postface 191

Glossary 195
References 205
Index 213

Participants

In Jaraci

House of Marinalvo

Marinalvo: priest of the Candomblé religion
Sultão das Matas: Marinalvo's principal *caboclo* spirit
Joãozinho: initiate in the house of Marinalvo, and childhood friend of Archipiado
Cravo: Joãozinho's *erê* spirit
Neuza: Marinalvo's mother
Delcir: Marinalvo's boyfriend
Sebastião: *ogã* (male ritual official) in the house of Marinalvo, responsible for sacrifices
Dudu: *ogã* and head drummer in the house of Marinalvo
Zita: *equede* (female ritual official) in the house of Marinalvo
Marta: "little mother" (ritual deputy) of the house
Celso: prospective "little father" (ritual deputy) of the house
Boiadeiro: Celso's *caboclo* spirit
Joana: initiate
Luisa: initiate
Gilberto: initiate
Rosilene: elderly initiate, and neighbor of Marinalvo's mother
Angélica: Marinalvo's housekeeper
Paulo: prospective *ogã* (male ritual official)
Almiro: a visitor to the house, from Rio de Janeiro
Chela: the house's dog

House of Edivaldo

Edivaldo: priest of Candomblé, neighbor of Marinalvo
Tupinambá: Edivaldo's *caboclo* spirit

Maria Eugênia: Edivaldo's female *exu* spirit
Taís: nickname of Wilson, resident in the house of Edivaldo
Corquisa: one of Taís's female *exu* spirits, enemy of Sete Saia
Sete Saia: the other of Taís's female *exu* spirits, enemy of Corquisa
Tupinambá: Taís's *caboclo* spirit
Sete Punhal: Taís's male *exu* spirit
Zezé: "little mother" (ritual deputy) and resident in the house of Edivaldo
Dinho: husband of Zezé, resident in the house of Edivaldo, but *ogã* (male ritual official) in the house of Biju
Toninho: brother of Edivaldo, and one of the latter's initiates

Others

Biju: priest of Candomblé
Pomba-Gira: Biju's female *exu* spirit
Luiz: priest of Candomblé
Zé-Pelintra: Luiz's male *exu* spirit
Oswaldo: priest of Candomblé
Biscó: Oswaldo's *egum* spirit
Seu Antônio: priest of the Umbanda religion
Dona Nega: owner of a small bar in Jaraci

In Fazendão

Dona Clara: elderly Candomblé priestess, who gave Marinalvo the priestly initiation
Dona Laura: "little mother" (ritual deputy) in the house of Dona Clara

In Matungo

Mané: priest of Candomblé, who gave Marinalvo his first initiation; now enemy of the latter
José: head of the religious organization that performs rituals for the *egum* spirits in Matungo

In Lobito

Gelson: priest of Candomblé
Pena Branca: Gelson's *caboclo* spirit
Márcio: friend of Archipiado, resident of Lobito, occasional visitor in the house of Gelson
Jorge: friend of Márcio
Rei das Cobras: *caboclo* spirit of a female initiate in Gelson's house
Trovezeiro: *caboclo* spirit of a priest who is Gelson's initiatic "brother"

Others

Archipiado: friend and research assistant of the narrator
Rory: American anthropologist, friend of the narrator
Xilton: priest of Candomblé, friend of Rory
Carlos de Barros: professor of anthropology at the Federal University of Bahia, friend of Archipiado
Miguel: friend of the narrator
Sérgio: priest of Candomblé
Pena Branca: *caboclo* spirit of Sérgio
Evaristo: nickname of the narrator

Pre-text

Laroiê Exu! Greetings Exu, crosser of boundaries!

Perspective 1

Henry Gates: Each version of Esu is the sole messenger of the gods (in Yoruba, *iranse*), he who interprets the will of the gods to man; he who carries the desires of man to the gods. Esu is the guardian of the crossroads, master of style and of stylus, the phallic god of generation and fecundity, master of the elusive barrier that separates the divine world from the profane. Frequently characterized as an inveterate copulator possessed by his enormous penis, linguistically Esu is the ultimate copula, connecting truth with understanding, the sacred with the profane, text with interpretation, the word (as a form of the verb *to be*) that links a subject with its predicate. He connects the grammar of divination with its rhetorical structures. In Yoruba mythology, Esu is said to limp as he walks precisely because of his mediating function: his legs are of different lengths because he keeps one anchored in the realm of the gods while the other rests in this, our human world (1988:6).

Perspective 2

Petr Bogatyrev: Let us place a still-life with apples alongside some real apples, and compare the real apples with the blotches of color on the canvas. The apple in the painting may seem almost comical, since the painted apple, in the opinion of the person comparing it to the real one, 'demands to be taken as a real apple'. . . . Another perception of paintings is possible: they may be perceived as living beings. Then we perceive every statue and painting as something mysterious, even frightening. Such a perception is not impossible: recall Gogol's story 'The Portrait' where the artist Čertkov perceived the portrait as a living man and went out of his mind in fear. Recall also Oscar Wilde's 'The Picture of Dorian Gray'.

It is not only the perception of the sign system of a work of art as living or real that results in this work of art being comical or frightening, but also the perception of one system of signs in reference to another system (1983:49).

Perspective 3a

Kenneth Burke: By the 'principle of courtship' in rhetoric we mean the use of suasive devices for the transcending of social estrangement. There is the 'mystery of courtship' when 'different kinds of beings' communicate with each other. Thus we look upon any embarrassment or self-imposed constraint as the sign of such 'mystery.' Quite as Sappho's poem on the acute physical symptoms of love is about the *magic* of love (the beloved is 'like a god'), so we interpret any variants, however twisted or attenuated, of embarrassment in social intercourse as sign of a corresponding mystery in communication.

If a woman of higher social standing ('a woman of refinement') were to seek communion by profligate abandonment among the 'dregs of society,' such yielding in sexual degradation could become in imagination almost mystical (a thought that suggests, from another approach, the strong presence of the Czarist hierarchy in Dostoevski's mysticism of the people). And a writer who gave particularized descriptions of sexual yielding under such conditions might fascinate in a way that mere 'pornography' could not. The work might be prosecuted as pornography; but it would really embody (roundabout and in disguise) much the same rhetorical element as shapes the appeal of Shakespeare's *Venus and Adonis* (which treats of a hot-and-cold relationship between persons of different classes, here figured as divine and mortal, while the real subject is not primarily sexual lewdness at all, but 'social lewdness' mythically expressed in sexual terms) (1962:732).

Perspective 3b

Kenneth Burke again: Over and above all the qualifications, *mystery* is equated with *class distinctions* (1962:646).

Perspective 4

Judith Irvine: There is no reason to suppose that these arguments apply only to cases of spirit mediumship and possession . . . For example, one could look at other types of spokesmanship—message-bearing, interpreting, quoting, and so forth—in all of which cases the audience must suppose that the speaker's message has some source external to himself or herself. Another possibility would be the case of role-switching. In spirit mediumship the roles taken by the medium are particularly divergent (associated with spirit and human identities), but less drastic sorts of role-switching also suggest an audience who concur that the switcher is now acting in some different capacity. Yet another example would be the attribution of insanity, especially in the insanity defense, where juries must decide whether defendants are personally responsible for their actions (1982:257).

Perspective 5

Joel Achenbach: [Shirley MacLaine] came in person. I managed to get a brief interview.

She said her most recent book, *It's All in the Playing,* was a compendium of revelations that came to her while playing herself in the TV movie based on her previous best-seller, *Out on a Limb.*

'It uses the experience of playing myself to explore—well, the notion that we're all the writers, directors, producers, and stars of our *own* drama. You can play your part *in real life* just as you can play your part in a movie.' . . .

Naturally I had to ask Ms. MacLaine the obvious question: Would there soon be a movie based on her book about playing herself in the movie based on her previous book?

She hesitated. Then she said, 'I don't think so.'

But later, her publicist, Stuart Applebaum, refused to rule anything out: 'Nothing is impossible' (1988:115).

Perspective 6

John Donne: Or that the common Enemie find the doore worst locked against him in mee (quoted in Alvarez 1973:149).

....

Perspective n

N: Etc. (n:n).

I

Exu

Epistemon started to speak. He had seen the devils, he told them, he had spoken familiarly with Lucifer, he had had a rollicking time in hell and in the Elysian Fields. The devils, he testified, were such excellent fellows and jovial company that he regretted Panurge's recalling him back to life so soon.

"I enjoyed seeing them immensely."

"How so?" Pantagruel asked.

"They are not so badly treated as you suppose," Epistemon explained. "The only thing is that their conditions are changed very curiously . . ."

Rabelais, *Gargantua and Pantagruel*,
Book 2, Chapter 30 (1936:II, 180).

1. The Lips of Pomba-Gira

On my second-last night in Brazil I walked across the dunes to Jaraci to take leave of friends there, and after the human farewells wound up in the company of two *exuas*, Pomba-Gira and Sete Saia. An *exua* is a female *exu*, one of a class of originally African deities who have found a new home in Brazil.

This Pomba-Gira has a rather shy disposition, and Sete Saia taunted her for her "fineness." But after some bottles of sweet red wine were fetched from the long-suffering Dona Nega, who operates a small store-cum-bar nearby, Pomba-Gira began to sing and dance. Sete Saia joined her. They passed successive bottles to me and the two other men present. We drummed on chairs and clapped, and the *exuas* took spells from dancing by sitting in our laps.

I had been in Brazil almost twelve months, over two field trips, and my farewell had already included several hours of drinking. Yet I reacted as any *gringo* might if a reputedly diabolical female spirit sat in his lap. My uncertainty made me tentative.

Pomba-Gira got up and disappeared behind the curtain that divides the small dirt-floored house into two rooms. She returned with a long piece of white lace decorated with gold thread, which she gave me. She said to come out to the house of Exu, so that she could show me what she wanted me to do with the lace.

She went inside the small shed that stands at the front of the yard, and pointed out the pitchers, dishes, and spiky metal constructions that belong to the *exus* of various people I knew in Jaraci. Each group of objects is called a "seat"—the place where a spirit has been "seated." Her own "seat" consisted of a tall pitcher with a clay dish on top. She told me that when I got back to my land I should buy a similar pitcher and tie the lace round it, with two bows.

I was standing at the door. "Would you like to kiss me?" she said. "Yes," I said.

In Brazil there is a folk saying:

Mulher de bigode
Nem o diabo pode.

"Not even the devil can (bring himself to kiss) a woman with a moustache." The folk are not always right.

Pomba-Gira said it was the first time she had ever kissed "matter." I had been keeping company with *exus* long enough to know that they do not expect their utterances to be judged by the standards of an objectivist theory of meaning. It may or may not have been the first time.

But this was less important than her recognition that something out of the ordinary had taken place, a conjunction of incommensurables.

* * *

I begin this account of interaction between spirits and humans in Candomblé with the *exus*, because in this Brazilian religion every major undertaking or ritual has to begin with them. The honoring of the *exus* is also one of the two factors that give the religions sometimes called "Afro-Brazilian" their unity.

These religions are very diverse, in both their doctrines and their rituals. Each initiatic lineage is independent, and not responsible to any superior body for the maintenance of conformity to a set of common traditions. It is true that most states in Brazil have one or more umbrella organizations, usually called "federations." Their function, however, is primarily to mediate between individual religious centers and the wider Brazilian society, in particular the organs of government. They may discuss doctrine and ritual, but any synthesis they arrive at is intended mainly for the consumption of outsiders, and would be difficult to impose on member houses.

There is also a national, though somewhat factionalized, umbrella organization called CONTOC—"Conference of the Tradition and Culture of the Orixás." This body provides representatives to the International Congresses of Orisa Tradition and Culture. The membership criteria of CONTOC provide some idea of what basic elements the adherents of the Afro-Brazilian religions perceive themselves as having in common.

To participate in CONTOC a *terreiro* (the usual word for "religious center") must, first, have members who "receive," or go into trance with, the African deities, most frequently known as *orixás*. Second, the house must have an *exu* who has been ritually "seated."

These criteria distinguish the religions which may be called "Afro-Brazilian" from the various other religions in Brazil which involve trance or trance-like states. Some of these latter religions, such as the Assembly of God and other Pentecostal denominations of Christianity, are unlikely to be confused with the Afro-Brazilian religions. But there is also a category of religions known by the term "Spiritism," whose relationship to the Afro-Brazilian religions is more complicated.

In Brazil "Spiritism" generally denotes those religions that derive at least part of their doctrine and practices from the work of the nineteenth-century French spiritist Hippolyte Léon Denizard Rivail, known more frequently by his pseudonym Allan Kardec. Kardec regarded himself as a scientist, and some of his followers in Brazil reject any intrusion of the Afro-Brazilian religions into Spiritism as incompatible with his principles. Such people practice what is called "Kardecism" or "pure Spiritism," in which the *exus* and *orixás* have no part to play. But Kardec's ideas have spread well beyond Kardecism—in part, no doubt, because they provide a Portuguese vocabulary (in translations of his works from French) with which to conceptualize dealings with the spirit world. Various religions have grown up in Brazil which combine Kardecist notions with others that trace their historical roots to Africa and to Brazilian folk traditions. These religions may still go by the name "Spiritism" (or by other names, such as "Umbanda"), but they are accepted as Afro-Brazilian, at least for the purposes of participation in CONTOC, as long as they have a seated *exu* and members who receive the *orixás*.

In the north-eastern state of Bahia, where I did my field work, the dominant Afro-Brazilian religion is called Candomblé, though Umbanda is also widespread outside the capital, Salvador. Candomblé is regarded as more African than Umbanda, partly because of its use of African languages in liturgical chants and special-purpose vocabularies. The main language of Umbanda is Portuguese. Candomblé is divided into "nations," according to the putative origin of different initiatic lineages in parts of Africa speaking different languages. The main nations are Queto (regarded as a subgroup of the "super-nation" called Nagô), Gege, and Angola, associated respectively with Yoruba, Ewe, and the Bantu languages.

For CONTOC, however, the idea of "nation" has a slightly different sense. Queto, Gege, and Angola are nations, but so is Umbanda, and so are the Afro-Brazilian religions of other states, such as Xangô of Pernambuco and Mina of Maranhão.

I base these observations on conversations with a member of CONTOC, a "father-of-saint" called Xilton. ("Father-" and "mother-of-saint" are probably the most commonly used terms for the heads of Candomblé *terreiros*.) It was Xilton who was responsible for my being in Bahia.

* * *

I had arrived in Rio de Janeiro in December of 1987, intending to carry out my field work on the outskirts of that city. However, before I left my hotel for "the field" I wanted to see an old friend called Rory, who had been doing field work in Bahia. He was in Rio for a couple of weeks before leaving the country to return to the United States. When I called him he said he had come to Rio with a Bahian father-of-saint called Xilton, who had been helping him with his research. They persuaded me to stay in the city until Rory's departure, so that we could spend some time together. Xilton would be attending to clients, and Rory would be doing some last minute field work.

A few days later we drove to São Cristóvão, where Xilton was to perform an "obligation of Exu" for a young fashion designer, to help him overcome certain problems in his life. An obligation is a ritual offering to a spirit entity.

In the car a dispute occurred between Rory and Xilton. Rory complained about racism in Brazil. Xilton hotly defended Brazil as a racial democracy. Rory is a Black aristocrat, from one of the best North American universities. Xilton, partly of African descent, looks white and Iberian, and has become a member of the Bahian middle class through his own efforts. Rory attempted to refine his argument by explaining their difference of opinion as a difference of culture. He intended the term in its anthropological sense. Xilton became even more offended, however, since he took it to mean something like "level of education."

Rory was due to leave Brazil in a couple of days.

We arrived in São Cristóvão, at the house of a friend of Xilton's. Xilton began the preparations for the obligation of Exu, chopping up large quantities of raw vegetables and setting out plates of white and yellow manioc flour. The client took a herbal bath prepared by a neighbor, and changed out of his beautiful hand-printed shirt into an old T-shirt.

The obligation began in the back yard, with the dismemberment of two guinea fowl. These black and white speckled birds had been brought, tied up, by Xilton's client. Xilton untied them, since they have to be free for the sacrifice, and explained that one was male and one female, since Exu is the divinity of sexual union. The client held one bird in each hand. Then Xilton took them by the feet and swept them up and down the length of the client's body. He proceeded to kill one bird at a time, first breaking its wings, then its legs, then pulling out its neck. Xilton is one of those fathers-of-saint who believe that, while sacrifices for the other gods may be performed with a knife, those for Exu must be done by hand.

He placed the dead birds at the bottom of a large enamel bowl, and the various other elements of the obligation on top of them. He tore the client's T-shirt to shreds, and added it. He produced a spool of white thread and wound it around the head and body of the client to produce a kind of net, the end of which he held in his left hand. Then he took a pair of scissors, cut through the threads, and dropped them into the bowl.

Rory and I watched, and the neighbor clapped slowly. She did this, she said, to avert from us the negative influences departing from the client's body. Rory and I were vulnerable, since we had not taken the necessary precautions, such as a herbal bath.

I do not know why Xilton let us witness what is normally a private ritual that is supposed to entail risks for the uninitiated observer. Perhaps he himself does not believe. Perhaps he regarded Rory and me as belonging to some category that is not subject to the influence of Brazilian spirits. Perhaps it was an experiment—he wanted to see what effect it would have on us.

Or perhaps he knew what effect it would have, and subsequent events were part of the working out of that effect.

The motivations of a father-of-saint are often more difficult to understand than those of other people. They are also potentially more dangerous. This no doubt accounts, in part, for his power. Xilton said he found me transparent.

I was a little surprised when, after we had seen Rory off at Galeão airport a few days later, Xilton invited me to visit him in Bahia for the annual festival of the washing of the Church of Bomfim, due to take place in just over three weeks.

It is also surprising, though less so, that at the end of three weeks I found myself on the bus heading for Bahia. I had spent Christmas and New Year among strangers in Espirito Santo. I had not got into the field in Rio. I was tired of not knowing anyone. At least in Bahia I would know Xilton.

* * *

For those who know Brazil, Salvador (or, as it is more commonly known, Bahia) has become a legendary city, a land of the imagination produced by generations of novelists, songwriters, poets, ethnographers, historians, artists, musicians. It is for this reason that I originally intended to avoid doing my field work there. I did not want to be beguiled by a phantom. A large part of the city's population—probably at least eighty percent (Brissonnet 1988:40-41)—lives in poverty. But in the Bahia of the imagination people's everyday lives are made to take on a significance that transcends the ordinariness or deprivations of their material circumstances.

For example, in the drawings of Carlos Bastos that illustrate recent editions of the guide to Bahia written by the great novelist Jorge Amado (1982), the ordinary people of Bahia, selling food and drink on the streets, carrying loads on their heads, or participating in festivals, occupy the same space as Catholic saints in swirling robes, *orixás* in full skirts and long frilly drawers, and naked *putti* bearing African ritual objects. This space consists of a hilly peninsula adorned with tiled roofs, high-rises, exuberant baroque churches, huts on stilts, and the most famous public elevator in the world; it is flanked on one side by palm-fringed Atlantic beaches, and on the other by the sailing boats and islands of the Bay of All Saints.

Mundanity is doubly transcended. People interact with, and may become, supernatural beings; and their lives are played out against a background so much like its representations that it has the potential to transform the most banal acts into performances. I use the trope of "performance" not in order to make life in Bahia interpretable in terms of the common sociological metaphor of social life as drama, but because it accords with Bahian folk theories of human motivation. I frequently heard people's behavior explained in terms of *estrelismo*, "star-ism," "the desire to be a star."

Bahian *estrelismo* has a paradoxical relationship to Bahian proxemics. A large part of the population of the city lives in crowded conditions, walks on bustling streets, travels on densely packed public transport. Other cities also have these characteristics. But in Bahia this closeness is not simply endured. Rather it is celebrated as a sign of social proximity, intimacy even, for example in festivals such as *carnaval*, which test the limits of human contiguity. There is an obvious tension between *estrelismo* and this ethos of closeness, since *estrelismo* implies a desire to distinguish oneself from the crowd.

* * *

Bahia is a city of multiple identities. For some the *genius loci* is Oxum, the goddess of love, beauty, wealth, and luxury, who carries a mirror of brass or gold and is associated with fresh waters, fish, mermaids, and butterflies. A popular song says that "everyone in this city belongs to Oxum." Others see the city's face in Our Lord of Bomfim, represented by a miracle-working crucifix in the church which bears His name. His body shines like porcelain, and His wounds are rose-red and heart-shaped. He is backed by the Brazilian flag. In Candomblé He is identified with Oxalá, father of the gods. The "Hymn of Bomfim" is virtually the national anthem of Bahia, played as many as four times daily by some radio stations, at the day's cardinal points: 6.00 a.m., midday, 6.00 p.m., and midnight.

But Jorge Amado (1982:15) advises the visitor to Bahia to make his first offering, of *cachaça* (uncured rum), to Exu, who guards the thoroughfares of the city.

The difference between the terms "Exu" and "the *exus*" requires explanation. In West Africa Exu's counterpart is a member of the pantheon of Yoruba gods called *òrìṣàs*. When people adopt this perspective in Brazil, Exu is thought of as one of the *orixás*, and as a single entity, though like all the *orixás* he has different aspects, often called *marcas*, or "brands" ("types," "qualities"). More frequently, however, Exu is singled out for special treatment. The little building where his ritual objects are kept is usually at the front of the *terreiro*, while the house or houses of the *orixás* are generally further back. There are variations in this arrangement, particularly when the religious center does not have much space. However, the principle which is always observed is that the ritual objects of Exu and those of the *orixás* should be kept separate. Similarly, it is uncommon for Exu to "manifest" (that is, to materialize in a human body) in the same ritual context as the *orixás*.

From this perspective Exu inhabits a different social world from the *orixás*. But for it to be a social world, with the same kinds of social differentiation as characterize the world of the *orixás*, Exu cannot live there alone. So the realm of Exu is populated by a multiplicity of *exus*, who are distinguished by sex, age, and status, as well as by names and personal qualities.

* * *

On arrival I found lodgings in the Pelourinho, a historic, cobble-streeted quarter of the High City. Xilton invited me to visit him, treated me very hospitably, and showed me through his house and *barracão* (literally "big shed"—the large hall that is the main public ritual space of a *terreiro*). On his household altar were representations of Catholic saints and a statue of Hotei, the laughing Buddha, with his back turned. Xilton said this brings good fortune and financial success. We attended the washing of the Church of Bomfim together, and I got sun-stroke.

A few days later I contacted Professor Carlos de Barros, an anthropologist I had met on my previous trip to Bahia. I had spent a month there in 1985, during which time I consulted a mother-of-saint about my prospects for the future. She performed a divination procedure called "throwing the cowries," and told me that the "paths were open" for me to come back.

Through Professor de Barros I got to know Archipiado, an anthropology student at the Federal University of Bahia. Archipiado called himself a militant atheist, but he had friends who were involved with Candomblé, and offered to introduce me to them. I resolved to wait a little longer before deciding whether to return to Rio.

We visited numbers of houses of Candomblé, in the city and on the island of Itaparica, but our participation was restricted to attendance at festivals. *Carnaval* came round. In Bahia they say it is the "festival of the devil blessed by God." (I have heard the city itself described in the same terms.) Archipiado and I spent six nights dancing and drinking in the streets. One night we met a childhood friend of his, called Joãozinho, whom he knew to be involved with Candomblé, and a friend from my previous stay in Bahia, called Miguel. The four of us snatched a few hours' sleep after sunrise, then went to the beach called Jardim de Alá, "Garden of Allah," to recuperate from our exertions and to prepare ourselves for the rigors of the coming night. We sat on the grass under the palm trees, drinking the milk of fresh coconuts, while Joãozinho entertained us with Candomblé stories. One of these stories concerned three *exus*, Padilha, Pomba-Gira, and Sete Facadas.

2. Padilha's Vow

This is the story of the three *exus*, which Joãozinho told while we were at Jardim de Alá.

They say that there was once, in a certain place, a woman who had two daughters. One was called Maria Padilha and the other was Pomba-Gira.

The family was more or less well off.

When Padilha was seven, with a well-formed body, her brother, Sete Facadas ("Seven Stabs"), felt sexually attracted to her.

Padilha and Pomba-Gira did not get on together, since Padilha was envious of the presents that were given to the younger daughter. Pomba-Gira was treated with affection, and Maria was left with the household tasks.

One time their mother was out, leaving them alone. Their brother began to caress Maria's body. She was fourteen when he took her virginity, by force, and she vowed she would kill him one day, with seven stabs, and drink his blood.

Long years passed. She grew up, became a woman. Her dream was to be very rich—much richer than Pomba-Gira, of whom she was envious. So she married a king, and became rich.

Pomba-Gira was quite rich, although she had never married. She had inherited the family's goods.

Although very rich, Maria Padilha nursed a hatred for her brother, and wanted to take vengeance on him. She would use her wealth to find him.

It happened that Maria abandoned all her riches and her husband, and went to live in a *brega* (brothel district).

One day, in the *brega*, she came across her brother, and quickly recognized him. She used all her beauty to conquer him, which produced its effect: he began to desire her as a woman, not recalling, however, where he knew her from.

He invited her to a drink, she accepted. She sat down, armed with a dagger, which she always carried with her. They talked. He did not notice the dagger.

She asked, "Do you know me?"

"No," her brother replied.

"You don't remember me?"

"No."

So she started to tell him her life, until he remembered her.

Then she asked, "Do you remember the oath I swore?"

"Yes," he replied. "But now, after so much time, you've grown up, and you wouldn't do that to me."

"I swore what I would do, and I'm going to carry out my pledge."

She killed her brother with seven stabs, and drank his blood. But, as bad luck would have it, she died on top of his body. A lady who lived in the *brega*, and who was the lover of Maria's brother, stabbed her in the back, and one more time in the stomach.

Her soul came to inhabit the *bregas*, and she swore that she would be Maria Padilha, and that she would govern hell.

Some time passed. Although they had been enemies, Pomba-Gira looked for her sister everywhere. Then she went to the *brega*, the last of the places in which she might be sought. Someone in the *brega* told her the story: that seven years ago her sister had been murdered, after killing her brother.

It was late, and, sadly, Pomba-Gira was crossing a bridge. (For this reason she belongs to Oxum.) The spirit of Padilha met her soon after the bridge, at a crossroad.

Seeing Pomba-Gira weeping, Padilha came to meet her. She asked her what was happening, and Pomba-Gira said she was living in a good place, and had come to find her sister, so that she could take her back there.

The spirit of Padilha refused to come with Pomba-Gira, and said that the place where she herself was living was more elevated, inviting Pomba-Gira to share her world with her.

However, Pomba-Gira knew that she was dealing with the spirit of Padilha, and because of her refusal to go with her, a fight started between them.

In the discussion on the bridge, as they were grappling with each other, Padilha pushed Pomba-Gira into the river, and she fell and hit her head on a stone.

Padilha took the spirit of her sister and carried it to hell.

Then Padilha came to be the woman *exu* who governs the *brega*, having various names: Lebara, Exu Apavenam, et cetera, including the name of Pomba-Gira herself (which leads her to be confused with her sister).

Leandra was the name of Pomba-Gira, daughter of the mother of Padilha, with a gypsy. She was rich, which caused Padilha's envy.

Pomba-Gira came to have other names: Dama-de-Prata ("Lady of Silver"), Dama-de-Ouro ("Lady of Gold"), et cetera.

Their brother, Sete Facadas, was called, when alive, Manuel.

Even though they are both *exuas*, Pomba-Gira and Padilha continue to be enemies. In any house of Candomblé where the *exua* of one daughter-of-saint is Pomba-Gira and the *exua* of another is Padilha, the two women do not get on together.

Tranca-Rua is the husband of Padilha. She has seven husbands, including Lucifer, king of hell.

* * *

Before and after the story Joãozinho made a disclaimer, saying that he "sold the fish for the price at which he bought it"—that is, that he was passing on the story as it was told to him, without making any claims as to its validity.

* * *

The three principal characters in the story set out on life with human names: Maria, Leandra, and Manuel. But Joãozinho refers to them more frequently by the names they acquired when they became *exus*: Padilha, Pomba-Gira, and Sete Facadas.

Some of the names he mentions—Pomba-Gira, Lebara, Exu, Apavenam—have roots in African languages, and in the religions of the people who speak those languages. Others—Padilha, Sete Facadas, Dama-de-Prata, Dama-de-Ouro, Tranca-Rua, Lucifer—are Portuguese, and derive from folk Catholicism (as in the case of "Lucifer"), or from popular traditions that may have originated in, or contributed to the development of, Macumba. The term "Macumba" refers to those Brazilian religions that specialize in dealings with "low" spirits, who may be called "devils" or *exus*. Macumba is associated in particular with the so-called "low spiritism" of Rio de Janeiro, though the term is also colloquially used to refer to all the Afro-Brazilian religions.

However, in Candomblé as practiced by Joãozinho and, from my observation, for many Bahians, these distinctions, and the cosmological differences they imply, are not significant. The names in the story refer to spirits who all belong to the same conceptual category, that is, the *exus*.

In formal, ritual contexts the *exus* are referred to, respectfully, as *exus*, or as "slaves" (of the *orixás*). Outside such contexts, however, they are often called, somewhat jocularly, "devils" (cf. Trindade 1985:67 and *passim*). This is a popular usage, the appropriateness of which has been disputed by some writers, on the grounds that it confuses the distinct characteristics of the Yoruba deity Ẹṣu and the Christian malefactor, Satan. But this association is an ineradicable part of the Bahian imagination. Moreover the "confusion" of Exu and the devil entails not so much a corruption of Exu by seeing him from the perspective of the Christian conception of evil, as rather a re-interpretation of the devil by seeing him in terms of Candomblé's own theodicy.

The difference between these two perspectives is most apparent if one examines the "orientational metaphors" (Lakoff and Johnson 1980:14) of their cosmologies. In Christianity heaven is metaphorically "up" and hell is "down," which results in the popular conception of a three-tiered universe, with the human world in the middle. Candomblé's universe is structured differently, as is apparent from Padilha's remark that her place, in hell, is "more elevated" than Pomba-Gira's place in the world of mortals. In Candomblé the various entities that populate the universe, and the "places" they inhabit, are conceptualized as lying on a continuum between matter and spirit. The lowest place in this schema is the world of mortals, which is identified with matter—the human being is often referred to simply as "matter." All spirit entities occupy places that are metaphorically "above" matter. These places are themselves hierarchically arranged, according to their degree of proximity to one pole or the other. The *exus* are closest to matter (cf. Costa 1980:99), for which reason it is considered more appropriate, and more efficacious, to call on them when one needs help in the material world, rather than to trouble the *orixás*, who are high on the spirit-matter continuum.

The *exus* may be "devils," with names such as Lucifer and Belzebu (Beelzebub), but they are also spirits, and therefore on a higher level than humans. For this reason they are owed and accorded respect. However, the difference between Candomblé and Christianity lies not only in the architecture of their cosmologies, but also in their attitudes towards evil.

In Candomblé the *exus* are not identified with absolute evil. Like human beings, they are capable of doing both good and bad. Humans may enlist their aid without "selling their souls."

Candomblé characterizes the behavior that is appropriate in dealings with the *exus* in terms of metaphors of inducement. One persuades the *exus* to do good, on behalf of oneself or others, by making offerings to them. One may also, of course, induce them to do evil to others, by the same means. This entails certain risks, however.

Candomblé may also employ metaphors of warfare in referring to relations with the *exus*, as Christianity does in talking about relations with the devil. But there is a difference. From the Christian perspective the devil, in whatever form he appears, is always the antagonist. For Candomblé, however, the danger is not so much from one's own *exus*, whose co-operation one hopes to ensure by means of offerings (though the *exus* are known to be somewhat unpredictable), as from the *exus* enlisted by one's enemies. If one petitions an *exu* to do harm to a third party, the risk one runs is that of retaliation, and an escalating war of the spirits.

The distinction I have drawn between Candomblé and Christianity is an idealization, for clarity of exposition. In practice the two models do not necessarily exclude each other. It is rather a question of which aspects of which model are emphasized in which contexts by which people for which purposes. Adherents of Candomblé are also Catholics, and numbers of important Candomblé rituals, including initiation, may require attendance at mass as part of the ceremonial cycle. (From the perspective of Protestantism, all the spirits of Candomblé are demons. It is not possible to be a Protestant and an adherent of Candomblé simultaneously. Sequential membership of these two religions, however, occurs regularly.) There are also some things that the Christian idea of the devil and Candomblé's notions about the *exus* have in common.

In Christian mythology Lucifer was cast out of heaven for his pride, for the individualism implicit in his disobedience to God. In Brazilian Portuguese one of the names by which the devil is colloquially known is "the individual."

The *exus* are the spirits most closely linked to the individual and his or her destiny. They are the guardians of public thoroughfares because it is they who may "open" or "close" the "roads" which constitute the individual's fate. If one experiences obstacles in one's life, one may make an offering to the *exus* to "open the roads." One could, alternatively, pray to the Catholic saints, but the saints are supposed to be impartial in their dealings with humans, so they cannot be relied on to help if one's roads are closed because other people are blocking them.

If one decides to deal with such people by performing a "work" for the *exus*, one becomes involved with a branch of Candomblé ritual sometimes called "the line of oil." (There is a link between Exu and oil. The offering made to him at the beginning of any ritual consists of a plate of yellow manioc flour cooked in oil.) Some fathers- or mothers-of-saint specialize in such works. Xilton told me about a fellow father-of-saint who performed only works intended to cause death, because they are the most highly paid. Popularly such practices are called "sorcery."

A parent-of-saint may also practice "the white line," which deals with works intended to do good rather than harm, and is often concerned with healing. The white line shows the influence of Kardecism, and its spirits and rituals are regarded as distinct from those of Candomblé. The white line and Candomblé are complementary, however, rather than incompatible, and for a parent-of-saint to practice both is not uncommon.

* * *

The individual is regarded, in most houses of Candomblé, as "belonging to" (the Portuguese expression translates literally as "being of") three of the *orixás*, or deities of the African pantheon. A parent-of-saint determines which three by throwing the cowries. These three are known, respectively, as the "owner of the head," the *juntó*, and the *adjuntó* (often pronounced *adé-juntó*). I have also heard the *adjuntó* referred to as *tojuntó*, *dijuntó*, and "the third." Sometimes there is also a fourth (occasionally called *quijuntó*), which the person has "by inheritance" from a deceased relative. The long initiatic process of Candomblé entails "seating" these *orixás* over a period of years—that is, setting up their ritual objects in the *terreiro*, performing sacrifices which induce the *orixás* to take up residence in these objects, and making regular offerings to them. A few large *terreiros* have individual houses for each of the *orixás*. In smaller *terreiros* all the *orixás* may be seated together in a single house, or in a room, called "the room of the saints."

Every *orixá* has a "slave"—that is, an *exu*—of the same sex as the *orixá*. These *exus* also have to be seated, in the house of Exu, usually situated at the front of the *terreiro*.

Initiates are divided into two categories: those who "receive saint"—that is, who go into trance; and those who do not. Initiates who receive saint are called "sons- and daughters-of-saint." Those who do not are called *ogãs*, in the case of men, and *equedes*, in the case of women. Initiates who complete all their obligations over a period of roughly seven years (the actual length of time is determined by divination) may "receive the *decá*."

This entails a ceremony in which their parent-of-saint gives them a tray of ritual objects that signify their right to open their own *terreiro*. They may now remove the objects pertaining to their *orixás* and *exus* and take them to their own house.

During this seven-year period sons- and daughters-of-saint will have learned to receive all their *orixás*. Ideally they also learn to receive all their *exus*, but this does not appear to happen in all cases. It seems to be sufficient to receive two *exus*, one male and one female, where this is possible.

This qualification is necessary because some people have *orixás*, with corresponding *exus*, who are all of the same sex. This is not very common, however. I met only one person in this position—a woman with three male *orixás*. Generally people have a combination of male and female *orixás*, and the preponderance of one sex or the other is taken as an indication of the balance of masculine and feminine characteristics in their personality.

* * *

Both male and female *exus* are associated with sexuality. Joãozinho's story implicitly equates hell with the *brega*, which, in the popular imagination, is considered to be the typical social setting of the *exus*.

The Brega used to be the main brothel area of Bahia. It was a district of poverty and crime that took its name from its principal thoroughfare, which runs steeply between the Low City and the High City. Even today people avoid this area by taking the Lacerda Elevator. The personage with the dubious distinction of having the street named after him was the sixteenth-century Jesuit Fr. Manuel da Nóbrega. In the vocabulary of contemporary Bahians the word *brega* is a common noun, used to refer to any low-life district. It is also an adjective, meaning something like "raffish," "disreputable," or "plebeian," its antonym being *chique*, or "chic."

Although there are both male and female *exus*, their common association with sexuality has a particularly masculine emphasis. Xilton once said to me, "Exu is the penis." This masculine emphasis can be seen also in their association with the *brega*. The sexuality of the *brega* is *public* sexuality, as distinct from domestic sexuality.

The link between men and public sexuality, on the one hand, and women and private sexuality, on the other, may be best demonstrated by considering certain aspects of Bahian dress codes. It is the fashion among Bahian males to walk the streets of the city with their penises raised to one side under their trousers, and often at least semi-erect. This phallic display is so much an accepted part of the Bahian way of life that there is even a rule about the side of the body on which the penis should be exhibited. If it is raised to the right rather than the left, this is cause for comment. By contrast the traditional costume of the women of the city, worn not only on ceremonial occasions, such as public festivals or Candomblé rituals, but also as everyday attire by the Baianas who sell dishes of African origin on the streets, is strikingly decorous. It consists of a turban, a full-length skirt over layers of petticoats, and a short-sleeved blouse decorated with lace, which has an opening high on the chest and is usually loose at the bottom, so that it falls vertically from the breasts and conceals their shape.

It is interesting that both male and female *orixás*, when they descend at Candomblé festivals, wear skirts that are variants of those of the traditional Baiana costume. (In some religious centers where it is considered improper for men to wear dresses, sons-of-saint are dressed in baggy pantaloons while they are in trance. But there are also many houses in which both male and female initiates wear the full skirts characteristic of the *orixás*.) This suggests that the *orixás* are comparatively "feminine" entities, by contrast with the *exus*, who are comparatively "masculine." And since the *orixás* are closer, on the spirit-matter continuum, to the pole of spirit, while the *exus* are closer to the pole of matter, it suggests also a link between femaleness and spirituality, and maleness and materiality.

There are, however, paradoxes in this arrangement. From a different perspective humans, who are equated with matter, are "female" in relation to all the spirits. Humans "give" offerings so that the spirits may "eat." "Giving" and "eating" are common Brazilian metaphors for the passive and active roles in intercourse (Fry 1982:67). Humans are also passive to the spirits when they go into trance. These paradoxes could be seen as indicative of a certain tension in Candomblé over the relative statuses of men and women. But their implications are broader than this. They suggest a contest over the kinds of value which may be attributed to different ways of being—over what is to be considered "up" and what is to be considered "down." It is this contest which is at the heart of the story of Padilha's vow.

* * *

It is also at the heart of Candomblé itself, and is summed up in the notion of *axé*.

Axé is Candomblé's ultimate value term, and has two main usages. In the first usage it is a "container" and in the second a "content" or attribute.

From the perspective of the first usage, it means something like "the ethos of Candomblé." For example an *exua* called Corquisa once said to me, "you were not born within the *axé*."

The sense of the second usage is harder to convey in English. It means something like "the quintessence of the ethos of Candomblé." In this usage things "have" *axé*, though not indefinitely. The term "presence" would express something of its intangible quality, but not its dynamism. *Axé* moves around. A thing that "has" *axé* at one moment may lose it the next. From this perspective *axé* has a lot in common with fashion. Like the *exus* and the stock market, it is not entirely predictable.

It is because of the mobility of *axé* that ritual objects in Candomblé require repeated sacrifices. Blood renews the *axé* of these objects, and helps to stabilize their value. There is a close link between *axé* and blood, for which reason the term is sometimes translated as "vital force." The ethos of Candomblé—*axé* in the first sense—is like an organism defined by and sustaining itself by means of the circulation of its animating force—*axé* in the second sense—among its parts.

But this image fails to account for the role played by human motivation in the circulation of *axé*. Since *axé* is Candomblé's ultimate value term, humans are necessarily interested in the way it moves around.

The ethos of Candomblé—*axé* in the first sense—is like any ethos in that it consists partly of certain conventionalized notions about the comparative value of the various phenomena that make up its conceptual world. It is these notions which give Candomblé the "flavor" that distinguishes it from other cultures.

But these notions are to some extent relativized, or opened to contestation, by *axé* in its second sense. The value of a thing may change if *axé* is attributed to it—or not attributed to it. Thus stones, in themselves, have little intrinsic value. But if a person finds a stone that seems to have *axé*, that stone may become an *otá*, the head of a god, the central item among the ritual objects that make up a "seat."

This is a fairly innocent example, because we are talking about stones, not about people. When, however, comparisons are made between people and their actions on the basis of the attribution of *axé*, the use of the term is bound up with the strategies humans engage in to define themselves, and is thus liable to be contested.

Such strategies can be divided into two main types. One strategy is to attribute *axé* to phenomena that are conventionally regarded as having little value. For example, I was told a number of times, by different people, that the poorest houses of Candomblé, constructed of scrap material and floored with dirt, have more *axé* than *terreiros* consisting of fine buildings. I take this to be an inversion of conventional values because most of the parents-of-saint I knew aspired to embark on ambitious building programs, if they had not already done so.

The other strategy is to attribute *axé* in accordance with conventional values. Occasionally I heard "much *axé*" attributed to certain parents-of-saint who have become highly successful in terms of such values—who are rich, famous, well connected, and established in buildings of almost palatial grandeur.

These considerations throw some light on the contest over values which takes place in the story of Padilha's vow.

* * *

The things that Padilha aspires to at the beginning of the story—material well-being, affection, and sexual purity—form a single complex of conventional values. The chastity that she defends against her brother's advances is a commodity she needs in order to acquire the other things that she wants. In Bahia, marriage patterns are popularly perceived as hypergamous. A girl from a family that is "more or less well off" values her virginity because she can use it to make a marriage that will improve her station. (The description of Padilha's family as "more or less well off" is ambiguous, since the family does not have a servant—the role Padilha herself is obliged to play. It is commonly said in Brazil that every family, even among the poor, tries to have a servant.)

In spite of her initial setback Padilha succeeds in acquiring the things she values, by making a good marriage. However, as the plot develops she trades in these things—material well-being, affection, and sexual purity—for the world of the *brega*, with its poverty, mercantile relationships, and sexual impurity. Moreover, she attributes greater value to this world. When she tells Pomba-Gira that her own world is "more elevated" than Pomba-Gira's, this is not just a claim that the world of the spirits is superior to the world of mortals, but also, since hell is equated with the *brega*, an implicit assertion that the *brega* has more *axé* than the world of conventional values. Pomba-Gira, of course, does not believe her, so their struggle on the bridge is a conflict between the personifications of two opposed sets of values.

Padilha wins, and takes Pomba-Gira's soul to hell, where the conflict continues to this day. But in spite of their ongoing fight the two sisters become identified with each other. Sometimes they are called by the same name, in which case they are thought of as a single *exua* who may act in accordance with two different sets of values. When people distinguish them, sometimes the values of the *brega* are attributed to Pomba-Gira and conventional values to Padilha, and sometimes the reverse. The two sets of values are really the same values, seen from different perspectives—from the perspectives of their acceptance and their rejection, or perhaps from the perspectives of innocence and experience.

The most interesting part of the story may be the reason behind Padilha's decision to "abandon all her riches and her husband" and set off for the *brega*. What is it about her vow to kill Manuel that makes it more important than maintaining her hold on the things she originally valued?

We have a clue in the fact that Padilha vows to drink her brother's blood. It is through drinking blood (though in real life it is the blood of sacrificed animals) that one acquires and periodically renews one's membership in the *axé*, the ethos of Candomblé. By seeking out Manuel and drinking his blood, Padilha renews her participation in a family drama, or a cultural game. Playing this game to the end is more important to her than her relationship to the king, who is an outsider to the game.

In the world of Candomblé, as in the story of Padilha's vow, there is often conflict, and there are sometimes cruel deeds. But the participants choose to remain within the *axé* because they know, so to speak, the taste of each other's blood. The world outside the family dramas of the *axé* is, by comparison, tasteless.

The fact that the three principals of Joãozinho's story end up in the *brega*-which-is-hell tells us something more about the contest of values in Candomblé. When people say that poor religious centers have more *axé* (in the second sense) than wealthy ones, they are implying that the wealthy houses have split the *axé* (in the first sense), so that it is no longer a single family, with a drama in which all can play. Padilha's desire to re-unite the siblings in the *brega*-which-is-hell is based on an identification of the *axé* with the ethos of closeness.

But, ironically, Padilha herself is not free of *estrelismo* ("star-ism," the desire to distinguish oneself from the crowd). Even in hell she wants to be the queen.

* * *

Joãozinho told me another story. The *orixás* were engaged in a battle with the *exus*, and had not been able to defeat them using conventional weapons. They called on Oxum, who up to that point had stayed out of the fray. Oxum subdued the *exus* effortlessly, by holding up to them her golden mirror. For this reason Oxum has a special relationship with the *exus*—and with Pomba-Gira in particular. She is the *orixá* most closely associated with "sorcery."

* * *

As goddess of the mirror, the bridge, and the kiss, Oxum personifies the conjunction of incommensurable worlds, and so, in a sense, participates in both sides. The surface of the fresh waters over which she rules is like a two-way mirror. The fish that swim below, in the dark world of dreams, see themselves reflected in the butterflies that flit above in the sun. The butterflies, looking down, find their reflection in the fish. Oxum herself is sometimes represented as a mermaid, with a tail that belongs to the below, and a head and torso that belong to the above.

When Oxum, who is the mirror, combs her flowing hair in front of her mirror, what does she see? Is it a woman, or is it a man? Is her skin white, or is it black? Does she see youth, beauty, love, wealth, and life; or age, ugliness, hatred, poverty, and death? Do her head and her tail see these things as different? Or does this creature of conjunctions have a simultaneous vision of what, for us mortals, are perspectival inversions or temporal transformations?

We divide up the world, through language, into the incommensurable realities of subject and object. But when we make ourselves the object of our own subjectivity we become paradoxical. Either we are obliged to see that these realities cannot be distinct, since subject and object both participate in the same action, the verb that unites them (cf. Durand 1969:236); or else we have to locate the subject outside of ourselves—which seems to be what happens in trance.

3. Corquisa

Just before dawn on the same night that I met Joãozinho, Archipiado and I encountered Marinalvo, Joãozinho's father-of-saint, in Praça Castro Alves, a square in the High City, overlooking the Bay. Marinalvo was with his new boyfriend—the fifth, he later told us, he had had during the five nights since *carnaval* had begun. Joãozinho introduced Archipiado and me to him, as "researchers." Marinalvo invited us to come to his *terreiro* for a festival in two weeks' time, and said to bring a camera.

Marinalvo eventually "initiated" me as an *ogã* in his *terreiro*, which is not in the city of Salvador itself, but in Jaraci, a beach-side suburb of a municipality that I shall call Fernando Pessoa, after the Portuguese poet whose centenary was celebrated in Bahia while I was there. Fernando Pessoa lies just outside the municipal boundaries of the city of Salvador—or, to give it its full name, Salvador da Bahia de Todos os Santos ("Savior of the Bay of All Saints"). Salvador is the capital of the state of Bahia. But Soteropolitans, or the people of Salvador, often refer to the city itself simply as "Bahia," and to themselves as "Bahians." In spite of the boundary that lies between the two municipalities, Fernando Pessoans tend to think of their town as a remote district of the capital—admittedly poorly served by public transportation to the city, but probably no worse than the distant suburbs that lie within Salvador's borders.

There are, however, ways in which life in Fernando Pessoa differs from life in the capital. In Jaraci, for example, the Afro-Brazilian religions were a part of people's everyday lives in a way that I never observed in the city. On any day of the week one might encounter, in the public places of Jaraci, various kinds of spirits "manifested" or "incorporated" in human vehicles—*erês*, or the child spirits of the *orixás*, playing pranks on the public or chasing each other in the street; *exus* drinking together in makeshift bars, and making passes at the women present; or *caboclos* (roughly, "Indian spirits") generally intent on getting their human vehicles from one place to another without the inconvenience of being conscious of the distance.

Six fathers-of-saint lived in the same small area of Jaraci where Marinalvo's *terreiro* is located. Five of them had their own *terreiros*, and four of them resided in the same short, unpaved street.

I liked Jaraci, and wanted to get to know its people better. But even after I was made *ogã*, I was still living in the city, and commuting to Jaraci, mainly for ritual occasions. Marinalvo also kept a watchful eye on me, to make sure I did not get too involved with people from other *terreiros* who attended his festivals. There is a certain competition among *terreiros* for members, and defections are not unheard of.

I went to Jaraci one day to talk to Marinalvo, and found out he had left for the country, to visit the family of another man he planned to make *ogã*. He had met Delcir during *carnaval*. The latter was already a member of a *terreiro* in the city, but was planning to transfer his allegiance to Marinalvo. The woman who was taking care of the *terreiro* told me that Marinalvo would be away for a couple of weeks.

There was a commotion outside, and I walked out to see what was happening. Free bread was being distributed from a van. Walking back from the van was a young man I had talked with a number of times during festivals at Marinalvo's *terreiro*. His name was Wilson, but he was universally known by his nickname, Taís. I struck up a conversation about the provenance of the free bread. Taís invited me to come with him to meet the people in the *terreiro* where he was living, just a few doors from Marinalvo's.

Taís and I became good friends, and through him I got to know many of the people from other *terreiros* in Jaraci. I had long since given up any idea of returning to Rio. Now I started to think about moving to Jaraci. Such a move would also enable me to think of myself as a properly professional anthropologist, taking up residence "in the field." This was complicated, however.

Most of the people in Jaraci have barely enough space for their own families. I did not imagine they would want the additional burden of an anthropologist prying into their private lives. I was offered a house in the "invasion," a short distance from Marinalvo's. An "invasion" is an area of land where people build, usually using scrap material, without having title to the property. The people of Marinalvo's *terreiro* were shocked that I would even contemplate the idea. The reason they gave was that in the invasion I would be vulnerable to thieves. I took this to be a way of saying they considered it an inappropriate location for a white foreigner.

I also had to consider Archipiado, who was helping me in the capacity of field assistant. From our place in the Pelourinho it had been fairly easy for him to get buses to his classes at the university. If we lived in Jaraci, transport would be a constant problem.

Eventually I found a place in a complex of multi-story apartment blocks in the center of Fernando Pessoa, about twenty minutes' walk from Jaraci. I located the apartment a few hours after my first encounter with Corquisa. Actually it may have been my second encounter; but during the first one I was ignorant of her presence.

* * *

It had been the feast day of St. Anthony of Padua, and I had gone to Jaraci to attend an offering of prayers to this saint in the *terreiro* of a father-of-saint called Biju. Biju had set up a small altar in one corner of the front room of his house—the same house where I wound up with Pomba-Gira and Sete Saia on my second-last night in Brazil. The altar was decorated with flowers and candles and a small statue of St. Anthony, dressed in the robe of a Franciscan monk and carrying the infant Jesus.

This thirteenth-century doctor of the Church, in spite of being connected by his name to the Italian city where he lies buried, was born in Portugal and educated at Coimbra. So the special devotion given to him by the colonizers of Brazil had patriotic overtones. One of the hymns we sang to him that night called him "the most beloved saint of the Brazilian people." He has even been made a general in the Brazilian army. There is a certain irony in this when one considers the way his statues represent him—with gentle features, bunches of madonna lilies, and a child in his arms. The connection with weapons has, however, carried over into Candomblé, where St. Anthony is equated with Ogum, the *orixá* of battle. (In a *terreiro* I visited in the Pernambucan city of Olinda, north of Bahia, where the first church dedicated to St. Anthony in Brazil was built, he is regarded as the "protector" of the *exu* called Tranca-Rua.) He is the patron saint of the poor, of prisoners, and of those looking for a partner. People also pray to him for the resolution of particularly difficult problems.

The ceremony consisted of prayers and hymns, in Portuguese sprinkled with Latin phrases, in honor of St. Anthony, the Virgin, and Our Lord of Bomfim. It was led by a father-of-saint from Jaraci called Luiz, who had the words written down in an exercise book. The last prayer asked for blessings on those present and on all people, on the sick, and on mothers. Special mention was made of mothers because of their long-suffering tolerance of the waywardness of their sons. During the last hymn to St. Anthony we pelted his statue with a fragrant mixture of rice and petals. Then people came up individually to make their requests of the saint. When my turn came I prayed that Archipiado's visa problems be resolved. He was due to leave shortly for a conference in Boston, and the American consulate had twice refused him a visa. Someone told me afterwards that petitions at the festival of St. Anthony should be on behalf of other people. I was relieved to have done, by chance, what was culturally appropriate.

Biju distributed cake and liquor, and we moved out into the yard. Biju's *terreiro* does not have a *barracão* ("big shed"), so the public rituals that involve dancing are held in the open air. On this occasion there was a samba circle, in the course of which Taís and the four fathers-of-saint who were present received their *caboclos* (Indian spirits), who danced, one at a time, in the middle of the ring.

I thought that the spirit Taís received there was his *caboclo*, Tupinambá. But he later told me that Tupinambá had only stayed for a short time, then "given passage" to Corquisa, who had not wanted to materialize under her true identity in a gathering of *caboclos*. The only way anyone could know it was an *exua* rather than a *caboclo* would have been by observing a slight quivering of the left side of the upper lip. Corquisa is one of Taís's two *exuas*, the other being the same Sete Saia ("Seven Skirts") who danced with Pomba-Gira on my second-last night in Brazil. Taís also receives a male *exu* called Sete Punhal ("Seven Daggers").

* * *

It was a few days later that Corquisa first revealed herself to me. I had gone to visit Taís at Edivaldo's, where he was living. Edivaldo is another father-of-saint, who lives just a few doors from Marinalvo. I wanted to ask Taís if he knew of any accommodation available in the area. We sat in the *barracão* behind the two-room house. Slivers of light from the morning sun pierced the palm branches of the walls and roof, traced arabesques on the smoke of our cigarettes, and scattered among the moving shadows on the dirt floor.

Edivaldo had been going about the household tasks of a father-of-saint. Suddenly he received his *caboclo*, who, like Taís's, is called Tupinambá. Shortly afterwards Taís quivered and closed his eyes. The head that had been Taís's tilted back, and another being looked out through half-closed lids. Corquisa had descended, and let out a horrible laugh.

"Good day, my lady," I said, kissing the hand that she proffered. She said she had some important matters to discuss with me, but first I had to get her something to drink. She would accept a cigarette while I went to the bar on the corner to get her some beer and *cachaça* (uncured rum), which, on my return, she proceeded to mix in a large beer mug.

The *exus* are said not to favor beer, which is the preferred drink of the *caboclos*. They like hard liquor, in particular *cachaça*, or wine. Perhaps Corquisa added the *cachaça* to the beer to make it tolerable. (In my observation these reported preferences were never followed very strictly. Corquisa, being a classy *exua*, told me that her favorite drink was champagne.)

She began our serious discussion by saying that she wanted to speak to Archipiado, that it would be in his interests to come and see her before his journey. To resolve his problems he would need to bring her seven bottles of beer, three kilos of sardines, a small bird, a condiment made of peppers, a bottle of vodka, and a drinking glass. He would also have to tell her the name of his boss and two friends who might have something against him.

I had told Taís about Archipiado's visa problem. But Corquisa, who must have been listening in, seemed to be under a misapprehension about what a visa is. She apparently thought it had something to do with his place of employment. Archipiado worked half-time—eighty hours a month, for a monthly wage of the equivalent of about $20—as a student intern in a government office. But his boss had nothing to do with the visa problem.

Then Corquisa began to sing:

A porta do inferno estremeceu,
As alma saiu prá ver quem era.
Quando ouviram a gargalhada na encruza
Era Corquisa, a Rainha do Cabaré.

The door of hell shuddered,
The souls went out to see who it was.
When they heard the cackle at the crossroad
It was Corquisa, Queen of the Cabaret.

As in the story of Padilha's vow, there is an association in this song between hell and the *brega*. The cabaret, located in the *brega*, is the place where assignations are made.

Corquisa went on to talk about her dwelling place in hell, and the various husbands she has there. One of them is Lasca-fogo ("[he who] spits fire"). She said that it is he who "gives the orders" in Brazil, because an *ebame* ("senior initiate") had "seated" him beneath the Catholic basilica in Brasília, which lies at the center of a crossroad of twenty-one "legs." Her own favorite crossroads are those with three, six, seven, and twenty-one legs. In connection with Brasília she mentioned that a well-known Bahian politician, former state governor and, at the time of writing, federal minister and presidential hopeful, "has great faith in us"—that is, the *exus*. (This politician is popularly rumored to have done away with a number of rivals by means of sorcery, carried out by a famous mother-of-saint with whom he was friendly.) Another of her husbands is Embarabô, the one who makes love the best. She began to stroke the beer-stein, and said that she wished every cock were as thick.

She once told me, later, that an *exua* finds sexual relations with other *exus* much more satisfying than relations with "matter" could ever be. A materialized *exua* would not have sex with material beings, unless it were in order to kill them. She added that an *exua* does not permit herself to be kissed on the face, only on the hand. However, on a different occasion she informed me that the *exus*, alone among the spirits, can have relations with human beings, but only "in spirit"—that is, in dreams.

When she arrived she had the manners of a *grande dame*. In the course of the morning and early afternoon, as an audience gathered, she retained her aloofness and irony, but lost some of her refinement.

She asked me to come out to the house of Exu, so that she could introduce me to another of her husbands, Arranca-toco ("[he who] pulls up the stump"). She opened the door of the shed at the front of the yard, to reveal the *assentamento* ("seat") of Edivaldo's *exu*. It consisted of a metal construction cemented into a clay pot. It had seven pointed vertical spikes at the top. The central spike was longer than the others, and formed the shaft of the construction, with two crossed diagonal spikes attached to it further down. The whole arrangement was spattered with congealed blood and feathers.

Corquisa proceeded to give me some advice. She said that I was not born within the *axé*. To be free within the *axé*, and to get "the men of the street" (a term that refers to the *exus*) to leave me in peace, I would have to make another offering. The purification ritual I had undergone during my initiation at Marinalvo's *terreiro* had been incorrect. There should have been a piece of onion in the herbal bath I used, and there should have been two red *acaçá* among the offerings. (*Acaçá* is a gelatinous white paste made of fine corn meal, formed into a kind of cake and wrapped in banana leaves.) She gave a long list of objects I would have to buy for the offering.

We returned to the *barracão*. She sang more songs:

Hoje eu vou sair para beber,
Vou beber, vou cair pelas calçada.
Eu bebo, estou cumprindo minha sina.
Eu bebo, sim, porque sou uma desgraçada.

Today I'm going out to drink,
I'm going to drink, I'm going to stagger along the pavements.
I drink, I am fulfilling my destiny.
I drink because I am a wretch.

Various members of Edivaldo's household had come to watch Corquisa. They included a young couple who lived in a room at the back of the *barracão*. The woman, who was expecting a child, was one of Edivaldo's daughters-of-saint, and the man was Biju's chief *ogã*. Corquisa asked me to give the child a mattress when it was born. In exchange she would make it her *ogã*. The child's mother, Zezé, said it would have nothing to do with Candomblé—it was going to be a "believer" (slang for an evangelical Protestant). The father-to-be, Dinho, said he could not commit the child in advance. It would have to make up its own mind when it was old enough to understand what was involved. When Corquisa talked about the fires of hell in which she lives, Dinho commented wrily that he thought hell was this world we humans live in.

I told Corquisa I would have to go soon, to continue with my house hunting. She said she was going to depart shortly as well. She sang some more songs, then gave a deep cackle. The body she had been using was flung violently backwards. Dinho rushed to stop it from falling, pressed down on its shoulders, and clapped above its head.

Taís looked dazed, rubbed his eyes, and mumbled something incomprehensible. I experienced a sense of relief I came to know well. At the time I thought I was simply glad to be back in the presence of a friend who was a known quantity. But in the course of my field work I got to know some of the spirits—Corquisa in particular—as well as I knew some of my human friends. On reflection I think this sense of relief, which I always felt when the spirits departed, had to do with the fact that in my dealings with humans the terms of the relationship generally seemed more negotiable than in my dealings with spirits. The spirits are often demanding. One learns, of necessity, to negotiate with them, but there are supernatural risks involved in frustrating them.

A few days later Archipiado and I were sitting with Corquisa in the front yard at Edivaldo's, outside the house of Exu. A woman passed by in the street, and called to her. Corquisa beckoned the woman into the yard, then proceeded to abuse her. The woman had asked Corquisa to send her a man, which Corquisa had done. But the woman had not paid the *cachaça* she had promised. Corquisa demanded to be paid by the coming Wednesday, otherwise she would take it out of the woman's hide. The woman asked if it could be Thursday, when she received her money. Corquisa at first refused the moratorium, then relented.

This was the first time Archipiado had met Corquisa. She told him about the "work" he needed to perform to ensure the success of his journey. She added some more details. As well as the items mentioned already, he would need to bring her a tongue, since the root of the problem was gossip. Also she would need not only the name of his boss, but also that of the boss's deputy, and the names of seven other people who bore him ill will, instead of the original two.

When we left, Archipiado was cross. He thought I was going too far in my relationship with the Jaracians, and implied that I was losing my objectivity. There was a history to this situation. Briefly, in the course of our visits to various houses of Candomblé, two different spirits had caused Archipiado to experience a short and unwilling trance.

* * *

Over time I got to find out more about Taís's background, and about his relationship to the various spirits he received. The following account is pieced together from numerous conversations. As usual, I am selling the fish for the price at which I bought it.

Taís was a relative newcomer to Jaraci, having arrived there about six months before my first encounter with Corquisa. He said he was born in Salvador, but grew up in the city of Ilhéus, in the south of the state of Bahia. At the age of seven he had been attending a Candomblé festival with his mother when Corquisa "grabbed" him. She demanded liquor. The people present did not want to give it to her, because the "matter" into which she had descended was only a child. Taís's mother said it was all right.

Seven years later he was attending a festival in a *terreiro* in the suburb of Salvador where his parents came to live, and *bolou*, or "rolled." This means he went into trance and fell on the floor in a position that indicated to the mother-of-saint that she should initiate him into her house. He spent a year in seclusion in the *terreiro*. The mother-of-saint had determined that his *orixás* were Iançã (goddess of lightning), Oxosse (god of the forest and the hunt), Oxumaré (goddess of the rainbow), and Obaluaiê (god of illness and curing), with corresponding *exus* Corquisa, Sete Punhal, Sete Saia, and Julemeiro (the latter being an *exu* "on the street" and a *caboclo* "in the house"). He said that after fourteen years as an initiate he would also have to seat Corquisa's husband Capa Preta ("Black Cape"), so that he would not cause trouble.

When he "made saint"—that is, was initiated as a son-of-saint—there had been a battle between his two *exuas* to take control of his head. Sete Saia had defeated Corquisa, and for the next seven years he had received only Sete Saia. Then Iançã, the "owner of his head," demanded that Sete Saia give way to Corquisa, saying that each of the two *exuas* would reign for seven years.

Corquisa's return seems to have coincided with a period of transition in Taís's life. There was, for example, trouble with Taís's mother-of-saint. At a festival for the seating of an *exu* at the *terreiro*, Taís had received Sete Saia at an inappropriate time. The mother-of-saint had tried to "suspend" her—that is, to make her leave Taís's body. She refused to go. Sete Saia is known to be tough. The mother-of-saint pushed her. She pushed back. The mother-of-saint slapped her face. She slapped back, harder. The mother-of-saint collected Sete Saia's ritual objects from the house of Exu and dumped them in the middle of the street.

Taís appears to have been dividing his time among three houses in the same suburb—that of his parents (his father is a Jehovah's Witness), that of his mother-of-saint, and that of his boyfriend. When he discovered that his boyfriend was going out with other men, their relationship ended.

It was during this unsettled period that Taís met Marinalvo at "Tropical," a night-club in the city, and subsequently went, at the invitation of a friend they had in common, to attend a festival at Marinalvo's *terreiro*. He stayed at Marinalvo's after the festival, and when I met him, had only been back to his parents' suburb for infrequent short visits.

There was trouble at Marinalvo's when the latter's most recent boyfriend started to get interested in Taís. Taís moved to Biju's. However, Biju was too possessive, so Taís moved to Edivaldo's. Thus Taís had close, if somewhat complicated, ties to the three *terreiros* in Jaraci that I myself also got to know best, at least partly as a result of his friendship.

When I met him he was planning to "seat" Corquisa—that is, to induce her, through sacrifices, to take up residence in her ritual objects—in the house of Exu at Edivaldo's. Because of my friendship with Taís I got involved in the arrangements for this festival, which was due to take place about six weeks from the time I first met Corquisa.

In the period that I knew Taís, Corquisa and Sete Saia continued to do battle over his head. Many people in Jaraci and in Taís's home suburb, which we visited together once, had met both Corquisa and Sete Saia, and generally adored one and hated the other. So the seven-year alternation of the two *exuas* seems to have been an imperfectly realized ideal.

I met Sete Saia a couple of weeks after my first encounter with Corquisa. She descended upon Taís as I was sitting talking to him at Edivaldo's. At first I thought it was Corquisa. She went to the room of the saints at the back of the *barracão*, to put on her *exua*'s garments, and when she emerged there were delighted shouts from members of the household: "Sete Saia! Sete Saia!" She began to dance, and Edivaldo's brother accompanied her on the drum. She said that she had "come in front of Corquisa," that Corquisa had "taken it up the ass" (that is, been overpowered). She dragged various people onto the dance floor with her, quivering her hips, lowering herself to the floor with knees bent—mimicking intercourse with the beer mug she had placed there. She said she is called Sete Saia because she has seven skirts of different colors, one for each day of the week. When she left, a rather sour Corquisa arrived, and made various derogatory remarks about her.

Corquisa belongs to the category of "upper class" *exuas*, who are supposed to be characterized by their haughty refinement and their love of luxury. Sete Saia is of the "lower class" of *exuas*, who are more raucous and earthy, and great partiers. Both *exuas* liked telling me about themselves, and Taís also gave me some details about their backgrounds. The various accounts are not always easy to reconcile.

It seems clear that one difference between them is age. Corquisa died at the age of sixteen or seventeen, whereas Sete Saia was already an "old whore" when she passed away. Taís once told me that Corquisa had died a virgin. However, she herself claimed to have been raped by Embarabô, and to have had relations with her mother's husband, Capa Preta. On one occasion she said she had been raped after she died. On another she said she had been raped before she died, but "the man up above" had restored her virginity. However, when she arrived in the world of the dead, she was told she could not become an *orixá* because she had taken to strong drink, as a result of having been brought up in a cabaret in the *brega*. So now she lives in a tomb in the catacombs, and comes out at night to seduce the *exus* who wander there.

I have already mentioned the class difference between the two *exuas*. Corquisa's mother was the proprietress of a cabaret in the *brega*, whereas Sete Saia was a common prostitute. This was not her original condition, however. Corquisa once told me that Sete Saia had been the wife of an ambassador, who cast her out when he found her having an affair with a servant.

The two *exuas* also differ in appearance. Taís told me that Corquisa is white, with long blonde hair and blue eyes. (Taken with the fact that she is sixteen or seventeen, the description makes her sound rather like Xuxa, the idol of square-eyed Brazilian sub-teens, who, while I was in Brazil, starred in a movie called "Super-Xuxa against the Low Astral.") On another occasion, however, Corquisa herself said to me, pointing to the eyes of the body in which she was materialized, "these eyes are mine." Taís has brown eyes. She added that the eyebrows were not hers—her eyebrows meet in the middle and extend further to each side.

Taís described Sete Saia as being of his "own color." This would mean that she was Black. Once, however, at a stall in the São Joaquim market, he pointed out to me a statue that he said looked just like Sete Saia—a buxom light-skinned *mulata*, bare-breasted, wearing boots, skimpy pants, cape, and tiara, with a string of pearls across her forehead. In her left hand she held what looked like a *xaxará*—a kind of cylinder of straw, which is the ritual implement of the *orixá* Obaluaiê, with the difference that this one had a skull on top. From her belt hung a sword. Her eyes were red, and white teeth showed between her smiling lips.

Taís knew what his *exuas* looked like because he saw them in his dreams. He said that all the spirits appear to people in dreams. This does not happen often, just when the spirit wants to leave a message. However, if the spirit wants to "eat"—that is, to receive a sacrifice—he or she may appear every night. All the spirits except for the *orixás* may also show themselves to people in broad daylight, on the street. The apparition lasts for a short time, then disappears.

Taís once said that Corquisa and Sete Saia are really the same *exua*, with different names. In fact, I found Taís, Sete Saia, and Corquisa adopting each other's characteristics so frequently that it became difficult for me to separate them completely. Corquisa would sometimes use Sete Saia's coarse mannerisms, just as Sete Saia would sometimes lapse into refinement. On one occasion, as Corquisa was drinking a glass of spirits, she said that when she drinks *cachaça*, it is not she herself but Sete Saia who drinks, since her own preferred drink is champagne.

I also recall a couple of times when the *exuas* acted as though they were Taís. Once Corquisa was telling me about herself, and said "*eu sou muito educado*" ("I am very refined"). But she used the masculine instead of the feminine form of the adjective. On another occasion I went with Sete Saia late at night to pester Dona Nega to open her little store-cum-bar to sell us some wine. Dona Nega asked who it was. Sete Saia replied "Taís," and whispered to me that she had to act like Taís in order not to upset Dona Nega.

False trance is a familiar phenomenon in Candomblé, and is known as *equê*, which Taís defined for me as "a type of theatre." The existence of *equê* does not mean that there is no such thing as genuine trance. But it does mean that people who go into trance have considerable room for maneuver. I did not regard it as necessary to consider the lapses in the performances of Taís's *exuas* as evidence of *equê*—although it may have been. I simply took it for granted that, since the three of them used the same body, they would find it hard not to get in each other's way.

* * *

Sete Saia was surprisingly disdainful towards Taís. Whenever she talked about him she called him *meu viado*, "my faggot." She often said she wished he were a man. I thought it would be pointless to tell her that this distinction is a cultural construction. It would be like telling her that she herself was a cultural construction.

Corquisa was generally more indulgent towards Taís. She too called him *meu viado*, but said that she adored him. One might expect that there would be a greater affinity between Taís and Sete Saia, since in the popular imagination there is a link between *viados* and prostitutes. But perhaps this link is, in reality, a situation of competition.

The most visible group of *viados* in Bahia are the transvestites, who, at the time of my field work, plied their trade in the area of the High City between the Praça Municipal and the church called the Ajuda. They flaunted their sexual availability much more openly than the female prostitutes. It is perhaps for this reason that they are feted during *carnaval*, and given positions of prominence on the floats of various parade groups. The rest of the year they lead a precarious existence, subject to alternating tolerance and harassment by the police and occasional violence from their clients.

Like Sete Saia, they are known to be tough. At one stage of his career Taís had associated with them occasionally, and learned some of their survival skills. He told me, for example, that when he was alone in the tougher parts of the city he carried a razor blade in his mouth. He proceeded to demonstrate the way transvestites use this instrument to defend themselves from aggressors. (Transvestites are often at the center of outbursts of violence that occur during *carnaval.*)

Taís once said to me that he could not be an *ogã* because—apart from the fact that he goes into trance—he *lacra.* An *ogã*, whatever his sexual practices may be, has to comport himself like a man, and a man does not *lacrar.* I found this statement somewhat puzzling, since *lacrar* means "to seal with sealing wax." However, Taís patiently explained that *lacrar* is one of the synonyms for *fechar.* I already knew about *fechação*, which is a kind of extreme form of *estrelismo* ("star-ism") of which the transvestites are the acknowledged masters. *Fechar* means literally "to close." However, in Bahia it also means something like "to draw attention to oneself through extravagant behavior." This usage is said to derive from the expression *fechar o trânsito*, "to close [halt] the traffic." Other verbs that have a primary meaning similar to that of *fechar* have acquired also its secondary meaning—for example *trancar*, which means literally "to bar," "to lock," "to bolt," and of course *lacrar*, "to seal with sealing wax." All these verbs are transitive in their primary usage and intransitive in their secondary usage. *Fechar* has other synonyms also. Their primary meanings have no relationship to that of *fechar*, but if they are used intransitively they have the same secondary meaning. These include *abafar* ("to choke," "to stifle," "to hush up"), *abalar* ("to shake up," "to shock"), *arrasar* ("to demolish," "to raze"), *desempenhar* ("to perform [a role]"). Finally there is also *desbundar*, which is intransitive and has a primary meaning quite close to the secondary meaning of the verbs we have been considering: "to exceed the limits."

The noun formed from *fechar*, in its secondary sense, is *fechação.* The transvestites have developed certain common kinds of *fechação* into virtual art forms. One of these is the *baixa* (literally "low one"). This is a stylized type of verbal abuse, which, according to Taís, no man, even the most shameless, would ever use. Women and *viados* use it if they have occasion to engage in public disputations.

This is a "secular" *baixa* that Taís reproduced for me:

> Que bobagem é essa, quer me xoxar, é? Quem é você, por ventura?—alça do meu sutiã, cós da minha calcinha, tapete da secretaria, escorregadeira do Maciel, pinico sem fundo, travesseiro que eu me deito com meu homem, resto de espermatozóide do meu homem, tunfo do meu boi!

> What nonsense is this? So you want to bad-mouth me, eh? Who are you, by chance?—strap of my bra, hem of my pants, carpet of the office, street where the whores walk in Maciel [a *brega*], bottomless chamber pot, pillow where I lie down with my man, remains of my man's sperm, used rag of my menstruation!

I call this a "secular" *baixa* because it makes no reference to the world of Candomblé. However, occasionally a *baixa* may be delivered at a religious center—for example, after the formal proceedings at a festival, when food and drink have been distributed and the atmosphere is not so serious. Taís reproduced for me a *baixa* he himself delivered at a festival at Marinalvo's. Someone had given offense to the *caboclo* of Edivaldo, the father-of-saint of the household in which Taís lived.

> Taís: Quem buliu com caboco, que eu vou dar uma baixa!
> Equede: Você não vai dar baixa aqui em ninguém!
> Taís: Quem é você? Quer me xoxar, é? Quer me jogar prá cima? Eu não lhe conheço como nada—porta de bater, cancela de receber, abiã sem quartinha, rodante sem pai e mãe, iaô raspada por iaô, exua mal assentada no fundo da minha casa!

> Taís: Who messed with the *caboclo*? I'm going to give them a *baixa*!
> *Equede* [female dignitary of the house]: You're not going to give anyone a *baixa* here!
> Taís: Who are you? Do you want to bad-mouth me, eh? Do you want to get into a fight? I don't even know who you are—door for knocking, gate for receiving [clients in a brothel], *abiã* [uninitiated person] without pot [vessel used to hold water during initiation], dancer [in the circular dance of Candomblé rituals] without father or mother [-of-saint], *iaô* [daughter-of-saint] shaved by *iaô* [a daughter-of-saint's head must be shaved by a

father- or mother-of-saint, not by a fellow daughter], *exua* badly "seated" at the back of my house [the *exus* should be "seated" at the front of a house]!

Edivaldo's *caboclo*, Tupinambá, whom Taís had been attempting to defend, then asked Taís to leave.

* * *

I moved to Fernando Pessoa shortly after Archipiado left to go to the United States for a month. (His visa came through some few hours before he had to catch his plane.) I began to spend most of my time in Jaraci, and in the other districts of Fernando Pessoa where the Jaracians had connections. A lot of the time I was in the company of Taís.

I wanted to ask Taís to come to my apartment to record Candomblé stories and songs. My conscience was troubled that, by just hanging out with the Jaracians and writing up field notes after the event, I was not doing "real anthropology." I had made some half-hearted attempts—I did not want to be intrusive—to do recordings in natural contexts, but the results were often incomprehensible, because of the drumming and other background noises that are typical of Candomblé.

However, I decided to leave this invitation until Archipiado's return. I did not want to provide grist for the gossip-mills of Jaraci. My caution, however, was in vain. The rumors sprang up anyway. They may have been started by Marinalvo, who was put out that I was no longer dependent on him for access to the world of Candomblé.

My relations with Marinalvo remained cordial—I was, after all, still his *ogã*, and known locally as the *ogã de ococi*, the "*ogã* of money." In Jaraci my small research grant made me a moderately wealthy man, so I was able to contribute to his festivals without too much strain on my limited budget. But there was increased tension between us.

The background to this tension can be considered from a number of angles. Marinalvo knew that I was one of those people who write books about Candomblé, through whom other houses have become famous. So one of the reasons he accepted me into his *terreiro* may have been his fondness for publicity. But he was not very helpful in giving me the kind of information I would need to "do anthropology." Perhaps he thought that by eking out the information he imparted he would be better able to control the flow of favors expected from me in return.

But the position I was in was not unique to me as a white foreigner.

Parents-of-saint have a reputation for wanting to control the lives of all the members of their *terreiros*. Let me give an example. Marinalvo had an elderly daughter-of-saint who lived in the same street. He passed on to her landlord's wife some information that caused the daughter-of-saint to be evicted. Subsequently Marinalvo was obliged to accommodate her and her family in the *terreiro*, at considerable inconvenience to himself. I can find no explanation for his behavior except that he wanted to demonstrate that he was in control of her life.

Some mornings I would meet Marinalvo in the street, after sleeping in Jaraci, usually at Edivaldo's or Biju's. He would always ask me, without any circumlocution, where I had spent the night. That such behavior is considered typical of parents-of-saint is indicated by a comment made to me by a friend: "I did not leave the house of my parents in order to be supervised by my father-of-saint."

My friendship with Taís made it possible for me to circumvent Marinalvo's supervision, at least to some extent. But it brought with it its own set of complications.

I knew that Taís wanted to hold a festival to "seat" Corquisa, about five weeks from the date I moved to Fernando Pessoa. Corquisa implied that I owed her something for having given Archipiado a successful voyage, even though he had not carried out the "work" she suggested. So I gave Taís an advance contribution towards the expenses of the festival, and also paid him for the recording sessions he did with me. I expected to have to make a larger contribution when the time came for preparations for the festival. But I did not expect to have to bear the whole financial burden on my own. I was accustomed to the situation in Marinalvo's house, where he drew on the resources of the various members of his *terreiro* who could afford to make a contribution to the mounting of any festival. I had also explained to Taís that my own financial circumstances were precarious, because a check I had received from overseas had proved to be invalid, as a result of a clerical error. (This was, in fact, true.)

The day of the festival came round. I was not in a good mood. Archipiado—who, by this time, had returned from the United States—and I had quarreled. In the aftermath I asked him, sarcastically, to tell me about the Brazilian idea of sincerity. Archipiado, never at a loss for words, said that the Brazilian, in order to appear easy to get on with, avoids confrontation, bluntness, and direct requests. This leads to the use of subterfuges and evasions to maintain the appearance of sociability. He contrasted this with what he called the American mania for frankness, which may be at the expense of another person's feelings. He also used this model to explain the fact that in Jaraci requests so often came via or on behalf of third parties, including spirits.

He left to go to the university, and I waited for Taís, who arrived with Edivaldo's sister. We set out for the São Joaquim market, the largest in Bahia, which consists of a maze of permanent stalls selling foodstuffs, household items, and the various requisites for Candomblé rituals and magical practices. Corquisa had earlier given me a note listing all the things she needed for the festival. This is a favorite practice of the spirits. I knew that I did not have enough money to buy them all. So, recalling that Archipiado had explained to me that direct refusal of requests is a solecism, I told Taís how much money I had with me, so that he could calculate which items on the list were essential, and which could be omitted if we ran out of cash. I expected that he would also have money from other sources.

He began by purchasing two brown hens and a black rooster from a man who had them trussed up in a wheelbarrow. This immediately used up sixty percent of my funds. Live fowls are more expensive than those already prepared for the table. It is taken for granted that the only reason for purchasing them alive is so that they can be used in sacrifices. We went on to buy tomatoes, dried shrimp, manioc flour, onions, a bunch of herbs, a knife for the sacrifice, and perhaps one or two other items. The money was running out, and I could feel the tension mounting.

Taís's lids began to droop, and he leaned against a wall with one arm. I could see what was coming. Corquisa did not announce herself, but I knew from the imperious tone of voice who it was. She said, threateningly, that if she had been in my position, she would have bought everything she had requested. We proceeded to a shop that sells earthenware goods. She selected a basin and a pitcher. She ordered me to reach over and get a small pot for her. I picked the wrong one. She commanded me, testily, to get the one she wanted. "Get it yourself!" I snapped.

She was quieter after this, and informed me that she was not Corquisa, but Sete Saia. She said that Corquisa had got pissed off and checked out. Also the festival would not be for Corquisa, as planned, but to "seat" Sete Saia herself. I was expecting to be blamed for Corquisa's anger, and was prepared to say I was no longer interested in having anything to do with the festival. After making a couple more small purchases, including some red candles—there was not enough left to buy the black, red, and white cloth she wanted, nor the roses—we went to a bar, where I had just enough money to buy her a shot of *cachaça*.

She said to me she understood what had happened. For one paranoid and superstitious moment I thought she was referring to my quarrel with Archipiado, although I had not mentioned it. She had said she was cross with him for not giving her anything in return for his successful voyage. I thought, "Has she been interfering in our lives?" But she had money on her mind. She said she knew that if my check had arrived I would have bought everything Corquisa had requested. But she, Sete Saia, had caused the problem with the check, so that Corquisa's festival would not work out. She wanted to be "seated" instead of Corquisa, in order to be able to kill the mother-of-saint who had dumped her previous *assentamento* in the street.

So she had "come in front" of Corquisa. She regarded Corquisa as a brazen upstart. Corquisa had wanted a lavish festival, but this was going to be a simple festival, which was fine with Sete Saia—she was not accustomed to luxury in any case. She added, tactfully, that Corquisa's anger was not with me but with Sete Saia herself.

She went on to talk about the various people she likes and dislikes. She adores Edivaldo's sister, with whom we had been doing the shopping, even though the latter is a woman, and women are worthless—as she, Sete Saia, is one to know. She does not like her *viado* (Taís), and often punishes him. When I asked why, she said she wished he were a man. One day she is going to make a man of him. I will come back to Brazil and find a man where there was once a *viado*.

While we were at the bar there was a sound of breaking glass and the pungent smell of over-fermented alcohol. Sete Saia said this was caused by her presence. I got used to breakages when I was in the company of Taís or his *exuas*. On another occasion I had been having lunch with Taís at a bar near my apartment. My glass, which was well away from the edge of the table, next to a Coke bottle, leapt off and smashed on the floor. Taís said this meant Corquisa was hovering in the vicinity. Neither Taís nor I had touched the glass. If its fall had been caused by the wind, I reasoned, the Coke bottle would have gone too. Shortly afterwards the waiter dropped and smashed a mirror he was carrying.

Eventually Sete Saia decided it was time to leave São Joaquim, and we hauled our purchases to the bus stop. She carried the largest shopping bag on her head. We were just in time for the Fernando Pessoa bus, and sat at the back. Sete Saia proceeded to sing *exua* songs. The other passengers smiled nervously.

Sou eu, sou eu,
Sou eu, eu não nego.
Sou eu, uma Sete Saia,
Que venho da loca da pedra.
Quem quiser saber meu nome
No precisa perguntar.
Eu me chamo Sete Saia,
Aqui ou em qualquer lugar.

It's me, it's me,
It's me, I don't deny it.
It's me, a Sete Saia,
Who come from the hole in the rock.
Whoever wants to know my name
Doesn't need to ask.
I'm called Sete Saia,
Here or in any place.

Juraram me matar
Na porta de um cabaré.
Eu me chamo Sete Saia,
A mulher de Lucifé.

They swore to kill me
At the door of a cabaret.
I'm called Sete Saia,
The wife of Lucifer.

* * *

That night I walked under a full moon, through the streets of Fernando Pessoa, past the shanty-town known as the "invasion," and across the dunes to Jaraci. There was a bonfire in the street outside Edivaldo's. I gave Taís the liquor I had brought from the Comprelucre supermarket in Fernando Pessoa, and went to the bar on the corner to buy more. He placed the bottles in the little shrine he had constructed in one corner of the *barracão*. It was made of branches of a palm called *nicori*, and banana leaves. The same foliage decorated the walls of the *barracão*. Inside the shrine seven red candles were burning.

In spite of Taís's obvious efforts, the festival seemed to be ill-starred. For a start, there were no drums. Edivaldo had lent them to Biju. He had asked for them to be returned the day before, but Biju had lent two of them to someone else. So the festival proceeded without any preliminary drumming and singing.

It began with the sacrifices. Taís had received Sete Saia, who dressed in a costume consisting of a turban, a piece of cloth wrapped round her waist as a skirt, and another wrapped round her chest. Most of the people I knew in Jaraci were there, except for Marinalvo. Taís had invited him, but he had sent apologies. We assembled at the front of Edivaldo's, by the house of Exu. On the ground were two earthenware basins, a pitcher, and a small pot.

The sacrifices were performed by two *ogãs* and another father-of-saint from Jaraci called Luiz. First they slit the throats of the two hens, and sprinkled their blood on the pitcher and the small pot. The hens were passed to Sete Saia, who pressed her mouth to their necks, to drink the blood. Then Sete Saia gave passage to Taís's *exu* Sete Punhal, who swaggered round bare-chested, rubbing his crotch. The sacrificers cut the throat of the black rooster and dribbled blood into one of the clay basins, which contained beer and oil. Sete Punhal then drank blood from the cut. The heads of the three birds were severed about three quarters of the way through, to let the blood escape, then tucked under their wings. The birds were placed on the ground while the sacrificers performed the *lobaça* oracle, to determine whether the spirits had accepted the offerings.

This divination procedure consists of throwing the two halves of an onion (*lobaça*). On the first throw the two halves landed with different sides up. This is an uncertain result, and requires another throw. Sete Punhal said to put some *cachaça* on the onion. I could not see the result of the second throw, but it must have been the same, because the onion was thrown a third time. Again, one half landed face up and the other face down. Finally, on the fourth throw, both halves landed face up. There was applause.

The sacrificers proceeded to cut off the heads, legs, and wings of the fowls. These parts were placed in the second earthenware basin, which would subsequently be taken and left at a crossroad, or in the forest, to "suspend the sacrifice." The bodies of the birds were taken to the kitchen.

The ritual objects of Taís's *exus*—the pitcher and pot of Sete Saia and the basin of Sete Punhal—were placed in the house of Exu. Biju counseled me that now I had to bless the sacrifice by leaving "money on the ground."

This expression refers to the payment of ritual assistants. I had spent almost all the money I had with me buying liquor for the festival. I went into the house of Exu and placed on the ground the few notes I had left. The sacrificers hurried in. There was some dispute, which I could not hear clearly from outside. I think they were arguing because the amount I had left could not be divided equally three ways. Luiz complained to Sete Saia—who by this time had returned, displacing Sete Punhal—that the amount I had left was very little.

Luiz is one of the six fathers-of-saint who live in the same small area of Jaraci. Three of the others were also present: Edivaldo, in whose *terreiro* the festival took place; Biju; and Oswaldo. Edivaldo had received his *caboclo*, Tupinambá, before the sacrifice, and Oswaldo had received an entity I did not recognize. (It was probably a spirit called Biscó, who is Oswaldo's *egum*. An *egum* is the spirit of someone who has died.)

After the sacrifice we returned to the *barracão*. Tupinambá gave passage to Edivaldo's Padilha, called Maria Eugênia—an *exua* of exquisite refinement, who dusts off a chair before sitting down, and drinks with her little finger crooked. Biju received his Pomba-Gira, who was quiet and mysterious. Luiz received an *exu* called Zé-Pelintra, who proceeded to sing a song about how he had murdered all the members of his family.

There was some desultory singing and dancing, but without the drums it seemed to lack enthusiasm. Sete Saia attempted to liven things up by doing the dance in which she mimes intercourse with a beer bottle. Zé-Pelintra obviously thought the bottle was a poor substitute, and they performed an erotic number together. Edivaldo's brother Toninho, who is also one of his sons-of-saint but was not in trance, came up behind Sete Saia, and they mimicked a threesome.

One of Biju's sons-of-saint was drinking heavily. He took Sete Saia's glass while she was out of the *barracão*, and received an earful of abuse when she returned. He put the glass down on the ground next to her, and was told it was bad manners not to return it to her hand. Suddenly he began to lurch about, and gave a deep and evil chuckle. He had received a very surly *exu*, who went around verbally accosting those in his vicinity. The *ogã* Dinho was prevailed upon to "suspend" this spirit immediately. Biju's son-of-saint was only recently initiated, and not very practiced in the etiquette of trance. He subsequently received his *caboclo*, who was better accepted.

The *ogãs* engaged in some verbal games, imitating the speech of different spirit entities—not just the general style characteristic of particular categories of spirits, but also the personal linguistic idiosyncracies of individual spirits who were familiar to the audience.

Each of the categories of spirits in Candomblé, except for the *exus*, has its own particular style of speech, which differs in various ways from the speech of mortals. The speech of the *exus*, by contrast, was described to me by Taís as "ordinary." (I analyze the speech styles of other spirits in later chapters.) It is interesting that, out of all the spirits, only the *exus* speak the language of ordinary human beings.

This does not mean, however, that the speech style of any particular *exu* is necessarily the same as that of his or her material vehicle. For example, an *exua* incorporated in a male body will often speak in a high-pitched voice. Also the language of an *exua* will tend to be either educated Portuguese, if she is "refined" like Corquisa, or street language, if she is "coarse" like Sete Saia. Interestingly this variation along class lines is not characteristic of the language of the male *exus*, whose typical speech style is the kind of slang associated with the *malandro* (a type of stylish con-man) of Rio de Janeiro.

I should add that the *exus* sometimes *do* use the same language as their "matter," as when Corquisa and Sete Saia dropped their falsetto and characteristic sociolects, and spoke in the voice of Taís.

The mastery of the various speech styles of the spirits of Candomblé requires considerable skill, so the *ogãs*' clever performance was a demonstration of their status as insiders in a somewhat exclusive speech community.

It was getting late, and the festival was coming to an end. I saw Sete Saia chewing on the hearts of the chickens that had been sacrificed, and told her I wanted to leave. She said that what I had given for the festival would bring me happiness, that the money I had spent would come back doubled. She added that whenever I wanted to make a request of her, either to help me or someone else, or to do someone harm, all I had to do was leave a note in her basin in the house of Exu. I appreciated this courtesy, since I knew that the *exus* never express thanks.

* * *

This event was the only *exu* festival I had the opportunity to witness in its entirety during my time in Bahia. Public festivals for the *exus* are much less common than those for the *orixás* and *caboclos*, of which I attended many. Often the sacrifices for Exu that I heard about were carried out in the context of private ceremonies.

Although its purpose was to "seat" Taís's *exus*, it struck me that, in terms of its format, this event had a good deal in common with festivals for the *caboclos*. Taís confirmed this observation in subsequent discussions. The literature on Candomblé has paid little attention to the pattern of these festivals, so I have devoted a later chapter to the subject. But let me make some preliminary remarks here.

Some *terreiros* in Bahia hold public celebrations only for the *orixás*, and others only for the *caboclos* (cf. Ribeiro 1983; Ferreira 1984). But many, perhaps the majority, mount festivals for both these categories of spirits. In some *terreiros* the *caboclos* have a single cycle of festivities in the course of the year. In others—and this seemed to be the common pattern in Jaraci—the *caboclos* have their special public festival, but also descend after most celebrations for the *orixás*. This practice is reminiscent of the Greek theatre, where tragedy would be followed by comedy; for the two kinds of festival differ not only in terms of the spirits being honored, but also in terms of their tone.

Festivals of the *orixás* are characterized by their formality. In spite of the drumming, dancing, and trances, they not infrequently reminded me of stately church services. They use a liturgical language, the meaning of which is at best only vaguely understood by the majority of participants. They have a fairly fixed structure, which allows little room for spontaneity or for interaction between the "celebrants" and the "congregation." The use of liquor, if it occurs at all in the course of the ritual itself, is highly controlled.

The tone of *caboclo* festivals is more effervescent. The spirits speak and sing mostly in the vernacular. There is more spontaneous interaction among the participants, both spirit and human—aided by the consumption of alcohol by all present. And the format is less predetermined, and more open to being influenced by the interactions that take place.

I should add that *caboclo* festivals themselves vary in their degree of formality. Public *caboclo* festivals are planned and fairly highly structured, though not to the same extent as festivals of the *orixás*. One of the characteristics of life in Jaraci, however, was the frequent occurrence of unplanned private celebrations, at which a variety of spirits might materialize, and which followed loosely the general format of *caboclo* festivals. Usually they took place inside a *terreiro*, but not always. Sometimes they would happen at a bar owned by one particular *ogã*.

The festival for the seating of Taís's *exus* was a planned, public festival, but had many of the characteristics of a spontaneous, private celebration. Since I had witnessed no other complete *exu* festivals with which I could compare it, I asked Taís, during one of our recording sessions a few days later, what are the regularly occurring components of such festivals. He described the following "ideal" pattern.

The festival begins with the sacrifice, which is followed by the songs of greeting that the *exus* sing as they arrive, or that the audience sings to welcome them. The *exus* then sing songs to "call" other *exus*—that is, to induce people who are not in trance to receive their *exus*. Next come the songs of provocation the *exus* sing to each other, or to members of the audience, challenging them to put on a livelier performance. The climax is the "*exus*' samba circle," characterized by enthusiastic singing, dancing, drinking, and flirtation, involving both audience and *exus*. The festival ends with a farewell song sung by the *exus* as they prepare to leave their "matter."

This is the same general pattern as a *caboclo* festival, except that there are fewer episodes, and the possibilities within each episode are more limited. Taís knew only a few songs for each episode, by comparison with the dozens he knew for the episodes of a *caboclo* festival. He gave me, for example, only two farewell songs. Moreover, the songs of the *exus* are less individualized. Some *exus* have their own songs, as the *caboclos* do, but most draw on a pool of songs appropriate to their gender, and insert their own names where this is called for in the songs.

The type of *exu* festival described by Taís, and the various kinds of *caboclo* festival I have described above, presumably have a common origin, perhaps in popular celebrations centering around the samba circle, which is a common feature of secular festivities. Taís said that many of the *exus*' sambas are identical to those sung by the *caboclos*. The evolution of *exu* festivals seems to be comparatively rudimentary, perhaps because they are less frequent and less public than *caboclo* festivals.

But my interest here is less in the history of these festivals than in the fact that their similarity suggests a certain affinity between the two categories of spirits they celebrate. Corquisa once said to me, "we [the *exus*] and the *caboclos* understand each other."

Both the *caboclos* and the *exus* are identified with marginal social groups—the *caboclos* with Indians and backwoodsmen, and the *exus* with the inhabitants of the *brega*. Both are also said to be "close to matter," so it is to the *caboclos* or the *exus* that one turns for help with problems in the material world. Both may give consultations, and both may perform "works." Both have a taste for partying, strong drink, and flirtation.

There are, however, important differences between them. The account of the *caboclos* in Part 2 will show some of the ways that they are distinct from the *exus*. For the moment I will mention just one distinguishing feature, which strikes me as somehow representative. The *caboclos* are capable of weeping, while the *exus* are not.

* * *

One of the last times I saw Corquisa was when she and Tupinambá, Taís's *caboclo*, collaborated in the performance of a love-magic rite on behalf of a couple who were soon to be separated. I had the impression that Corquisa undertook this "work" on her own initiative, without having been asked.

A friend of Taís's called Rita was visiting at the time, and she and I acted as ritual assistants. We began by cooking up a pot of white corn, the food of Oxalá, father of the gods, who was "owner of the head" of one of the parties, and a pot of *feijão fradinho*, a bean that is the food of Oxum, goddess of love, who was the "owner of the head" of the other party. Rita was set to work removing the heads from dried shrimp. I had to cut off the thorns from three white roses. Corquisa laid a straw mat on the floor, and on top of it a white cloth, on which the offerings would be placed. She also tied strips of white cloth around various items used in the rite, such as the knife and the bottle of lavender water.

The first part of the "work" consisted of building up a cruciform pattern of offerings on the mat. Corquisa began at the bottom of what was to become a cross, and put there a glass containing the three roses. Above this she placed a saucer with a burning candle. Next came a glass of red wine, then a plate with two lighted candles, between which she poured a small quantity of honey and red wine. These four items constituted the shaft of the cross. Corquisa then sprinkled Rita and me, and the offerings, with lavender water.

There was a break in the proceedings while the names of the couple were written, together, on slips of paper. Corquisa bound one slip with a strip of cloth around the right leg of a reluctant dove, which had been languishing in a paper bag. She also tied its wings. She placed another slip in the middle of the plate with two candles, and covered it with honey. Rita and I brought four more plates. Corquisa put one—a large serving dish—above the plate with two candles, where it was to form the center of the cross. The slip of paper she placed on this dish was different from the others. On one side were the names of the couple, the names of their *orixás*, and their *orixás*' salutations: *Oraieieu* for Oxum, and *Cheueu Babá* for Oxalá. On the reverse side the names of the couple had been written on top of each other, so that the letters intermingled. Over this slip of paper Corquisa heaped the white corn, then added a small quantity of *feijão fradinho*, and the three roses.

She proceeded to put down two smaller plates, one on either side of the serving dish, to form the arms of the cross. She placed a slip of paper on each, then a quantity of white corn, topped by a smaller quantity of *feijão fradinho*. Finally she set down a large plate at the head of the cross, placed on it a slip of paper, covered this with *feijão fradinho*, to which had been added the dried shrimp and a quantity of *agua de flor* ("flower water"), and topped off the arrangement with three boiled eggs, laid out in a horizontal line.

The time had come for the *lobaça* divination. Corquisa asked for a "male" onion, and cut it in half. She threw twice. The first time one half landed face up, the other face down. The second time both halves fell face up. She took another slip of paper and placed it on the face of one half of the onion. She covered this with honey, laid the other half on top, put the onion in the middle of the plate with two candles, and poured more honey over it. She said that the onion represented sadness, of which the couple would have much. She added that the roses represented love, and the dove happiness.

Rita, who had asked if she could add a note of her own to the central dish, to help with a problem in her romantic life, observed that this "work" was so powerful it was dangerous—it would bind the couple together so tightly that they would never be able to escape from their relationship, unless they carried out another work to undo this one. She added that she had once commissioned a "work" of this kind, with the result that her boyfriend became insanely jealous. She could not go out with either women or men without arousing his suspicion.

Corquisa announced that she was leaving, to make way for "the Indian," who would complete the "work," but she would return in three days to "raise" the *ebó* (the technical term for a "work"). This would entail taking it to the sea. Three days would be necessary to allow the *ebó* to rest. She began to sway back and forth on her chair, and closed her eyes.

The eyes that opened again were those of Tupinambá, who immediately asked, in a deep *caboclo* accent, for something to drink. This being provided, he went into the room where the *ebó* was laid out, lifted up each of the plates of food, and replaced it. He then took the dove and removed the strip of cloth which bound the slip of paper to its leg. He tied the cloth around the paper in such a way that it formed four loops, and placed it on the serving dish in the center of the *ebó*, so that its loops made a cross. He took the glass of wine, and poured it over the ribbon. He went about his work in a much more casual way than Corquisa, taking an occasional swig from his glass of vodka, chatting with Rita and me, singing snatches of *caboclo* songs, putting us at ease.

He untied the dove's wings and took it to the window. He gave it a poetic farewell, linking its two wings to the couple on whose behalf the rite was being performed, its release to their freedom from trouble, its joy in flight to their future happiness.

He let it go, and it flew away.

He asked for some more vodka. The three of us sat and drank, resting. He began to sway. I pressed on his shoulders and clapped above his head.

Taís asked if he had been sleeping. We explained the events of the day. He went to see the *ebó*, and remarked how beautiful it was.

II

Caboclo

It is always the colonial view of the jungle that provides the means for representing and trying to make sense of the colonial situation. Emptiness and absence become assimilating presences. The nebulous becomes corporeal and tangible. And in this dreadful object-making, as shadows of things acquire substance, a veil of lifelessness, if not death, is drawn apart to reveal the forest not merely as animated but as human . . .

And the truth of the matter, the savagery of the Indians? Each person's opinion contradicts the next and each opinion contradicts itself in a surfeit of ambiguous images—a montage of bits and pieces of possibility colliding into one another, no less chaotic than a page from Casement's diary and no less indebted to the surreality of the colonial unconscious with its phantoms of various shapes and guises stalking each other in the thicket of their differences. Indeed, to Alfred Simpson, the defining quality of the forest Indian was precisely the imprecise in a wild medley of difference. 'At all times they are unchangeable and unreliable, betraying under different circumstances, and often apparently under the same, in common with so many of their class, all the opposite traits of character.' Except stinginess and, perhaps, servility.

Michael Taussig, *Shamanism, Colonialism, and the Wild Man* (1987:77, 91)

4. Order and Progress

Brazil, like the continent in which the *orixás* originated, and like Australia, the land of my birth, lies on the surface of that half of the planet usually considered to be the "bottom." There the stars of the night sky—represented on the Brazilian flag, with the Southern Cross at their center—are different from those seen in northern latitudes, and the cycle of the seasons is reversed, if considered from a northern perspective. However, the solar festivals introduced to the southern hemisphere from Europe are celebrated on the same dates as in the Old World. So, for example, Christmas coincides, in the south, with the height of summer, rather than with the winter solstice; and the feast of St. John, celebrated in Brazil, as in Europe, with fires, marks the southern mid-winter, rather than the turning point of summer.

The southern hemisphere has, of course, its own festivals, in addition to those brought from Europe. Some of these are secular occasions, such as the public holidays that affirm a national identity; and some derive, whether historically or whimsically, from the religious celebrations of the original inhabitants of the hemisphere. In the *caboclo* festivals of Bahia these two kinds of event, with their differing symbolic import, are made to coincide.

Although I attended *caboclo* festivals in Candomblé houses from March to August, the "official" day for their celebration is the second of July, the date of the independence of Bahia. The national colors of green and yellow predominate in the decorations used for these festivals, and any *terreiro* that can afford it adorns the *barracão* and the hut of the resident *caboclos* with strings of Brazilian flags. To understand the link between *caboclos*, Bahian independence, and the national flag, we need to consider certain recurrent themes of Brazilian history.

Brazil celebrates its independence on the seventh of September, the date on which, in 1822, the Portuguese prince Dom Pedro, subsequently the first emperor of Brazil, declared the nation's autonomy, and thus his own independence from his father, João VI of Portugal. As a result of a certain resistance on the part of administrators loyal to the Portuguese crown, the revolution came late to Bahia. On the second of July, 1823, the new government staged a triumphal entry into Salvador—with the help, it is said, of certain Indian tribes.

Indians had a long symbolic association with Brazilian nationalism. An earlier, unsuccessful independence movement, called the *Inconfidência Mineira* and led by the hero Tiradentes, had designed a flag that pictured an Indian breaking his chains.

The flag of the new nation did not incorporate an Indian motif. It consisted of a yellow diamond on a green background, with the imperial coat of arms at the center. When Brazil was declared a republic in 1889, only the central blazon was changed, to be replaced by a blue circle embellished with the constellations of the southern sky, and a white arc containing the words *ORDEM E PROGRESSO*, the Portuguese translation of Auguste Comte's motto, "Order and Progress."

Each of these turning points in Brazilian history was accompanied by a certain utopian rhetoric, based on the notion of the establishment of a new social order, in which *communitas* (to use Victor Turner's [1979] term) would replace the old structures of domination. It scarcely needs to be said that the historical facts belie the rhetoric. Brazil has always been, and remains, a highly stratified nation under the control of an elite—what Roett (1984) calls a "patrimonial society."

Nonetheless the aspiration reflected in the rhetoric is real enough, and it is this sentiment that Brazilians celebrate when they parade the yellow and green—the colors of spring, of the new beginning. There are numerous patriotic dates on the Brazilian calendar that provide the opportunity for expression of this sentiment. But for Bahians the most important of them is undoubtedly the second of July, the day when the flag and the *caboclo* are linked.

Although this link is generally rationalized in terms of the help given by the Indians to the army that liberated Bahia from Portuguese domination, there is a deeper connection. The flag is an abstract symbol of the same utopian aspirations that the Indians embody, at least in the popular imagination, in a real, concrete community. The strength of this symbolic link can be seen from the fact that *caboclo* festivals held in states other than Bahia also habitually use the Brazilian flag as a decorative motif, and may take place on a date close to the second of July, which is then thought of more as the "day of the *caboclo*" rather than as the day of the independence of Bahia.

The term *caboclo* (which in Candomblé is usually pronounced without the *l*, as *caboco*) is said to come from the Tupi word *kari'boka*, meaning "deriving from the white" (Ferreira 1975:242). Thus its primary meaning is "mestizo," "a person of part Indian and part European descent." But it may also be used to refer to any Brazilian Indian. The difference between these two uses of the term in ordinary Brazilian Portuguese has carried over into Candomblé, where there are two basic categories of *caboclo* spirits: those called *boiadeiros*, or "cowboys," "backwoodsmen" (Boiadeiro is also the proper name of one particular *caboclo*), who wear hats of leather or straw, and sometimes also fringed leather jackets and knickerbockers; and those called "Indians," who often wear feather headdresses, and may be costumed in feathers, fur, or hide.

These are the only types of *caboclo* I myself saw at the festivals I attended. However, I have heard of others. There are, for example, various foreign *caboclos*, such as the King of Hungary (who is the *caboclo* of a famous Bahian mother-of-saint called Olga of Alaketu [Santos 1984]), and Italian and Japanese *caboclos*. There are also *caboclos* of the "village of the sea," such as the sailor *caboclos*.

Taís once said to me "*caboclos* are infinite," in contrast with the *orixás*, of whom there is a fixed number. It seems that in spite of the nationalistic overtones of the utopian sentiments with which the *caboclos* are associated, these same sentiments are capable of creating a sense of universal brotherhood, into which non-Indians and non-Brazilians can be incorporated. Perhaps the etymological link between the *caboclo* and the blending of races makes the *caboclo* tradition the obvious symbolic vehicle for the incorporation into Candomblé of foreign elements.

I have called the sentiments motivating the tradition of the *caboclos* "utopian." But we could also think of them as "carnivalesque," in the sense in which this notion has been elaborated by Mikhail Bakhtin. In his work on Rabelais, Bakhtin has developed a "carnival principle," which underlies not just the carnivals of the Middle Ages and Renaissance that provided imagery for Rabelais, but any manifestation of the "nonofficial, extraecclesiastical and extrapolitical aspect of the world, of man, and of human relationships (Bakhtin 1984:6). Carnival celebrates "temporary liberation from the prevailing truth and the established order"; it marks "the suspension of all hierarchical rank, privileges, norms, and prohibitions" (1984:10).

Structurally, at least, one could say that Candomblé as a whole has traditionally stood in a "carnivalesque" relationship to official Brazilian culture. Like the folk celebrations of the Middle Ages, the festivals of the African gods were originally the popular, "nonofficial" counterparts of the feasts of the church. In Candomblé every *orixá* corresponds to a Christian saint, and was traditionally celebrated on a date close to that of the saint's day, with dancing, drinking, and feasting. (It is worth recalling also that the colonization of Brazil began during the lifetime of Rabelais; so the possibility of a historical link between Candomblé and the European folk traditions of that era is not implausible. Cf. Williams 1979:9.)

However, since the early decades of this century certain leaders of Candomblé, aided by anthropologists and other sympathetic intellectuals, have struggled to make Candomblé an "official" religion, with a status on a par with that of the Catholic Church. Their strategy for doing this has entailed attempting to divest Candomblé of its carnivalesque elements, and emphasizing its orthodoxy as an African religion. The result has been the evolution of a notion of degrees of "purity" in Candomblé. Religious centers that are "pure" are those that have tried to discard all that is "folkloric" and "syncretistic," and to incorporate as much as possible that is African (cf. Dantas 1982; Birman 1980:6–31; Frigerio 1983; on the prejudice against syncretism, cf. Berling 1980:4–9).

Perhaps the most extreme example is a famous *terreiro* called Ilê Axé Opô Afonjá, which in its process of re-Africanization has been largely purged of Christian iconography. (But even this *terreiro* has not been able to remove all traces of syncretism. Its ritual calendar is still tied, at least in part, to the feast days of the church [Maia 1985:99].) The mother-of-saint of this *terreiro*, Stella Azevedo, wrote a short paper called "Syncretism and Whitening" for the Third International Congress of Orisa Tradition and Culture, which I attended in New York in 1986. After stating that freed slaves, through a desire to "whiten" themselves, adopted practices that syncretized Catholicism and "traces of Africanism," she concludes with these words: "But, in the present times of total liberation, it is worth remembering that these maneuvers ought to be abandoned, with all people assuming the religion of their roots" (1986:2).

I am not unsympathetic to the political motivation behind these remarks. I recognize that the re-Africanization of Candomblé, based on the idea of throwing off white domination, has considerable symbolic significance for the Movimento Negro Unificado—a loose affiliation of Black activist groups in Brazil, concerned with political and economic justice for Blacks, and the fostering of a positive Black identity.

However, the re-Africanization movement in Candomblé has a number of consequences that in some ways undermine the aspirations that inspired it. To begin with, it promotes comparison between *terreiros* on the basis of the degree to which they are "orthodox" or "traditional." These terms are frequently encountered in the literature on Candomblé, but it is hard to know what justifies their usage. Since Candomblé, unlike the Catholic Church, has no central body responsible for the formulation of doctrine and the regulation of practice, and every initiatic lineage is, in effect, a law unto itself, there is no basis for judging any *terreiro* as more or less "orthodox" than any other. Moreover, if one takes "traditional" to mean "based on long-standing custom," there would be grounds for arguing that "syncretistic" *terreiros* are more "traditional" than the re-Africanized ones, since, as Mother Stella herself points out, syncretism historically *preceded* the re-Africanization movement (cf. Mott 1988).

Another consequence has been a certain bias in anthropological studies of Candomblé—a tendency to write about it as an "abstract corpus of beliefs deriving from Africa" (Frigerio 1983:45), rather than as a living social form embedded in the realities of contemporary Brazil. But in terms of my present concerns the most interesting consequence lies in the paradoxical fact that the re-Africanization movement, while aiming to counter white domination, has in some sense capitulated to it. In seeking the status of an "official" religion for Candomblé, the re-Africanized *terreiros* have conformed themselves to the dominant culture's idea of what a religion should be—often with the assistance of anthropologists.

From the perspective of the dominant culture, a religion should have a systematized metalanguage corresponding to the notion of theology or philosophy. Roberto Motta has pointed out that for the Afro-Brazilian religions "anthropology itself becomes transformed into a rationalizing metalanguage, through its search for origins and its classificatory endeavors. Hence the almost symbiotic relationship that is established (the Bahian examples are celebrated) between researchers and fathers- and mothers-of-saint" (1987:79). Further, a "religion" should not be involved with "charlatanism" and "black magic," so the re-Africanized *terreiros* dissociate themselves, at least officially, from such practices. A religion should, instead, be respectable. I would find it hard to count the number of times that I have seen the so-called "orthodox" *terreiros* praised—usually, of course, by white writers—as "dignified."

In all of this, it could be argued, the re-Africanized *terreiros* have overlooked the fact that the "carnivalesque" elements they have abandoned have been, historically, powerful weapons for countering the domination of white culture.

Moreover, some of these elements, in particular the kind of rhetorical play that is characteristic of the *caboclos*, have probably as much affinity with African traditions (cf. Gates 1988:53) as the body of beliefs that is alleged to be "orthodox." But this affinity is at the level of pragmatics rather than semantics.

Lapassade and Luz have written an interesting Marxist-Freudian analysis of Quimbanda—the Afro-Brazilian religion most closely associated with black magic—as a "counterculture," which they see as any cultural form that contests the ideology of the dominant classes. Quimbanda lacks respectability not just because of its association with black magic, but also because of the predominance in its rituals of "sexual provocation, slang, obscenities, *cachaça*, cigars, etc." (1972:xxiii). Quimbanda is a religion of Rio de Janeiro; but Lapassade and Luz point out that the religious practices closest to it in Bahia are those associated with the *caboclos* (1972:6).

It is not surprising, then, that the *caboclo* tradition has been largely suppressed in the re-Africanized *terreiros*. According to Frigerio (1983:22), Engenho Velho and Gantois no longer celebrate the *caboclos*, although apparently they once did. And Ilê Axé Opô Afonjá, although it cultivates the *caboclos*, holds no public ceremonies for them.

If it is true that the festivals of the *orixás* have a structurally carnivalesque relationship to the saints' days of the church, it may seem that the additional carnivalesque rituals of the *caboclos* are redundant. But the point is, I think, that Bakhtin's "carnival principle" is relative. So, while the festivals of the *orixás* are carnivalesque in relation to the "official" religious celebrations of the church, in the world of Candomblé itself the *orixás*' rituals are "official." The *caboclos* provide the carnivalesque element *within* Candomblé—and thus, I suppose, are doubly carnivalesque in relation to the dominant culture. (It is worth noting in this connection that the ritual of the *caboclos* is the only Candomblé celebration that is linked to a secular rather than a religious holiday. This suggests that the nation-state is structurally carnivalesque in relation to the church.) One could go further, and say that the world of the *caboclos* has its own "official" side, in the *caboclo* festivals that are celebrated publicly, and that within this world the carnivalesque side is provided by spontaneous private *caboclo* festivities.

* * *

Bakhtin's "carnival principle" provides a useful analytic tool for understanding the symbolism of the *caboclos'* world, so I will treat it in some detail here, before going on to a consideration of the various facets of that world.

The carnival principle is closely linked to all the other major themes in Bakhtin's *oeuvre*—to his ideas about heteroglossia, dialogism, reported speech, and novelization. All of these notions are particular formulations, in different domains, of Bakhtin's general strategy for understanding the multi-dimensionality of human experience. This strategy entails, essentially, viewing the human being as non-hermetic, a perspective opposed to what he calls "the bourgeois conception of the completed atomized being" (1984:24). Let me trace Bakhtin's use of this "principle of permeable boundaries," as we might call it, in the various domains in which he has elaborated it.

In his writings on carnival, Bakhtin maintains that one of its most salient characteristics is its use of imagery involving what he calls the "grotesque body."

> Contrary to modern canons, the grotesque body is not separated from the rest of the world. It is not a closed, completed unit; it is unfinished, outgrows itself, transgresses its own limits. The stress is laid on those parts of the body that are open to the outside world, that is, the parts through which the world enters the body or emerges from it, or through which the body itself goes out to meet the world. This means that the emphasis is on the apertures or the convexities, or on various ramifications and offshoots: the open mouth, the genital organs, the breasts, the phallus, the potbelly, the nose. The body discloses its essence as a principle of growth which exceeds its own limits only in copulation, pregnancy, childbirth, the throes of death, eating, drinking, or defecation. This is the ever unfinished, ever creating body, the link in the chain of genetic development, or more correctly speaking, two links shown at the point where they enter into each other (1984:26).

In the domain of linguistics Bakhtin has developed a model very different from that of linguists whose theories are premised on the notion of a solipsistic, hermetic "ideal speaker-hearer." He views language rather in a "grotesque" light, as one of those experiences through which "the world enters the body or emerges from it, or through which the body itself goes out to meet the world." For Bakhtin language has to be seen as a form of human interaction with the world—in particular, of course, interaction between people (1988:ch. 6). Hence the crucial importance in his writings of the idea of dialogue.

But it is not just the human *experience* of language that Bakhtin views in this grotesque light. He sees language itself from the same perspective. If we regard a person's linguistic production as a corpus, or body of utterances, it is a grotesque, non-hermetic body, because it is pervaded by, and pervades, the utterances of others. Pomorska has summarized the point nicely when she says that one of Bakhtin's outstanding ideas is

> his discovery that *quoted speech* . . . permeates all our language activities in both practical and artistic communication. Bakhtin reveals the constant presence of this phenomenon in a vast number of examples from all areas of life: literature, ethics, politics, law, and inner speech. He points to the fact that we are actually dealing with someone else's words more often than our own. Either we remember and respond to someone else's words (in the case of ethics); or we represent them in order to argue, disagree, or defend them (in the case of law); or, finally, we carry on an inner dialogue, responding to someone else's words (including our own). In each case someone else's speech makes it possible to generate our own, and thus becomes an indispensable factor in the creative power of language (1984:ix).

In developing the concept of heteroglossia, Bakhtin has attempted to relate his micro-sociological insights about dialogue to a more macro-sociological perspective. We could think of heteroglossia as a kind of "macro-dialogue"—Bakhtin's response to the Saussurean *langue* (language as a macro-social fact).

Bakhtin sees two kinds of social forces at work in language, which he calls "centrifugal" and "centripetal." The centrifugal forces are those that attempt to fix, standardize, centralize, and unify language. Socially, they are the institutions (political, academic, ecclesiastical, commercial) that produce codifications of pronunciation, spelling, grammar, style, and rhetoric, and attempt to impose the use of one kind of language rather than another. These are the forces that decontextualize the sign, that emphasize its "reiterability," its identity with itself from one context to another. The centripetal forces are those that contextualize the sign, that give each instance of it a particular, unique meaning. Socially, they are the dialect groups, social classes, generations, professional bodies, movements, schools, circles, etc., that use the sign in varying, contradictory, and intersecting ways. Bakhtin sometimes uses "heteroglossia" to mean the tension between the centrifugal and centripetal forces, and sometimes to refer to the centripetal forces only (cf. Bakhtin 1981:272). This is not necessarily contradictory, since from a certain perspective the centrifugal forces could be seen as *included* in the centripetal forces.

In any case, for present purposes what is interesting about the notion of heteroglossia is Bakhtin's emphasis on the non-hermetic nature of language as a macro-sociological phenomenon. He views language in the same way as the grotesque body, as "ever unfinished, ever creating"—and as being inextricably linked to the organic and social life of the world.

In his literary studies Bakhtin has developed a theory of the novel that characterizes it not as a particular period genre, but as any literary form that uses language in a way that is heteroglot or carnivalesque. The novel is "non-hermetic," because, like the grotesque body, it has permeable boundaries. Holquist says of Bakhtin's ideas about "novelization" that

> literary systems are comprised of canons, and "novelization" is fundamentally anticanonical. It will not permit generic monologue. Always it will insist on the dialogue between what a given system will admit as literature and those texts that are otherwise excluded from such a definition of literature (1981:xxxi).

The novel can be contrasted with the usual notion of a genre, in that genres are "constituted by a set of formal features for fixing language that pre-exist any specific utterances within the genre" (Holquist 1981:xxix). Genres are, in effect, the literary equivalent of the "bourgeois conception of the completed atomized being." But the novel is "best conceived of either as a supergenre, whose power consists in its ability to engulf and ingest all other genres (the different and separate languages peculiar to each), together with other stylized but non-literary forms of language; or not a genre in any strict, traditional sense at all" (Holquist 1981:xxix).

From this perspective it is possible to speak of "the novelistic principle," defined by Holquist as "the proclivity to display different languages interpenetrating each other"; or of "novelness," characterized as a "consciously structured hybrid of languages" (Holquist 1981:xxix). The "novelistic principle" and "novelness" may, of course, have a part to play in genres other than the one conventionally defined as the novel—perhaps even in the genre called "ethnography."

The thrust of Bakhtin's *oeuvre*, then, is to show that entities considered from one perspective to be fixed, bounded, and completed—the body, social structure, language, and literary genres—can be seen, alternatively, as having an existence that is constituted by their interpenetration and incorporation of each other.

There is an important aspect of all this that is only partially explored in Bakhtin's work, and that deserves some elaboration. The two perspectives that Bakhtin differentiates—what we might call the "hermetic" and the "non-hermetic" perspectives—tend to be associated with different orientational metaphors, with the hermetic perspective being considered "up" and the non-hermetic perspective being considered "down."

To understand why this should be so, it will be helpful to consider Mary Douglas's reflections on body symbolism. Douglas's thesis is that "bodily control is an expression of social control" (1973:99). She goes on,

> Social intercourse requires that unintended or irrelevant organic processes should be screened out. . . . Socialization teaches the child to bring organic processes under control. Of these, the most irrelevant and unwanted are the casting-off of waste products. Therefore all such physical events, defecation, urination, vomiting and their products, uniformly carry a pejorative sign for formal discourse. . . . The more refinement, the less smacking of lips when eating, the less mastication, the less the sound of breathing and walking, the more carefully modulated the laughter, the more controlled the signs of anger, the clearer comes the priestly-aristocratic image (1973:101–2).

In other words, the "refined," hermetic body is considered "up," and associated with the higher, controlling strata of society, because of its connection with conscious control, located in the head; and the "coarse," non-hermetic body is considered "down," and associated with the lower, controlled strata, due to its link with "lower" bodily functions.

* * *

The *orixás* are African aristocrats, who sometimes wear the crowns—fringed or cowrie-studded, as in Africa, or cruciform, as in Europe—of royalty. When they descend into "matter," they keep their mouths and eyes closed.

I have only once heard an *orixá* speak, and that was in the most famous re-Africanized *terreiro* of Fernando Pessoa, where the Xangô of the father-of-saint delivered an oration in Yoruba, on his feast day. Generally the *orixás* do not talk, though I have occasionally seen them whispering instructions to the drummers at a festival. Nor do they eat, drink, or smoke—at least not in a material fashion. They consume "spiritually" the offerings that are made to them. As far as one can see, they have none of the needs or functions of the grotesque body. During rituals they wait patiently for their turn to dance, and perform with movements that, while often vigorous, are highly stylized and controlled.

The *orixás'* bodily functions are performed for them by their *erês*, or "child spirits," to whom they usually "give passage" when they depart from their material vehicles. The *erês* are the most uncontrolled and "grotesque" of all the spirits. They are hungry, obscene, thieving, boisterous, gossipy, and undiscriminating (cf. Trindade-Serra 1979). They are also the spirits who are kept most private.

Erês, *exus*, and *caboclos* have certain affinities with each other, which distinguish them as a group from the *orixás*. When they "manifest" they all keep their eyes open. They all speak. They all interact, in their materialized state, with human beings. They all have a taste for oral pleasures, whether it be for food, drink, or tobacco. They all have some link with eroticism. (In the case of the *erês* this involves obscenities and indecent gestures and pranks; for the *exus* and *caboclos* it entails flirtation.) In other words, they are all associated with the "grotesque body."

There are, however, differences among these three categories of spirits. In the case of the *erês*, the grotesque body is simply unsocialized, or inadequately socialized; in the case of the *exus* it is socialized but perverse, unpredictable, and therefore to some extent antisocial; in the case of the *caboclos* it is transformed into a vehicle of sociability. This is achieved through the "euphemization" of the grotesque body.

I borrow this notion of "euphemization" from Gilbert Durand, author of a major anthropological study of fantasy. According to Durand the purpose of fantasy is to "euphemize" our awareness of death and of the ravages of time (1969:127), by linking these negative images to others that are positively valued, and thus attenuating the differences between the two kinds of imagery (1969:313). So, to take an example from Bakhtin, a recurrent theme of the carnival imagery of the Middle Ages was the linking of death and birth (1984:24–26). As Durand points out, the tomb is typically euphemized as a cradle, or as a happy dwelling place (1969:313).

The grotesque body is the body that is subject to aging, death, and decay. But the *caboclos*, who are the spirits of dead Indians and backwoodsmen, are perpetually youthful and vigorous, and dwell in a forest land of beauty and abundance called Aruanda. (The name probably comes from the city of Luanda, in Angola [Cacciatore 1977:53].) In their behavior the functions of the grotesque body are euphemized in various ways. For example, when they dance the samba they like to make eyes and to flirt, but genital sex is apparently beyond their ken. Taís was horrified when I told him about a friend who claimed to have made out with the *caboclo* of his father-of-saint. He said the *caboclos* are only interested in booze and samba, not in sex. For the *caboclos*, the sexual function of the body is euphemized by being displaced upwards to the eyes.

There are other euphemizations of bodily functions in the symbolism associated with the *caboclos*. Among the abundant offerings of tropical fruit at a *caboclo* festival I attended at Marinalvo's, the central items were three pumpkins prepared in a particular way. I saw a member of the *terreiro* gouging a hole in the top of a pumpkin and stuffing it with dried tobacco leaves and honey. Someone else jokingly compared the hole to an *idi*, which, in the African vocabulary of Candomblé, means "anus." They were euphemizing the anus by linking it to the mouth. The mouth itself may also be euphemized. *Caboclos* typically smoke cigars, but sometimes place the burning tip inside their mouth, and blow smoke out the other end. When they direct the smoke at a member of the audience at a festival, it is supposed to have curing properties. The mouth is the organ that consumes and destroys the world, but here it is euphemized as an organ that reverses the process of decomposition.

Durand's view of the euphemism as a kind of oxymoron, the equation of signs with opposed values, can be extended to other aspects of the *caboclo* character, in particular their social status and their speech. The *caboclos* are primitives and rustics, and so, from a "civilized" perspective, at the bottom of the social scale. But they are also regal beings: chiefs of Indian tribes, or lords of the realm of wild nature, with names such as King of the Forests, Sultan of the Jungles, King of the Snakes. This oxymoronic status is reflected in their speech, which is that of refined bumpkins. The *caboclos*' characteristic way of talking has been misunderstood by at least one anthropologist as "murky" and "corrupt" (Landes 1947:189), so it merits an extended treatment here.

* * *

Brazilian Portuguese can be divided, approximately speaking, into three sociolects (Couto 1986:64). (There are, of course, numerous overlaps, sub-differentiations, and regional variations. But consideration of these is outside the scope of my present concerns.) There is literary Lusitanian Portuguese, which is used in Brazil only in writing, or by a learned elite on occasions where formal speech is required. Then there is standard urban Brazilian Portuguese, which differs from the Portuguese of Portugal in certain typical ways, such as in the pronominal system (Couto 1986:38-39), but which is the norm for ordinary middle-class speech. Finally there is the language of the lower classes, which Couto refers to as *o português caboclo*—"*caboclo* Portuguese," "backwoods Portuguese" (1986:45, 64)—even though it is spoken not only by peasants but also by "workers, . . . slum-dwellers, marginal groups, etc." (1986:57). This way of speaking is conventionally considered to be "non-standard" (though Couto presents a vigorous case in its defense). It should be noted, however, that it is not the language spoken by the *caboclo* spirits of Candomblé.

Some of the characteristics of this sociolect are worth mentioning, since they recur in my transcriptions of names, songs, etc. In its grammar, plurality is sometimes indicated only on articles, and not on nouns, adjectives, and verbs, as it would be in the standard dialect (Couto 1986:45). Thus, in a line from one of Corquisa's songs, *As alma saiu prá ver quem era* ("The souls went out to see who it was"), the definite article (*as*) has the usual ending in *s*, which indicates plurality, but the noun *alma* ("soul") does not; also the verb *saiu* ("went out") is the usual third person *singular* form of the perfect tense of *sair*.

One of the most characteristic features of the phonology of this sociolect is that final *r* is dropped. Thus when Sete Saia called herself "the wife of Lucifer," she pronounced the name of her husband as "Lucifé."

This sociolect, while it may be considered "*caboclo*" from the perspective of speakers of the middle-class dialect, is "standard" for many of the adherents of Candomblé, who have an image of the *caboclos*, the true backwoodsmen, as speaking a language even further removed from middle-class Portuguese than their own. In fact the speech of the *caboclo* spirits probably bears little resemblance to the actual linguistic usage of rural people, but is rather a stylized form of verbal art specific to Candomblé.

Not all *caboclo* spirits speak in exactly the same fashion, but the ways in which they transform the normal sociolect of Candomblé are selected from a fairly narrow range of options. Let me illustrate some of these options with a sample of *caboclo* talk reproduced for me by Taís. The background to this speech is that Toninho (Edivaldo's brother and also his son-of-saint) had spoken disparagingly of his own *caboclo*, Boca da Mata ("Mouth of the Forest"). So the *caboclo* had "manifested" and smoked all of Toninho's cigarettes, then left the following message, to be passed on to Toninho when he "awoke":

> Bom dina prá quené de bom dina, e bona
> noite prá quené de bona noite. Eu chó
> vim aquine prá dijene quene meu cavalo

> não cu-manda em choneu, que jeu
> cu-peguei a chua intaba, man diche prá
> que ene não me cu-xingache. Me
> cu-xingou, e daine que eu fine.

In standard Portuguese this would read

> Bom dia para quem é de bom dia, e boa noite para quem é de boa noite. Eu só vim aqui para dizer que meu cavalo não manda em mim, que eu peguei o seu cigarro, mas disse para que ele não me xingasse. Me xingou, e daí que eu fiz.
>
> Good day to whomever it is a good day, and good night to whomever it is a good night [this formula is a line from a *caboclo* song]. I just came to say that I do not take orders from my horse [literally, "my horse does not command me." "Horse" refers to a spirit's material vehicle], that I took his cigarette, but said for him not to abuse me. He abused me, and so this is what I did.

The phonological transformations in this passage are probably the ones that occur most commonly in *caboclo* talk. First, alveolar grooved fricatives are palatalized. Thus *sua* ("his") becomes *chua*. Second, an *n* is inserted where a syllable boundary occurs between two vowels. So *dia* ("day") becomes *dina*. This also happens across word boundaries, and in cases where the vowel before the boundary is nasalized. Thus *só eu* becomes *choneu*, and *quem é* becomes *quené*. Third, *-ne* is added to stressed final syllables (and sometimes replaces a final consonant). Thus *aqui* ("here") becomes *aquine*. Fourth, *l* and *r* are changed to *n* when they occur between vowels. Thus *ele* ("he") becomes *ene*.

These transformations, although not always consistently applied, are more or less "standard" in *caboclo* talk. There are other transformations as well, which do not occur in this passage, most of them less common. In addition, *caboclos* occasionally make random phonological substitutions that seem to be open to the free play of fantasy.

The first transformation described above is probably the most distinctive single characteristic of the speech of the *caboclos*. All the other transformations occur also in the speech of *erês*. (*Erê* talk has an additional set of potential transformations of its own, which further distinguish it from the speech of the *caboclos*. A stop may be replaced by any other stop, a fricative by any other fricative, and an affricate by a labiodental fricative.)

The phonological substitutions that occur in *caboclo* speech play with some of the phonological features that have been most labile in the evolution of Portuguese as a whole. They seem to be intended to exaggerate the kinds of difficulties that people who do not speak middle-class Brazilian Portuguese might have in attempting to master the standard dialect.

The grammatical features of *caboclo* talk require less commentary, because in general the *caboclos* follow the grammatical rules of the ordinary dialect of Candomblé (as in the passage quoted above). Occasionally, however, a *caboclo* will alter a verb form in a way that transfers a person-marker from one tense or paradigm to another where it is inappropriate.

Lexically, *caboclo* talk is, again, not very different from the standard dialect of Candomblé. Although the *caboclos* are "Indians," or of Indian descent, they sprinkle their speech with the same items of African vocabulary as the human members of Candomblé—for example, the word *intaba* ("cigarette") in the passage above. They do, however, have a few tricks that make their vocabulary distinctive. One of these is to use the prefix *cu-* before other lexical items. *Cu* means "ass," "anus," "buttocks" when used by itself. But I have heard *caboclos* use it in front of verbs, oblique pronouns, and, above all, proper names.

While on the subject of proper names, it is worth mentioning that *caboclos* use the polite form of address *seu* ("Mr." "Sir") in front of the first names of both men and women. They seem to be incapable, at least linguistically, of distinguishing between the sexes (although they have no dificulty in the samba circle). They also address both men and women as *o senhor* ("sir") or *seu moço* (literally "sir boy"). They may even change a feminine name to the corresponding masculine form. For example, I heard a person called Lucrécia addressed as "seu cu-Lucrécio."

There are a few miscellaneous lexical items that are typically associated with *caboclo* talk. One of these is the term *só-eu* ("I alone"), which is used instead of *mim* (the first person singular pronoun used with prepositions). There is also a set of *caboclo* interjections, such as *iê iê iê*, *ré ré ré*, and *rítia,*

rítia. These may perhaps be imitations of Indian war-cries. They are generally made when a *caboclo* has just arrived, and are followed by an announcement of his identity—for example, *Sou eu, Caipó*, "It's me, Caipó."

This is a typical opening formula in *caboclo* discourse. Alternatively a *caboclo* may use a conventional greeting, such as *Bom dia* ("Good day"), followed by the name of a person he wishes to address, then a phrase such as *Já chegou Raio do Sol* ("Raio do Sol [or whatever the *caboclo*'s name happens to be] has arrived"), or *Só vim aqui prá dizé* . . . ("I just came here to say . . .").

Caboclo talk is distorted in a way that is meant to imitate the speech of bumpkins. Some of the reasons for calling it the speech of "refined bumpkins" are evident from the foregoing discussion. For example, the *caboclos* are typically polite, as we have seen in the forms of greeting and address they use. This can be contrasted with the slightly threatening speech style of the *exus*, who might start a conversation with a formula such as *Colé* [*qual é*] *velho*?—roughly, "What's up, man?" But to obtain further insight into the *caboclos*' "refined" side, we need to see them in the context of a *caboclo* festival.

* * *

A *caboclo* festival consists of a number of episodes, each with its characteristic songs. I describe these episodes below, and give at least one typical song for each. Taís helped me work out the division into episodes, and provided their titles. Not every festival will include all episodes, and their order is also somewhat variable.

1. *Reza de matança de caboco* ("Prayer for a *caboclo* sacrifice")

A public *caboclo* festival generally begins with a private sacrifice, which may be in honor of a *caboclo* who is already "seated," or for the birth—that is, the "seating"—of a new *caboclo*. The following song was sung for a newly "seated" *caboclo* at a sacrifice at Marinalvo's.

Graças a Deus, orai meu Deus,
Louvado seja Deus, orai meu Deus,
Bendita seja a hora, meu Deus,
Que um Boiadeiro nasceu.

Thanks to God, pray my God,
Praised be God, pray my God,
Blessed be the hour, my God,
That a Boiadeiro [or whatever the name of the *caboclo* happens to be] was born.

2. *Abrimento da festa de caboco* ("Opening of the *caboclo* festival")

The public part of a *caboclo* festival may begin with the usual ritual of the *orixás* (which has been extensively described in the literature—see, for example, Bastide 1978b, and Carneiro 1967). This is a respectful acknowledgment of the status of the African deities, but is usually dispensed with much faster than it would be at an actual *orixá* festival. The *orixás* are not expected to descend, and if they do, they are "suspended," without being given the opportunity to dance. When the *orixá* ritual is concluded, the leader of the drummers and singers opens the *caboclo* festival proper, with a song such as the following:

Ô abre a sala de Angolá
Como simbuca lelê;
Ô abre a sala de Angolá
Como simbuca lelê Congo.
Vamos querequê bambatoisar,
Vamos querequerê bambatoisar.

Oh open the room of Angola
As *simbuca lelê*;
Oh open the room of Angola
As *simbuca lelê Congo*.
Let us *querequê bambatoisar*,
Let us *querequerê bambatoisar*.

Taís glossed *bambatoisar* as "to throw a party." Megenney translates *bamba* as "anyone who is admired because of some capacity possessed," and *quêrêrêquêxê* as "*reco-reco*," a wooden scraper used as a musical instrument (1978:148). Thus the meaning of the last two lines of the song may be something like "let us play the wooden scraper and put on a good performance." The meaning of the second and fourth lines is more obscure. Taís said *simbuca* means "gourd," so perhaps these lines refer to the musical instrument known as the *berimbau*, which has a hollow gourd attached to its lower end.

The references to Angola and the Congo may have to do with the fact that the *caboclos*' mythical land of Aruanda is thought to lie in that region of Africa. The *caboclo* festival itself is supposed to have originated in the Congo-Angola branch or "nation" of Candomblé (Carneiro 1981:62–63, 133–136).

3. *Salva de chegada* ("Arrival greeting")

As the music continues, the *caboclos* begin to arrive, and as they do so they sing a greeting song, such as the following:

Ô boa noite, senhor,
Boa noite, senhora,
Sou eu, Sultão das Matas
Que cheguei agora.
Eu cheguei com Deus
E Nossa Senhora.

Oh good evening sir,
Good evening ma'am,
It's me, Sultan of the Forests,
Who arrived just now.
I arrived with God
And Our Lady.

Ô salve Deus,
Ô salve a patria,
E salve os homens.
Salve todos que estão aqui.
Ô salve Deus,
Salve a patria,
Salve os homens,
Sou cavaleiro,
Sou caboco do Brasi.

All hail to God,
All hail to the fatherland,
All hail to men.
Hail to all those who are here.

All hail to God,
Hail to the fatherland,
Hail to men,
I'm a horseman,
I'm a *caboclo* of Brazil.

(Sung by Boiadeiro.)

4. *Homenagem ao caboco do dono da casa que chegou* ("Homage to the *caboclo* of the head of the *terreiro* who has arrived")

After the arrival of the *caboclo* of the parent-of-saint in whose *terreiro* the festival is taking place, those present sing a response to his greeting, such as this:

Ele já chegou,
Ele já chegou,
Ele já chegou na aldeia,
Ele já chegou.

He has now arrived,
He has now arrived,
He has now arrived in the village,
He has now arrived.

(The *caboclos* live in "villages.")

5. *Salva de apresentação* ("Greeting of introduction")

After a *caboclo* has greeted the audience, he sings a song in which he introduces himself, for example:

Sou caboco, sou guerreiro,
Me criei nas imburana.
Eu me chamo Sete Flecha,
Rei das cobra cainana.

I am a *caboclo*, I am a warrior,
I grew up in the *imburanas*.
I am called Seven Arrows,
King of the *cainana* snakes.

According to Taís, *imburana* is a type of leaf used by the *caboclos* in making a bed. A *cainana* snake is a species that flies.

6. *Cantiga de entrada* ("Entry song")

After enough *caboclos* have materialized there is a pause, during which they leave the *barracão* and go to the private quarters of the *terreiro*, where they dress in their *caboclo* costumes. When they return, a song such as the following is sung:

Para maiongombé
Elé panzué
Epara maiongombé
Elé panzué caboco
Toté toté de maiongá
Maiongombé.

Taís was only able to guess at the meaning of this song. From Castro (1971:82) we learn that the term *maionga* is connected with the clothes used in rituals.

7. *Rezas e salvas de agradecimento* ("Prayers and greetings of thanks")

The next episode consists of various expressions of respect by the *caboclos* who have "manifested." They give thanks to the *orixás* in general and to the *orixá* of the parent-of-saint of the *terreiro* in particular. They express gratitude to the *caboclos* of all the senior initiates, giving special attention to the *caboclo* of the parent-of-saint. They also ask the blessing of the dignitaries present, such as visiting parents-of-saint.

For the *orixás*, songs such as this one are sung:

Chegando aqui nesta aldeia
Eu me ajoelho para salvar,
Para salvar esta junça que é de ouro,
Para salvar meu pai Oxalá.

Arriving here in this village
I kneel down to pay my respects,
To pay my respects to this *junça*, which is of gold,
To pay my respects to my father, Oxalá.

Oxalá is the father of the *orixás*. *Junça* is the plant *Cyperus esculentus* (Ferreira 1975:806), which is known in Bahia also by the name *Espada de Ogum*. Taís was not able to explain its connection with the rest of the song.

The next song is of the type sung in honor of the senior *caboclos*:

Vou tirar meu chapéu,
Implorei a meu Deus.
Tupinambá é pai
E seu filho sou eu. Isa!

I will take off my hat,
I have implored my God.
Tupinambá [name of a *caboclo*] is father
And I am his son. Isa!

(*Isa*! is one of the interjections used by the *caboclos* as an expression of their "Indian-ness.")

When asking blessings from the dignitaries, the *caboclos* sing songs such as this:

A bença, a bença meu painé,
Bença pai, bença mãe,
A bença meu painé.
Ô toma bença aos mais velho, menino;
Deixa de ser mal criado, menino.

Bless me, bless me father,
Bless me father, bless me mother,
Bless me father.
Oh ask a blessing from your seniors, child;
Don't be bad-mannered, child.

Following the expressions of respect, the festival moves on to the episodes that form its core: the sambas. There are three principal types of samba at a *caboclo* festival: the *samba de sotaque* ("banter samba"); the *samba de roda* ("circle samba"); and the *samba de barravento* ("*barravento* samba," for calling other *caboclos*). I treat them here as separate episodes (some of which include subepisodes), in the order Taís considered typical. However, in my observation it is not unusual for the three types of samba to blend into each other.

8. *Samba de sotaque* ("Banter samba")

Sotaque means "accent," but is also used to refer to mocking, provocative speech. In this second sense it could be glossed in English as "banter," or as "Signifyin(g)"—to borrow a term current among African-North Americans (Gates 1988:46). *Sotaques* occur in many contexts in Candomblé. Typically they make use of sly, indirect, allusive language. If unwelcome visitors arrive at a *terreiro*, the members of the house may speak about them derisively, in their presence, using African vocabulary that will be incomprehensible to the visitors if they are outsiders to the world of Candomblé. If they are insiders, they are expected to take up the game and respond with a counter-*sotaque*, so confirming their insider status and justifying their presence.

The *sotaques* of the *caboclos* are more stylized, in that the songs that convey them, the allusions they contain, and the range of songs that can be used as responses, are stock formulae, in which the referential (signifying) function is typically less important than the indexical (Signifyin[g]) function (cf. Silverstein 1977; Gates 1988). Their purpose is also somewhat different. A *caboclo sotaque* is most commonly an indirect accusation that another *caboclo* does not match up to the standards of the ideal *caboclo* character—that he is not sufficiently courageous, generous, or spirited. In context, this means that the *caboclo* so accused is not contributing sufficiently to the effervescence of the festival, so the *sotaque* is really a challenge to get into the spirit of the occasion (to "get down," we might say).

Here is one *caboclo* sotaque:

Caboco não dorme em cama,
Cochila no pé do pau,
Com seu arco e sua flecha,
Tocando seu berimbau.
Que foi que eu disse?
Tocando seu berimbau.
Diga de novo:
Tocando seu berimbau.

A *caboclo* does not sleep in a bed,
He snoozes at the foot of a tree,

With his bow and his arrow,
Playing his *berimbau*.
What did I say?
Playing his *berimbau*.
Say it again:
Playing his *berimbau*.

The stylized nature of the allusions in the *caboclo sotaques* is evident from the fact that, to the outsider, this song appears to be quite innocent. But when one *caboclo* sings it to another, it implies that the *caboclo* to whom it is addressed is the kind who sleeps in a bed, and does not know anything about bows, arrows, and *berimbaus*. (The *berimbau* is a musical instrument, of African origin, consisting of a wooden bow that is strung with wire and has a hollow gourd attached to the lower end. It is typically associated with the dance called *capoeira*.) In the context of the festival, this is a challenge to participate more actively.

The *caboclo* being addressed may respond in one of two ways: with an equally provocative counter-*sotaque*, or with a peace-making *sotaque*. The following song is an example of the first type:

Eu sou caboco
Mas sou teimoso.
Cada caboco conhece a sua insaba.
É um caboco espiando outro.
Só quero ver
Quem arranca o toco.

I am a *caboclo*,
But I am stubborn.
Every *caboclo* knows his *insaba*.
It's one *caboclo* spying on another.
I just want to see
Who pulls up the stump.

Taís said that *insaba* means "leaves." The implication of the third and fourth lines is that a *caboclo* is supposed to mind his own business. According to Taís, the "stump" of the last line refers to the *jurema* pot, which used to be made of a stump. (*Jurema* is the sacred drink of the *caboclos*.) So the last two lines are perhaps a challenge to see who puts on the better performance once the *jurema* has been drunk.

The following is a peace-making *sotaque*:

Eu disse, camarado,
Que eu vinha
Aqui na sua aldeia um dia.
Mas eu disse, camarado,
Que eu vinha
Salvar na sua aldeia um dia.
Camarado, amigo meu,
Amigo de coração,
Amizade de caboco
Não se troca por um tostão,
Porque eu sou caboco,
Sou seu irmão.

I said, comrade,
That I would come
Here to your village one day.
But I said, comrade,
That I would come
To salute you in your village one day.
Comrade, my friend,
Friend of my heart,
The friendship of *caboclos*
Should not be exchanged for a farthing,
Because I am a *caboclo*,
I am your brother.

The tension in *caboclo* society is not between classes—*caboclo* culture is essentially egalitarian, since forest life does not provide much scope for the accumulation of capital—but between insiders and outsiders, and between members of different generations. There are some *sotaques*, such as the song just transcribed, that are used between *caboclos* who are inhabitants of different "villages," and others that are used between younger and older *caboclos*. The next song is an example of the latter type. Taís called it a *samba de guerra de caboco*—a "*caboclo*'s war samba."

A younger *caboclo* may sing:

Vamos guerriar, caboco,
Vamos guerriar, guerreiro.

Let us make war, *caboclo*,
Let us make war, warrior.

To this the older *caboclo* to whom it is addressed replies:

Vamos fazer paz, caboco,
Vamos fazer paz, guerreiro.

Let us make peace, *caboclo*,
Let us make peace, warrior.

(It should be mentioned that provocations do not come only from the younger *caboclos*.)

Another sub-type of the *samba de sotaque* is the *samba de teste*, or "test samba." A *caboclo* uses this kind of *sotaque* to challenge others to prove that they are really in trance, and not just "giving *equê*." The challenger may burn gunpowder on the palm of his hand, or dance on live coals, to show that his body is resistant to pain, and the song he sings provokes others to submit themselves to the same "test":

Ô queima polvora
Quem pode queimar.
Meu ponto é seguro,
Ninguém pode achar.

Oh burn gunpowder,
Whoever can burn it.
My stall is secure,
No one can find it.

The imagery in this song is taken from the world of street vendors, who use magical substances to protect their stalls from the spells of rival vendors. The *caboclo* giving this *sotaque* implies that his body is protected from the effects of gunpowder in the same way that a stall is protected from black magic.

9. *Samba de roda* ("Circle samba")

The episode of the "circle samba" may begin with a song of the type that Taís called *abrimento de uma roda de samba*, or "opening of a samba circle."

Ô dono da casa
Me dê licença,
Me dê o seu salão
Prá eu invadiá.
É meia hora só
E eu dou já.

Oh head of the house
Give me permission,
Give me your room
To invade.
It's just for half an hour
And I'll give it back.

What happens in a samba circle is that people form a circle, and one or two dance in the middle (cf. Teixeira 1986:ch. 3.2). The composition of the circle at a *caboclo* festival varies. It may include just *caboclos*, or *caboclos* and various members of the audience, or everyone present. If the dancing in the center is done singly, the dancer performs, then indicates with his or her foot the person or *caboclo* who is to dance next. If two people dance in the middle, one of the dancers is a *caboclo* who stays there, drawing members of the circle into the center to take turns dancing with him. An audacious *caboclo* may lie on the ground, with his head propped on his hand, admiring the view thus obtained of a woman who is dancing.

Apart from dancing, the main activities of this episode are flirtation and drinking, and this is reflected in many of its songs. A song that contains reference to these interests belongs to a sub-type that Taís called *samba de cachaceiro*, or "boozer's samba." The following is a boozer's samba in the form of a dialogue between father and son. Both parts are sung by the same *caboclo*.

(Father): Meu filho.
(Son) : Sim, ô meu pai.
(F): Onde você estava, José?

(S): No samba, meu pai.
(F): Tinha muita moça bonita, José?
(S): Tinha, meu pai.
(F): Tinha muita cachaça, José?
(S): Tinha, meu pai,
De meia noite prô dia.
(F): O velho 'tava lá, José?
Fora de lá, ô José,
Fora de lá, ô José!

(Father): My son.
(Son) : Yes, father.
(F): Where were you, José?
(S): At the samba, father.
(F): Were there many pretty girls, José?
(S): There were, father.
(F): Was there much *cachaça*, José?
(S): There was, father,
From midnight till daylight.
(F): The old man [father of the girl] was there, José?
Away from there, José,
Away from there, José!

If *jurema* has been prepared for the festival, it is during this episode that it is distributed. According to Sangirardi Jr., the term *jurema* designates various plant species, all with mildly hallucinogenic properties, of the genera *Mimosa*, *Acacia*, and *Pithecelobium* (1983:91). It is recorded as being used in *caboclo* rituals of Candomblé as early as 1905 (1983:194). The drink called *jurema* is based on an infusion of parts of the plant, with the addition of honey, herbs, alcohol, and other substances. *Jurema* made with the root or with the bark of the stem is reddish, the color of wine. The plant may also be mixed with tobacco and used for smoking (1983:195). Taís gave me a recipe for *jurema* that does not differ substantially from Sangirardi's. Taís said *jurema* should also contain the blood of sacrificed animals, and a magical powder called *pemba*. It should be served in a pot with feathers round the edge.

A *jurema* song may be sung:

A jurema boa
É no pé do pau.
Aqui mesmo eu bebo,
Aqui mesmo eu caio.

The good *jurema*
Is at the foot of the tree.
I'll drink right here,
I'll fall right here.

"The foot of the tree" may refer to the fact that the *jurema* pot used to be made of a stump.

During this episode the *caboclos* may embrace (ritually, not erotically) members of the audience. The type of song sung for this formality was called by Taís *Salva de agradecimento aos presentes*, "Greeting of thanks to those present." The following song of this type is in the form of a dialogue, both parts of which are sung by the *caboclo*:

—O senhor olhou prá mim?
—Olhei, sim senhor.
—O senhor gostou de mim?
—Gostei, sim senhor.
—Então me dê um abraço.
—Eu dou, sim senhor.

—The gentleman looked at me?
—Yes sir, I did.
—The gentleman liked me?
—Yes sir, I did.
—Then give me an embrace.
—Yes sir, I will.

10. *Samba de barravento* ("*Barravento samba*")

The third type of samba is the *barravento* samba, which has the purpose of "calling" other *caboclos*. *Barravento* refers to the state of vertigo that precedes trance. (The term is said to be derived from the name of a strong wind [Cacciatore 1977:64].) The person experiencing a *barravento* partially loses consciousness and muscular control, and begins to lurch. With the onset of the trance state proper, bodily control returns.

During this episode the *caboclos* attempt to make members of the audience who are not in trance receive their *caboclos*. They have various techniques for doing this. One is called a *bagunfamento*. To *bagunfar* someone, a *caboclo* takes a sip of alcohol or water and sprays it over the person concerned. Another method is to blow smoke at a person. Sometimes a look, a song, or a gesture such as pointing with the foot, is sufficient to cause a *barravento*.

If the *caboclo* doing the calling knows that a particular member of the audience receives a *caboclo*, but has not yet done so at this festival, he may sing a song which addresses that *caboclo* by name, such as this one sung to call Trovezeiro (the name of any *caboclo* may be inserted):

A lua lá no céu brilhou,
As mata escureceu.
Cadê um Trovezeiro de Aruanda,
Que até agora não apareceu?
Ai moré moré moré,
Ai moré moré moré moré.

The moon there in the sky shone,
The forests grew dark.
Where is a Trovezeiro from Aruanda,
Who has not yet appeared?
Ah moré moré moré,
Ah moré moré moré moré.

(*Moré* may have some connection with the Moré tribe of the Guaporé River.)

The *caboclos* who are already in trance may also try to call the unknown *caboclos* of visitors to the *terreiro*, using a song such as this:

Na minha boiada
Me falta um boi.
Ou me falta um,
Ou me falta dois.
Na minha boiada
Ainda me falta um boi.

In my herd
There is a bullock missing.
There is either one missing,
Or two missing.
In my herd
There is still a bullock missing.

Once all the *caboclos* have been called, earlier samba episodes may be repeated, until the maximum of participation and effervescence has been achieved.

11. *Salva de despedida* ("Farewell salutation")

Finally the hour comes for the *caboclos* to depart. Before they leave the *barracão* they sing leave-taking songs, such as this:

A minha cabacinha
Eu deixo aqui no chão.
Meu arco e minha flecha
Eu dou prá meu irmão.
O meu capacete
Eu dou prá guardar.
Adeus camaradinhos,
Até quando eu voltar.

My little gourd
I am leaving here on the ground.
My bow and my arrow
I give to my brother.
My headdress
I am giving for safekeeping.
Farewell, dear comrades,
Until I return.

The "refined" side of the *caboclo* character is evident in many of these songs. They uphold the "refined" values of piety towards God and the *orixás*, patriotism towards the fatherland, respect for one's elders and betters, good manners, friendliness, generosity, and courage. They allow themselves to have a good time in the samba episodes, having paid their respects to everyone, and having requested permission to "invade" the house. But their dancing, drinking, flirtation, and provocation, are not motivated by boorish sentiments. They are rather manifestations of the *caboclos'* generosity, of their desire to draw everyone present into the happy land of Aruanda.

* * *

Some *caboclo* names and songs had their origins in the romantic literature about the Indians written in the nineteenth century, for example, the novels of José de Alencar, and the poetry of Gonçalves Dias (Brown 1986:65). So I was surprised by the paucity of *caboclo* mythology current in Candomblé. My friends in Jaraci often told spontaneous stories about the *orixás* and *exus*, but rarely about the *caboclos*.

At my request Taís gave me some background about the *caboclos'* world, and told me the one *caboclo* narrative he knew.

The *caboclos* have always lived, he said, in the land called Aruanda. Aruanda used to be located in the Congo, but when the Congo was destroyed the *caboclos* were expelled, and moved to Angola, to a new Aruanda. In the process they became to some extent acculturated—or, as Taís put it, "domesticated." Traditionally, the only intoxicant they would drink was *jurema*, and they smoked only cigars. Today they also drink beer (or, it seems, whatever is available), and smoke industrially manufactured cigarettes (though they always tear off the filters). Their belief system also underwent some modifications. In ancient times they worshiped the moon, whom they called Lovely Maiden, and the sun, whom they called Eternal Fire. They considered an eclipse to be a war between Our Lady and God. When they moved to Angola they deified their warrior-king, who was known as Tupã. Later they began to worship a younger god called Tupim, who had also been a chief of Aruanda. Tupim was blind, having been bitten by a *cainana* snake in a battle with another village. It was at this time that the *caboclos* began to revere Jesus and the Virgin Mary. (Numerous *caboclo* songs make reference to Bom Jesus de Maria, "Good Jesus of Mary," or Bom Jesus da Lapa, "Good Jesus of the Grotto." The grotto referred to is presumably the one at the pilgrimage site of Bom Jesus da Lapa, in the west of the state of Bahia.)

Taís's story concerned a *caboclo* called Sultão das Matas ("Sultan of the Forests"), who, as it happens, is the *caboclo* received by Marinalvo.

The traditional social organization of the *caboclos*, as described by Taís in this story, would have delighted the heart of Lewis Henry Morgan, for they lived in a state of the most pristine "primitive promiscuity." They grew up without knowing the identity of their biological parents, and had to respect any older person as "father" or "mother." This meant that relationships sometimes occurred between brothers and sisters, since they were unaware that they had the same genitors.

Sultão belonged to the village of the Carajás. However, many people were dying in his village, and he had to move to the village of the Tupãs, with whom the Carajás were always fighting. The Tupãs were also known as "Redskins." In this village Sultão fell in love with an Indian maiden, who, unbeknown to him, was his sister. The god Tupã allowed this to happen. Eventually Sultão decided to return to his own village, but he kept the name of Redskin. His bride was accepted by the Carajás, and Sultão created peace between the two tribes.

The theme of incest is a recurrent one in Candomblé mythology. We have already seen an example of it in the *exu* story about Padilha and Sete Facadas, and it is common also in stories about the *orixás*, since, according to some accounts, all the junior *orixás* have the same father, Oxalá, and are the children of only two mothers, Oxalá's wives Nanã and Iemanjá.

The prevalence of this theme is no doubt related to the fact that the incest taboo is one of the greatest sources of conflict within any *terreiro* of Candomblé. A *terreiro* is essentially exogamous, in that its members are regarded as having acquired, through their initiation, a "consanguineal" relationship to each other, either as brothers and sisters, or as parents and children, and sexual relations between them are forbidden. (In theory this taboo applies to people of the same sex as well as to people of opposite sexes.) The pivot of these relationships is the parent-of-saint.

This situation causes conflict for two reasons. First, it happens from time to time that members of the same *terreiro* fall in love with each other. Second, the primary loyalty owed to the parent-of-saint causes strain on members' relationships with people outside the *terreiro*.

From the perspective of a *terreiro* member, then, the social organization of the *caboclos* is utopian, in that brothers and sisters may have relations with each other, and do not owe loyalty to any particular parent, since they do not know the identity of their biological mothers and fathers. The *caboclos'* world inverts the prevailing social order of Candomblé, and this is another factor that contributes to its carnivalesque atmosphere.

* * *

So far I have treated the mythological world of Candomblé as arranged vertically into a number of realms that lie on a continuum between matter and spirit. However, there are some aspects of Candomblé lore that do not fit very neatly into this vertical arrangement. It was never clear to me, for example, just where the world of the *caboclos* lies on the spirit-matter continuum. Obviously they are on a lower level than the *orixás*. Equally obviously they cannot be on a level lower than the *exus*, since the *exus* are the spirits who are closest to matter. One might conclude that their world lies somewhere in between—an inference that seems to have been drawn by the systematizers of Umbanda (cf. Brown 1986:54–64). But I never heard the members of Candomblé actually say this.

What they did say was that the *caboclos* are inhabitants of the forest. This suggests that the "vertical" perspective, which has probably come to Candomblé from Western metaphysics, via Kardecism and Christianity, coexists with a perspective that is more "horizontal," and that associates spirit entities with different geographical locations or aspects of nature. This perspective has certain affinities with the cosmology of the African religions to which Candomblé has historical ties (cf. Lépine 1982:16–20). But the idea of the forest as a primordial, utopian realm also has obvious similarities to the Judaeo-Christian origin myth recounted in Genesis.

What is significant about the forest, whether seen from the vertical or the horizontal perspective, is its relationship to the dichotomies that distinguish the other realms. Essentially, the forest is underdifferentiated. It could be seen, from a vertical perspective, as synthesizing the opposed realms of matter and spirit between which it lies; or, from a horizontal perspective, as lying outside of, or preceding, the division of the world into distinct realms. In fact, the forest does not fit simply into either of these perspectives, because it relativizes the very distinctions on which they are based.

I am not able to elaborate this point by reference to *caboclo* mythology, because of its paucity. But there are other forest-dwellers in the spirit world of Candomblé, and the stories that concern them may serve as illustrations.

The two myths I am going to recount concern Oxosse. Oxosse is an *orixá*, and thus, presumably, an inhabitant of the realm of spirit. But he is also god of the hunt, and so makes incursions into the forest. It is no doubt for this reason that he is considered by some to be the *orixá* most closely associated with the *caboclos*.

Taís told me that Oxosse was once in the forest and came upon Ossãe, the *orixá* of leaves and herbs. He thought Ossãe was a woman, and possessed and killed him. The *exus* carried this story to the king (Oxalá) in his castle, but, being tricksters, they inverted the roles. They said that Ossãe had possessed Oxosse. Thus there is a Candomblé song in which the king asks Oxosse if he is *odé*, and Oxosse replies that he is as much a man as the king. The punch-line here involves a pun. *Odé* means "hunter," a title conventionally given to Oxosse (Augras 1983:112). But Oxosse hears *adé*, an item of African vocabulary used to refer to a man who plays the passive role in relations with other men (cf. Birman 1988:237–39).

As for Ossãe, when he descends at a Candomblé ritual, he wears a covering of leaves, to hide the defilement of his body. According to Taís, Ossãe is *metá-metá*. This term means something like "half and half," and is used to characterize spirits that have two different natures. They may be both male and female or both human and animal, or they may belong to two different spirit realms. In the case of Ossãe, he is male for six months of the year, and female for the other six months. When he is male his whole body is covered with leaves. When he is female his top half is that of a woman, and his bottom half, which is covered with leaves, is that of a man.

On another occasion, Taís said, Oxosse went to hunt for food for his wife Oxum. He came across the serpent Oxumaré, struck her, and put her in a sack. (Oxumaré, though half male/half female, is generally considered to belong to the *aborôs*, or masculine *orixás*. But Taís consistently referred to Oxumaré using the feminine pronoun.) He brought her home for Oxum to cook. As he took her out of the bag, she began to sing. Oxum was horrified, because she had never seen a talking snake, and ran away. Oxosse proceeded to cut up Oxumaré, and put the pieces in a pan. While he was cooking and eating her, Oxumaré continued to sing. When Oxosse went to sleep, the pieces reunited in his stomach. Oxumaré burst out and fled. Oxosse tried to shoot her, but she grabbed his arrow and gave it back, saying, "You cannot kill me, because I am Oxumaré." She escaped to the castle, where she told the king what had happened. The king commented drily that Oxosse was "eating" all the animals of the forest. From that time Oxosse became known as Caçador, or "Hunter."

There are two puns here. As I have mentioned earlier, "eating," in Portuguese, can refer to taking the active role in sexual intercourse. And "hunting" can mean "cruising," "looking for sexual encounters."

Oxumaré realized she could no longer live on the ground, because of the danger from Oxosse, so she decided to ascend to the sky, as a rainbow. Oxumaré is also *metá-metá*. Her top half is male and her bottom half female for six months of the year, and her top half female and her bottom half male for the other six months.

These two myths have to do with a lack of discrimination in eating and in sexual relations—two areas in which the daily life of Candomblé is fraught with taboos. Such behavior is only possible in the forest, and not, of course, in the castle, the world of the spirit. The *orixás* whose natural habitat is the forest—Ossãe, Oxumaré, and also Logum-edé—are all *metá-metá*. In a literal sense this means that they are half male and half female. But it suggests also an ambiguous relationship to the realm of spirit. They are *orixás*, yes, but they also participate in the same oxymoronic world that is inhabited by the *caboclos*.

5. Of Keys

Before I became an *ogã* in Marinalvo's *terreiro* I was an *abiã*. A Jaracian defined *abiã* for me as a kind of spy—someone who goes from *terreiro* to *terreiro* participating in the rituals, without having made any "obligations." I was an *abiã* because my saint had not yet accepted any particular *terreiro*, out of the many I visited, as the appropriate place for me to make offerings to him.

However, I have a feeling he may have come close to accepting the *terreiro* of Gelson, in a district of Salvador called Lobito.

A student colleague of Archipiado's, Márcio by name and Marxist by persuasion, lived in Lobito and was a friend of Gelson. He invited us to a *caboclo* festival at Gelson's, but did not come with us. We were accompanied instead by his friend Jorge. Márcio was probably at the monastery of St. Benedict, attending a meeting of the Movement for the Defense of Slum-dwellers, in which he played a leading role.

It was a Monday, the final night of Gelson's annual three-day *caboclo* festival. What struck me on our arrival was color. On the ceiling of the *barracão* strings of paper pennants formed enormous yellow stars against a green background. The walls were draped with alternating panels of green and yellow fabric, and a Brazilian flag hung in front of the drums.

A young *ogã* directed us to the only chairs on the right-hand side of the *barracão*. We were complete strangers in this *terreiro*, but the members of Gelson's house engaged us in a way that gives this festival a bright place in my memories.

Archipiado probably has rather different recollections of it.

After a time the three drummers began to play, and Gelson entered, through the door that leads to the private quarters of the *terreiro*, followed by his daughters- and sons-of-saint—about a dozen women and two or three men. Gelson was dressed in a loose tropical shirt and casual trousers, and the women in full skirts made from bright printed fabrics. The emphasis on color and variegation is typical of a *caboclo* festival. At a festival of the *orixás* the members of a *terreiro* generally wear white.

The opening rites were performed. White and yellow manioc flour was offered to the *exus*, along with a jar of water mixed with *cachaça* and other substances. Gunpowder was burned, to remove evil influences. Then Gelson poured small quantities of white *pemba* onto his hand and blew it towards those present. *Pemba* is a magical powder that comes in the colors of the various *orixás*. White *pemba* belongs to Oxalá, the father of the gods, and is supposed to bring good fortune.

The first *roda* began. *Roda* means "ring" or "wheel," and in Candomblé refers to the circular formation in which the initiates dance, in a counterclockwise direction. This was the *roda* for the *orixás*. Some of Gelson's children-of-saint fell into trance during the songs for their particular *orixá*, and were led out of the *barracão* by the *ogãs* and *equedes*. At a festival for the *orixás* they would have returned dressed in the costume of their saint. However, on this occasion the *orixás* must have been "suspended" after they left the *barracão*. All the dancers exited after the first *roda*, and there was a short break.

The dancers returned to begin the second *roda*, for the *caboclos*. Gelson was the first to be "grabbed." He began to lurch, regained his balance, and was helped to remove his shirt and shoes by one of his *ogãs*. He left the *barracão*. One by one, other dancers were "mounted" by their *caboclos*, and exited.

After an interval the *caboclos* returned, led by Gelson's Pena Branca ("White Feather"). He wore a long war-bonnet of white feathers, a skirt of white feathers over shorts of silver *lamé*, and bands of white feathers around one ankle and both wrists. He was bare-chested. On public occasions men in trance generally wear a strip of white cloth bound around their chests. But for Pena Branca, whose "horse" is powerfully built and handsome, this convention was evidently outweighed by artistic considerations.

Other *caboclos* followed: Trovezeiro ("Thunderer"), Raio do Sol ("Sunbeam"), Sultão das Matas ("Sultan of the Forests"), Tupiniquim (the name of an Indian tribe, also colloquially used to mean "Brazilian"—this *caboclo* wore a fabric resembling the skin of the Brazilian jaguar), Boiadeiro ("Cowboy"), Mutalambô, Sete Serras ("Seven Saw-blades"), Sete Espadas ("Seven Swords"), and Rei das Cobras ("King of the Snakes"). Some of the Indian *caboclos* are distinguishable by the colors of their costumes or headdresses: black and white for Trovezeiro, yellow and green for Raio do Sol, blue and green for Sultão das Matas.

As the dancing and singing proceeded, individual *caboclos* announced themselves and were welcomed. During this episode of the festival a couple of events took place that merit commentary. First there was the suspension of a new *ogã*.

Pena Branca and Trovezeiro lifted up, on their linked arms, a man dressed in white, and carried him to the four sides of the room. Then Pena Branca took the man in his arms and brought him to a seat of honor next to the drums.

The word "suspend" is used in a number of specialized ways in Candomblé. To suspend a spirit means to bring the spirit's human vehicle out of trance, or to prevent the spirit from materializing in a person; to suspend a sacrifice means to take it from a ritual space and deposit it in a liminal space, such as the forest, the sea, or a crossroad. But when people speak of the suspension of an *ogã*, they mean that a spirit has chosen a man to occupy the status of *ogã*.

At first I thought the use of the term "suspend" in this context had to do with the physical elevation of the new *ogã*, which is usually done on a chair. But when I misused the term in this way I was corrected.

Pena Branca's decision to dispense with the chair in the act that symbolizes the suspension added a personal, *caboclo* touch. He had a genius for ritual aesthetics.

The second special event, which occurred some time later in the same episode, was a *bolação*, or "rolling." A young man went into trance, but instead of staying upright he fell to the ground and lay face down, with his feet pointing towards the private quarters of the *terreiro*. He was wrapped in a white sheet by a group consisting of *caboclos*, *ogãs*, and *equedes*. They lifted him up and held him, full length, at waist level, then carried him, head first, to the four directions—first to the front door of the *barracão*, then to the opposite wall, where the dignitaries and drummers sit, then to the right wall (the men's side), and finally to the left wall (the women's side). Each time the party stopped they rocked the young man's body twice. After this they took him out to the private quarters of the *terreiro*.

Jorge said that the young man had been taken into seclusion to have his head shaved—that is, to be initiated. He added that if the young man had "rolled" with his feet facing the front door of the *barracão*, he would not have been taken in.

This "rolling" is supposed to be a spontaneous event, which leads to a certain fear of Candomblé among people whose familiarity with it is limited. It is a widely held assumption that if you fall into trance in a *terreiro*, you may wake up weeks later and find yourself "shaved, clipped, and spread with butter," as Archipiado was accustomed to say. But it seems clear that the taking in of a novice is pre-arranged, and that "rolling" in the correct direction is simply the public confirmation of the novice's intentions. The young man who "rolled" at this festival already had close ties with the *terreiro*, since his mother was one of Gelson's daughters-of-saint.

The suspension of *ogãs* and *equedes* is also supposed to be a spontaneous decision on the part of a spirit that "manifests" at a festival. Usually, though not always, the material vehicle of this spirit is the parent-of-saint of the *terreiro*. Sometimes those chosen appear quite genuinely surprised by their suspension. On other occasions they arrive at the festival in the white costumes appropriate to their new rank, which suggests that the suspension has been arranged in advance.

After these two events the *caboclos* continued with their songs of greeting and respect, their *sotaques*, and their calling of other *caboclos*. One, named Rei das Cobras ("King of the Snakes"), came and asked me for beer. A boy was sent to fetch it from a nearby bar. Then Archipiado asked the *caboclo* to open a beer-bottle with his teeth. Rei das Cobras, whose human vehicle is a woman, performed this *caboclo* stunt without hesitation, and went away.

However, he later came back and said something to Archipiado that I did not hear, as I was busy lighting a cigar for another *caboclo*. When I asked Archipiado what Rei das Cobras had said, he replied that he could not tell me. I wanted to know why, and he said, "Because."

Another *caboclo* came and asked Archipiado why he did not let himself be "cut"—that is, with the cicatrices that signify initiation—in order to "cure" himself.

Various *caboclos* offered us swigs from their bottles of beer or vodka. Pena Branca had a large German-looking beer-stein, which he passed to us. The liquid was effervescent but did not taste like beer, and had a reddish color. I wondered, in the light of subsequent events, whether it might have been *jurema*. Trovezeiro gave us sips from a smaller mug containing the same substance.

If *jurema* was in use at the festival, it may also have been contained in the cigars the *caboclos* were smoking. From time to time a *caboclo* would come and blow smoke at us.

Twice Pena Branca motioned me to dance with him. At other Candomblé festivals where I was obliged to dance, I felt excruciatingly self-conscious and awkward. But on this occasion it seemed as though my feet were sparks in a world that sparkled. I followed Pena Branca's steps, and elaborated my own.

The first time this happened Pena Branca had been dancing alone. The second time, he had formed the *caboclos* and the audience into an enormous samba circle. This is the only festival at which I have seen a samba circle formed by everyone present.

At one stage of the proceedings, while we were sitting in our places, I noticed that Archipiado was slumped back in his chair, with his head tilted backwards and a glazed look in his eyes. I thought he must have been suffering from the effects of liquor, but jokingly clicked my fingers over his head, as if to chase off any spirits that might be hovering there. After a few minutes he got up, lurched about on the dance floor in the manner of someone experiencing a *barravento*, and staggered towards the front door, where he fell to the ground. I ran to help him, but the young *ogã* who had shown us to our seats said he would be all right, and took him out through the back door to the private quarters of the *terreiro*. He returned after a time, and seemed subdued.

The climax of the festival came after the *caboclos* trooped outside to the "hut" where their ritual objects are kept. A construction of this type is sometimes referred to as the *terreiro*'s "Aruanda." This one conformed to the ideal type, in being in the open air, circular, and thatched. It resembled a large cage, with a roof supported by rough-hewn poles spaced a short distance apart.

The *caboclos* returned, in procession, bearing mangos, papayas, pineapples, passionfruit, bananas, custard-apples, watermelons, canteloupes, sugar cane, apples, oranges, corn, peanuts, star-fruit, and jack-fruit. These they placed on a straw mat that had been laid out in the middle of the *barracão*, over the tiles that are known as the *terreiro*'s "foundation." Beneath lies the "precept" or "mystery"—a secret collection of objects that the parent-of-saint buries there when the *terreiro* is founded.

The *caboclos* sat round the edges of the mat, with Pena Branca and Trovezeiro at its head, and responded to the chants Pena Branca led, first with a kind of "war-cry" called *ilá* (cf. Cacciatore 1977:143), then picking up the tune. Pena Branca's charisma and exuberance seemed to evoke an ungrudging allegiance from his band of "primitive anarchists." I was sufficiently under his spell to think that the chants, which I too was singing, were outside of time, primordial.

Eventually the singing stopped, and the fruit was distributed to members of the audience. This seemed to conclude the formal proceedings, although the *caboclos* remained materialized, and had not sung their farewells. Meat was prepared on a barbecue in the front yard, and an enormous cake, in the form of the Brazilian flag, was brought into the *barracão*. It covered the whole surface of the small table on which it was carried, and had green, yellow, and blue frosting, with stars and the motto *ORDEM E PROGRESSO* picked out in silver dragées. I trust that the shade of the father of positivism was duly appreciative of this tribute.

Most of the guests trickled away after they had eaten. Jorge, however, was in no hurry to leave, and Archipiado and I knew that there would be no buses back to the city until just before dawn, so we stayed as well. We wondered if there was to be some epilogue to the festival.

Eventually the *caboclos* went out to the hut again, carrying an enormous basket, which they filled with offerings and covered with a white cloth. The skull of a bullock that had been sacrificed on the first day of the festival was also brought into the *barracão*. Then Pena Branca led a short expedition, which we joined, to a hill that lies north of the *terreiro*. The basket was placed on the ground and covered with branches that we broke from bushes growing there.

The route we took back completed a clockwise circle. When we arrived at the *terreiro* a woman was called to hold a metal pot of water above the gate. We all had to pass under the pot in order to enter the yard. I looked up and noticed that the bullock's skull was now suspended above our heads, in a tree.

The *barracão* was in the process of being cleaned, so the festival was clearly over. The *caboclos* went out to the private quarters at the back, to be suspended. A visiting father-of-saint emerged again. This man had been initiated in the same *terreiro* as Gelson, and was therefore the latter's brother-of-saint. It was he who had been incorporated by Trovezeiro. He presented us with mementos of the occasion—a small blue-eyed doll dressed as Pena Branca, and a little clay hut, with a straw roof and a bag inside containing candy. We asked him to give our thanks to Gelson, and took our leave. Jorge walked us to the bus stop.

* * *

When we awoke, around midday, I asked Archipiado what he remembered of his *barravento*. He did not recall anything of the period of trance itself, but said he realized beforehand what was happening, when he started to feel dazed and experienced a chill running up and down his spine. He had tried to indicate to me that he wanted to leave, but was immobilized. The next thing he remembered was sitting on a sofa in the private quarters behind the *barracão*, where the young *ogã* offered him water to wash his face.

He had a complex set of reactions to the experience, mostly of shame. He knew that Jorge would talk about the incident to their mutual friend Márcio, and did not doubt that Márcio would bruit it abroad among their student colleagues. He seemed to regard trance as something marginal and atavistic that would compromise his reputation—as atheist, materialist, scientist, and anthropologist.

At the time I wondered why he should feel this way, considering that there are respected anthropologists who have also experienced trance, such as Diana Brown (1986:12) and Larry Peters (1981:Ch. 3), to mention only two recent examples. In fact, there are numerous illustrious figures in the history of the social sciences who have not regarded their private religious proclivities as incompatible with objective scholarship.

On reflection, however, it has occurred to me that perhaps all these luminaries were confronted by the same dilemma as Archipiado, and simply developed acceptable strategies for resolving it in their writing.

The scientific community is undoubtedly resistant to the intrusion into its discourse of non-objectivist perspectives, whether these derive from beliefs that presuppose alternative epistemologies (cf. Stoller and Olkes 1987:ix–xi, Stoller 1989:39), or from scholarly challenges to any kind of epistemological dictatorship (e.g., Feyerabend 1978, 1985). This resistance has certain consequences for the genre conventions of social scientific writing. In the present context the most relevant of these consequences is that a boundary must be recognized between objectivist and non-objectivist modes of discourse. An author may observe this convention by writing different kinds of books (for example, ethnographies and ethnographic novels, or, as in the case of Peter Berger, social scientific works and theological ones), or by framing non-objectivist discourse within an objectivist theoretical context.

This convention forces on the scholar whose interests exceed the boundaries of objectivism a certain schizophrenia, since s/he is obliged to act as though s/he were two different people. So Archipiado was probably correct in his intuition that it is not a simple matter to integrate experiences such as trance into the public, professional persona of the social scientist.

There were other dimensions of Archipiado's concern as well. In spite of the growth in recent years of a number of middle- and even upper-class *terreiros*, the Afro-Brazilian religions are still associated predominantly with the poorest sectors of Brazilian society. So when a Black Brazilian anthropologist such as Archipiado goes into trance, this is probably more stigmatizing than it would be for a white foreign anthropologist (like, say, Diana Brown—although it should be noted that Brown makes only the briefest passing reference to her trance experience). This was particularly likely in Archipiado's case, because of his family history.

Archipiado was not born in Bahia, but in the state of Minas Gerais. His mother's father, of Bahian slave origins, had moved to Minas to become a teacher of foreign languages, and there married Archipiado's grandmother. Their daughter, Archipiado's mother, married a white businessman of part Brazilian Indian descent. Archipiado described his mother, whom he never allowed me to meet, as someone with a very forceful disposition. In Minas she had some contact with an Afro-Brazilian *terreiro*, which was a cause of some family tension. Her husband was an atheist, and tore down all the religious pictures she put up around the house. Eventually Archipiado's parents separated, and his mother moved to Bahia, leaving her four sons and one daughter with their grandmother.

The children's circumstances were harder there, but Archipiado spoke of the time spent at his mother's mother's with a certain nostalgia. From her he learned a good deal of Brazilian folklore, some of it African in origin (such as the story of the talking skull, which is also told by Black communities in the United States [Ekunfeo 1986:6–9]), and some European (such as beliefs concerning the magic powers of the pentacle, and of a knotted cord called "St. Francis' rope").

After several years his mother sent for the children to join her in Bahia. They lived in a one room house in one of the poorer quarters of the city. One of Archipiado's strongest memories of this time is the prevalent stench of a tidal channel. His mother set to work building extensions to the house and constructing other small houses that she rented out. The family's circumstances improved, and they moved to a better location, where his mother continued with her building projects. One brother opened a bar, other brothers were apprenticed to a mechanic, their sister married a lawyer, and Archipiado, the youngest, was left to play the role of family servant, at the same time as he was acquiring an education. He went to one of the city's better schools, where he passed the exams that enabled him to enroll at the university.

His mother, although not a member of any *terreiro*, was accustomed to receiving a turbulent *caboclo* named Sete Espadas ("Seven Swords"). This entity called himself "the man with three balls," and used to harangue family members whose behavior displeased him. Archipiado's mother does not drink or sing, but her *caboclo* would swig pure *cachaça* and sing *caboclo* songs, in a rough masculine voice. A series of incidents put an end to the appearances of this domineering spirit. On one occasion when he materialized, the family members simply deserted the house, leaving him to rant to the walls. Another time, after a fight between Archipiado's mother and his step-father, who was also involved in the Afro-Brazilian religions, Sete Espadas had raged through the house, breaking whatever was at hand. After this the family members persuaded Archipiado's mother to stop receiving her *caboclo*. So she turned her hand to cartomancy. By means of the Tarot cards she was able to predict dire outcomes for family members who persisted in disapproved courses of action.

Archipiado liked to present himself as conventional, dressing conservatively and speaking standard Portuguese, in compensation for a family background that he regarded as exotic. (It was probably not as anomalous as he thought, but certainly it made him hard to pigeonhole, in terms of regional affiliation, race, and class.) Since trance played an important part in the history that created Archipiado's perception of his family, I should have been less surprised that he was disconcerted by his experience at Gelson's.

I went on to ask him about what it was that the *caboclo* Rei das Cobras had told him. I was interested for a couple of reasons. I thought it might have had something to do with his subsequent *barravento*, and I suspected that it somehow concerned me. He refused to tell me, and also would not say why he could not do so. He asked me why it was so important to me to know. I replied that the information might be some kind of key. I added that I was not going to get up until he told me.

He said that was up to me, took a shower, and got ready to go out. He went to open the door, but it was locked. I had hidden the key. He realized he could not leave, but was intransigent in refusing to divulge what the *caboclo* had told him. He said Rei das Cobras had asked him not to betray the secret. I inquired how he could reconcile this with his posture as atheist and scientist. He replied that he was a Brazilian, then lay down and ignored me.

It did not take me long to realize that what I had intended as a joke had gone too far. He had once teasingly compared our friendship to the relationship between the United States and Nicaragua, or the United Kingdom and the Falklands. Since I am neither American nor British I did not consider this comparison appropriate, though it hurt me. Now I began to understand that perhaps it was more apt than I thought.

We went out to lunch. I was no longer interested in pursuing the subject of Rei das Cobras, but even so, Archipiado hardly spoke a word. Fortunately, by the evening, when we met again, his rage had passed. He was with a group of student colleagues, including Márcio, who had already told them all the story of Archipiado's *barravento*, having heard it from Jorge. But Archipiado was able to make light of it.

* * *

About three weeks later we went to another festival at Gelson's. It was a ritual of the *orixás*, of the type called *saida de iaô*—the coming-out ceremony of a new initiate. The young man who had "rolled" at the *caboclo* festival would emerge from seclusion and call the name of his particular *orixá*, which is supposed to be revealed in a dream or vision. This time both Márcio and Jorge accompanied us.

As we came through the gate Archipiado asked about the significance of the bullock's skull, which was still hanging in the tree. Márcio and Jorge laughed, and said he would find out. When we entered the *barracão* I noticed that the audience consisted largely of women, whereas at the *caboclo* festival men had predominated.

The woman who had received Rei das Cobras came and chatted with us before the festival started. But nothing was said about her *caboclo*.

Archipiado left the *barracão* several times in the course of the ceremony, to avoid falling into trance. At the *caboclo* festival Jorge had said that every time Archipiado attended a Candomblé ceremony in the future, his *orixá* would get closer and closer to him. Archipiado was determined to see that this did not happen.

After the ritual Archipiado and I were talking to members of the *terreiro*, asking questions about aspects of Candomblé that puzzled us. One young man was being friendly and helpful, until Márcio told him "not to give the gold into the hands of bandits." Márcio intervened in a similar fashion in another conversation shortly afterwards.

We went outside to get something to drink, and Márcio asked me to buy him a Coke. Archipiado told him this was an exploitation. Márcio replied that he was justified in exploiting the system. When I gave him the Coke I told him it was a present from the system.

We all walked to the bus stop. Márcio accused Archipiado of being compromised by his association with the bourgeoisie, rather than being active, as he himself was, in proletarian movements. Archipiado retorted that he preferred Nietzsche to Marx, and that in any case the revolution had never started from the bottom up. Márcio, obviously nettled, tried to think of examples to refute this assertion, citing Lenin, Mao, and Che Guevara.

For some reason religion came into the conversation. Márcio said that all religions are the opium of the people, except for Candomblé. Subsequently I came across the following quotation from the poet Abdias do Nascimento:

> When they say that religion has been the opium of the people and has been the instrument of social immobilization, this is not applicable to the African religions. It is not applicable to Candomblé, to Umbanda, nor to any of the branches of the so-called Afro-Brazilian religions, because these, to the contrary, have been [the means of] cultural resistance, have provided the parameters for our identity (quoted in Silva 1986:3).

I was annoyed and frustrated by Márcio, but not exactly angry. He had been prone to excitable moods since the recent departure of his Harvard-educated white American boyfriend. But his obstructiveness made me think it would be useless to attempt any further research at Gelson's *terreiro*. He and I subsequently repaired our friendship, and he invited me back to Lobito. But by that time my *orixá* had evidently developed a preference for Jaraci.

* * *

In this period I encountered in the city an acquaintance from my previous trip to Bahia. At that time Sérgio had been a son-of-saint in a distant northern suburb. Now he was a father-of-saint, and had opened his own house of Candomblé, not too far from the center of town. He invited me to his forthcoming *caboclo* festival.

So a week after the *saida de iaô* at Gelson's, Archipiado and I made our way to Sérgio's *terreiro*, which he had created from an apartment with no usable outdoor space. This necessitated certain compromises. The house of Exu was a back room at the end of a corridor, and the Aruanda of the *caboclos*, symbolized on this occasion by a bower of palm branches in which offerings of fruit and liquor had been placed, was located in a space created by the stair-well.

In the small *barracão* there was standing room only. As at Gelson's *caboclo* festival, the audience was predominantly male.

Archipiado and I crouched in front of the men who had arrived early enough to get a seat on the concrete bench that ran along one wall, but we were obscuring their view. A policeman directed us to the corridor leading to the room of Exu, where there was more space, but it was difficult to observe the proceedings, especially for Archipiado, who is about a foot shorter than I.

The atmosphere was palpably different from that of Gelson's festival. Members of the audience reacted touchily when they bumped into each other, and the *caboclos* also seemed more aggressive. Sérgio's *caboclo*, Pena Branca, carried a silver spear, which he periodically waved at members of the audience. Other *caboclos* also had spears, which they used, at one point, to prod a man who had fallen into trance on the floor. They all danced violently, throwing themselves around the *barracão*, and their greetings were belligerent. When *caboclos* embrace people they commonly bump chests. These *caboclos* did so with considerable force. Pena Branca greeted one man so roughly that they both lurched into the center of the *barracão*, colliding with an *ogã* and spilling the cup of wine he had been pouring.

This was the first festival at which I saw *caboclos* perform the gunpowder test. Several of them poured gunpowder onto their upturned palms and lit it with their cigars. One of them showed the black mark on his palm to the audience.

The *ogãs* distributed earthenware cups, inscribed with the words *LEMBRANÇA DO CABOCLO PENA BRANCA* ("Memento of the *caboclo* Pena Branca"), and the date. Periodically they brought around a clay pitcher, and half-filled the cups with sweet red wine.

About half-way through the evening I began to feel faint. This could not have been the effect of the wine, as I had drunk only two or three half cups. My hands and feet started to go numb, and I felt I was losing control of my arms and legs. Archipiado later told me he had experienced the same sensations before his *barravento* at Gelson's. In theory I was not worried about the possibility of falling into trance, but this did not seem like the appropriate place to do it. So I walked around in the corridor, exercising my arms and legs to restore circulation, and tried to concentrate. The strange feeling went away.

After the formal proceedings were over there was a reception on the porch of the building next door. Each guest who came up the steps was greeted by a spear-waving Pena Branca, who wore an upright headdress of white feathers and a feather skirt over white knickerbockers. Some were scared off by his threatening appearance, and ran back out into the rain. I had a strong sense of *dejá vu*, as though flashing back to a forgotten dream.

Pena Branca embraced each guest who made it up the steps, then posed a question, which the guest had to answer before proceeding. He asked me where I had seen him before. I was taken aback, and, momentarily confusing Pena Branca with his horse Sérgio, I mentioned the circumstances under which I had been invited to the festival. Pena Branca did not seem at all impressed, but let me pass.

As we were sitting eating, Archipiado reminded me that at the end of the *caboclo* festival in Lobito, after we had returned from the hill, he had asked Pena Branca when we could see him again. Pena Branca had replied that he would come back to Gelson's *terreiro* in a year's time, but that we would see him "round about."

* * *

In her fine study of the *terreiros* in the Baixada Fluminense, on the outskirts of Rio de Janeiro, Patrícia Birman notes the implications of different expressions used to refer to the behavior of spirits that induce trance. For her informants the most important distinction was between the terms *descer*, "to descend," and *virar*, "to turn." To say that a spirit "descends" implies that it belongs to the "entities" of Umbanda; to say that it "turns" means that it is one of the "saints" of Candomblé (Birman 1988:98, 192).

This distinction did not seem to be relevant in Bahia, perhaps because Umbanda is not widespread in Salvador, and so not in such competition with Candomblé as it is in Rio. Many *terreiros* in Salvador have incorporated elements of Umbanda, without regarding this as a threat to their identity as houses of Candomblé.

When generalizing about the inhabitants of the invisible world, people I spoke to in Bahia often referred to them all as "spirits." The term "entities" was used in the same sense, but less frequently. These "spirits" or "entities" are divided into various categories. One category is that of the "saints" or *orixás*. But there are expressions in which the word "saint" loses its association with a particular class of spirits. For example, *receber santo*, "to receive saint," and *dar santo*, "to give saint," can be used, regardless of the type of spirit involved, to mean, respectively, "to go into trance" and "to appear to go into trance."

The operative distinction in Candomblé of Bahia seems to be between expressions in which a spirit is the logical agent and those in which a human being is the logical agent. In most cases the logical agent is also the grammatical subject. The one important exception occurs with the use of *receber*, "to receive," which is perhaps the most common of all Bahian terms for referring to trance. In expressions using *receber*, the person who receives saint, or a particular type of spirit, is the grammatical subject, but the logical patient.

All the expressions in which a human being is the logical agent have slightly pejorative overtones. These include, for example:

dar santo ("to give saint")
cair no santo ("to fall into saint")
virar no santo ("to turn [over or around] into saint")
incorporar o santo ("to incorporate the saint")
rodar com o santo ("to circle with the saint").

By treating the human being as the logical agent, these expressions imply that he or she is "giving *equê*"—that is, faking a trance state. However, they are often used jocularly, whether or not there are any grounds for suspicion that the trance is false.

In the expressions that are used to refer to a legitimate trance state, the logical agent is a spirit. These expressions include, for example:

descer na (cabeça da) pessoa ("to descend into [the head of] the person")
baixar na (cabeça da) pessoa ("to come down into [the head of] the person")
rodar na cabeça da pessoa ("to circle in the head of the person")
pegar a pessoa ("to grab the person")
apanhar a pessoa ("to catch the person")
incorporar (-se) (n)a pessoa ("to incorporate [in] the person")
materializar (-se) na pessoa ("to materialize in the person")
manifestar (-se) na pessoa ("to manifest in the person").

People tried to make distinctions within these two sets of expressions, according to the types of spirits that they could be used with, but there were variations between the observations of different individuals, and inconsistencies in particular individuals' habitual usage. Taís, for example, said that *exus* do not "descend," because it is the *orixás* who come from above. He said the *exus* "come walking," which implies that they are on the same level as human beings. But Corquisa herself told me that when she arrives she "descends," and when she leaves she "ascends." And Taís often spoke of his *exuas* as "coming to earth."

There are, however, a few expressions that can apparently be used only with particular categories of spirits. *Caboclos*, for example, are the only ones of whom I have heard it said that they *montam (n) a pessoa* ("climb [on] the person") or *montam nas costas da pessoa* ("climb on the person's back"). This was in a conversation in which the behavior of *caboclos* was contrasted with that of *orixás*, who were said to "descend into the head of the person."

The verb *encostar*, "to lean" (which in standard Portuguese would be reflexive, that is, *encostar-se*) is used only in reference to *eguns* ("spirits of the dead") and, sometimes, *exus*. When *eguns* and *exus* "lean on" people, however, they do not cause trance, but a disturbed emotional and physical condition. This is typical behavior for *eguns* that have not been "educated" by means of offerings, but *exus* do it only if they are malicious.

In addition to these various expressions that refer to a relationship between only two parties, Candomblé also has a number of "triangular" expressions. These involve not only a person who goes into trance and a spirit, but a third party as well, who is in some sense the spirit's auxiliary. These include, for example:

virar a pessoa no santo ("to turn the person [over or around] into saint")
chamar o santo da pessoa ("to call the saint of the person").

In these expressions the grammatical subject is usually a parent-of-saint, *ogã*, or *equede*, who in this case performs a legitimate agentive role.

What seems to be at issue in all the expressions I have discussed here is the question of control. According to the ideology of Candomblé, people cannot control their own spirits. However, parents-of-saint, *ogãs*, and *equedes* may control the spirits of others, because they have the authority to do so.

* * *

Kenneth Burke has remarked that "there is a point at which Mysticism and Materialism become indistinguishable. Both involve a narrowing of motivational circumference. Materialism accomplishes this by a deliberate elimination of purpose as a term. . . . Mysticism arrives at somewhat the same result unintentionally, in making purpose absolute, and thereby in effect transforming it into fatality" (1962:291).

Thus it is possible for adherents of Candomblé and social scientists to offer explanations of trance that involve essentially the same determinism. We have seen that the "correct" way of talking about trance in Candomblé is to refer to people as logical patients whose behavior is controlled by spirits. When social scientists give Durkheimian explanations of trance, as reflecting particular aspects of the social order, they transpose the "mystical" explanation to a "material" plane: trance reflects the subservience of women in a male-controlled society (cf. Matory 1988), or of clients in a society characterized by relationships of patronage (cf. Brown 1986).

There is an alternative explanation of trance that we could call "idealist." Burke notes that "the unadulteratedly idealistic philosophy starts and ends in the featuring of properties belonging to the term, *agent.* Idealistic philosophies think in terms of the 'ego,' the 'self,' the 'super-ego,' 'consciousness,' 'will,' the 'generalized I,' the 'subjective,' 'mind,' 'spirit,' the 'oversoul,' and any such 'super-persons' as church, race, nation, etc." (1962:171).

The notion of the "individual" that, according to Steven Lukes, is characteristic of modern Western cultures, is "idealist," in that the individual is a "sovereign chooser, he *decides* between actions, conceptions of the good, plans of life, indeed what sort of person to be. The will, choice, decision, evaluation and calculation are central to this picture; and the individual to whom these features are essential thinks and acts as an autonomous, self-directing, independent agent who relates to others as no less autonomous agents" (Lukes 1985:298). But Lukes admits that the distribution of this notion of the individual in the West is not uniform. For example, it is more likely to be characteristic of men than of women (Lukes 1985:299). We could go further and say that idealism is more likely to underlie explanations of the behavior of entities perceived as controlling than of entities perceived as controlled.

Yet adherents of Candomblé and social scientists may both offer idealist explanations of trance, even though people in trance are conventionally perceived as "controlled." This is made possible by the notion of transgression.

When a member of a *terreiro*, in describing a trance state, refers to the person in that state as an agent, it is implied that the person concerned is transgressing the norms of trance behavior, by "giving *equê*" (faking trance). Social scientists use a similar "idealist" explanatory strategy when they interpret trance as a protest against the prevailing structures of domination, and thus a transgression of the rules of a particular system of social control (cf. Fry 1976, Comaroff 1985).

It is paradoxical that all these explanations are based on the same agent-patient distinction, considering that the actual behavior of people in trance appears to subvert that distinction. It was, as I have mentioned earlier, often not clear to me where the boundaries lay between spirits (such as Corquisa) and humans (such as Taís), and such a boundary is necessary for agent-patient explanations of trance to be possible. I was able to use the same terminology that everyone else did to draw the necessary distinctions. But what I observed often contradicted the boundaries implied by the terminology.

This contradiction suggested the need for a different approach to trance. Although explanations of the phenomenon in terms of the agent-patient distinction offer useful insights, there are important aspects of it that they do not account for. One alternative way of looking at the matter would be to consider it in terms of what Michel Maffesoli calls "causal pluralism" (1985a:62).

Maffesoli, a French sociologist whose works have had a significant impact in Brazil, has elaborated his ideas about causality in the context of a theory of "ordinary knowledge" (a phrase that provides the title for the most general and systematic exposition of his ideas, *La connaissance ordinaire* [1985a]). Ordinary knowledge is a complex mixture of reason and imagination. What distinguishes these two terms is their relationship to systems of social control (rather than their hypostasization as "conscious" and "unconscious" aspects of the psyche). Reason is associated with the institutional discourses of pedagogy, the state, administration, and economics, while the imagination is linked rather to the "miniscule situations of everyday life" (1984:64), which, as we have seen in the case of trance behavior, subvert the categories according to which reason operates.

Reason is concerned with the differentiation and ordering of phenomena, because this makes possible the determining of causes and the attribution of responsibility. Systems of social control require such an attribution in order that entities may be held accountable for events (cf. Maffesoli 1985b:129, 133; 1985a:47, 59). The imagination is more global, and therefore placed by Maffesoli under the patronage of Dionysus, the "undivided" (1985b:135). From the perspective of the imagination, causality is so multiplex that cause itself seems to disappear, to be replaced by a sense of "participation" (1985a:133).

Maffesoli's distinction between reason and the imagination owes a good deal to Gilbert Durand's analysis of the "anthropological structures of the imaginary" (1962; cf. Maffesoli 1985b:130 and *passim*). Durand divides "the image" into two "regimes"—the "diurnal regime," which consists of the kind of imagery produced by reason, and the "nocturnal regime," which consists of the kind of imagery produced by fantasy. Reason is characterized by the imagery of antithesis, which not only separates terms, but also endows them with opposed values. The positive terms are those associated with the eternal, the disembodied, the absolute. Fantasy is characterized by the imagery of synthesis, which links the eternal to the temporal, the disembodied to the spatial, the absolute to the relative. This imagery is, to use Bakhtin's term, "grotesque." The world of fantasy is a kind of organic flux, in which entities with indefinite or provisional boundaries interpenetrate and transform into each other, constituting their ephemeral existence through their interaction.

Because reason and fantasy are inextricable in the texture of social life, social phenomena are paradoxical, contradictory, ambiguous, heterogeneous—and pluricausal. "For the same social fact there can be a multiplicity of causes" (Maffesoli 1985a:58). Recognition of this causal pluralism necessitates a particular kind of writing: "various angles of attack," "concentric approaches," "successive sedimentations," and the concatenation of "local" or "situational" theories that are inseparable from empirical observation. There can be no strict separation of theory and description (Maffesoli 1985a:27–29, 62).

Superficially, Maffesoli's position would appear to have a certain amount in common with post-modernism, that is, with "those discourses that recognize the futility of seeking an absolute foundation for knowledge" (Eilberg-Schwartz 1988:110). But there is an important difference. The central trope in Maffesoli's writings is not "knowledge" by itself, but the "conjunction . . . of knowledge and sociality" (1985a:227). For Maffesoli, knowledge is not isolated in an ideal realm of theory, a world of pure text, but is intimately linked to the sociability of daily life (cf. Jackson 1989:184). Writing is thus not a privileged activity that has as its purpose to create the maximum distance between itself and the everyday world, but a form of social interaction that is embedded in ordinary experience (1985a:204), hence a species of "ordinary knowledge."

Maffesoli's position may be made clearer by contrasting it with that of, say, Foucault, whose program could be summed up as a quest for an "extreme singularity" of thought, with "ill will" as the method (Foucault 1977:181–82). For Maffesoli, sociality is not only the principal object of study of the social sciences, but also the principal means of approaching that object.

For both the adherents of Candomblé and social scientists, trance is capable of being explained in terms of what counts for "rationality" in their respective milieux. But, like any social phenomenon, trance is embedded in an everyday world in which reason is suffused with fantasy. So an explanation of trance that simply replaced the rationality of Candomblé with the rationality of the social sciences would ignore a large part of what is interesting about the phenomenon. My own approach has been to attempt to create an account of trance from the perspective of "ordinary knowledge." This entails locating particular instances of trance within the events of daily life, and attempting to reproduce the interaction of reason and imagination in the way trance was interpreted by those involved in the events, including myself. My purpose has been "to actualize or, in a strict sense, imagine that which in one way or another is found disseminated in daily existence itself" (Maffesoli 1985b:13).

* * *

I have never seen a *cabocla* (female *caboclo*) that belonged to Candomblé, and Taís confirmed that it would be difficult to find one. Once I attended a festival at Biju's where a *cabocla* "manifested," but her "horse" was an Umbanda mother-of-saint who was a friend of Biju's. In other words, the *caboclos* of Candomblé, at least in their materialized form, live in an exclusively masculine world. But a world in which there is only one sex is a world that is sexually undifferentiated.

This is perhaps why it is difficult to locate the realm of the *caboclos* on the spirit-matter continuum. This continuum is premised on antitheses, and associated, as we have seen, with sexual differentiation. But the imagery of the forest world of the *caboclos* has less in common with what Durand calls the "diurnal regime" of antithesis than with the "nocturnal regime," which resists dichotomization. The *caboclos*' world is oxymoronic, euphemistic, universalistic, utopian, carnivalesque.

Since the imagery of the nocturnal regime is, according to Durand, synthetic, one might conclude that the realm of the *caboclos* synthesizes, in dialectic fashion, what is separated out in the imagery of the diurnal regime, and therefore lies at the midpoint of the spirit-matter continuum. But I would suggest a small modification to Durand's observations on the nocturnal regime.

Synthesis is based on the conjunction of opposites that are taken as given, whereas in the nocturnal regime nothing is given. Dichotomies are not naturally occurring phenomena, but creations of the differentiating, diurnal mind. Seen in this light the forest world of the *caboclos* appears not so much to be located at a particular point on the spirit-matter continuum, as rather to be its "negative space." This does not mean that it has the kind of simple relationship to the spirit-matter continuum that ground has to figure. It is a negative space of the type that Douglas Hofstadter has in mind when he writes that "there exist formal systems whose negative space . . . is not the positive space . . . of any formal system" (1980:72).

The nocturnal regime is in some sense incommensurable with the diurnal regime, yet depends on it, interacts with it, subtly suffuses it, and constantly relativizes it.

6. Villages

In contrast with the *exus*, whose natural habitat is the street world of the big cities, and with the *orixás*, who are often thought to live in royal dwellings, as befits their status, the *caboclos* live in "villages." It is thus appropriate that my formal incorporation into the "village" of Jaraci was accomplished with the complicity of a *caboclo*.

Maffesoli writes of the contemporary world as a "multitude of villages," all interconnected, and populated by "tribes" of fluctuating composition (1987:194–95). He acknowledges that this is "only a metaphor," but it is one that provides a useful perspective from which to consider Machiavelli's distinction between "the thinking of the palace and that of the public square" (Maffesoli 1985a:184). In terms of this metaphor, the palace and the public square are also "villages," or parts of villages. This means that the kinds of thinking that characterize them can both be subsumed under the rubric of "local knowledge" (cf. Maffesoli 1987:81; Geertz 1983).

The thinking of the palace may be more universalistic, because of the palace's concern with empire, but this does not make it more "true." It is linked to local practices and strategies—admittedly with far-reaching implications—in the same way as the thinking of the public square. It is these practices and strategies that give all thinking, including scientific thinking, its "village" quality (cf. Latour and Woolgar 1979:28–29).

For social scientists who adopt this perspective, writing is not so much a matter of what Latour and Woolgar call "fact production" (1979:254), which presupposes the possibility of some kind of knowledge that is not local, but rather requires knowing how to *be* in what one describes (Maffesoli 1987:81).

* * *

A couple of weeks after *carnaval*, Archipiado and I took up Marinalvo's invitation to attend a festival at his *terreiro* in Jaraci. We went in the early afternoon, with Joãozinho—Archipiado's childhood friend and Marinalvo's son-of-saint. Our bus turned off the main highway and took us a short distance down a tree-lined dirt road. We walked the last half-mile to Marinalvo's on foot.

The *terreiro* is located on the outskirts of Fernando Pessoa, where clay begins to give way to sand. One side of the street is lined with houses, and the other is covered with dense vegetation, which members of the *terreiro* exploit for the leaves and herbs required in rituals. The street dips down to a small valley at the foot of the dunes, where the poorest residents of Fernando Pessoa have built an "invasion," or shanty-town, with a spring at its center. The spring is the invasion's water supply. Marinalvo's street has piped water (at least intermittently), but once a year the members of his *terreiro* go in procession to the spring, to draw off pots of water for a ritual called "the waters of Oxalá."

On the dunes above the invasion, which undulate down to the sea, the wealthy of Salvador have built mansions that they use mostly on weekends or during vacations. Some local residents are employed there as caretakers.

Jaraci is not exactly rural. A few people cultivate small plots of land, but the economy is not agrarian. Those who are employed work in local service industries or in the few small factories in Fernando Pessoa, or commute to jobs in other municipalities. Yet Jaraci feels like a village. The sense of territory is palpably different from that of the metropolis.

When I visited *terreiros* in the city I always had the sense of being confined to spaces and times allocated to outsiders, and thus of being excluded from the inside world of Candomblé. The distinction between private and public seemed less rigid in the *terreiros* of Jaraci, because of their embeddedness in the local community. The members of any *terreiro* were involved in a network of neighborhood relationships, and were constantly visiting and being visited by friends who did not belong to the *terreiro*. There was no neat overlap between the spatial boundaries of the *terreiro* and social boundaries. This meant also a certain blurring of the distinction between public and private information. Much of what happened in any *terreiro* rapidly became public information in Jaraci.

But perhaps this way of stating the matter reflects certain preconceptions about the meaning of public and private that I brought to Jaraci. It might be more accurate to say that the Jaracians drew the boundaries in a way that was unfamiliar to me.

When we arrived at Marinalvo's, he and other members of the *terreiro* sat and talked with us, first in the back yard, then in the kitchen, where we were invited to lunch. The conversation focused on sexual practices. Marinalvo described his own in graphic detail, and proceeded to interrogate us about ours.

I was disconcerted. I was not accustomed to such intimate revelations between people who hardly knew each other. Also, we were in the presence of a female dignitary of the *terreiro*.

As far as Marinalvo was concerned, the topic of conversation was a public matter. His own sexual practices were well known in Jaraci, and no one seemed to pay them much heed or regard them as in any way unusual, except for his mother, Neuza, who lived a few doors away. She had threatened to kill him if she found him in bed with another man.

Later, when we met this frail but determined woman, she confided to us that she would not mind so much if Marinalvo settled down with one of his nice middle-class boyfriends. What she objected to was his practice of making out with all the young ruffians of the district.

She was the only person I met in Jaraci who considered it necessary to find causal explanations for anyone's sexual habits. She said that as a child Marinalvo had had an intestinal worm, of the kind called in Brazil *caseira*. At the time I considered this explanation outlandish. But it made sense later, when Archipiado told me that "everyone knows" the cure for *caseira* is *pica* ("cock"). As explanations of sexual tastes go, this seemed as good as any other.

In any case, in Jaraci I found myself obliged to drop my received notions of what constitutes public and private information, and to adopt those that were relevant in the local community. I had picked up from my university training the idea that all religious practices are open to public scrutiny. It was hard to sustain this position in Jaraci, where I came to understand that one's life could depend on keeping certain religious information secret.

Marinalvo left us to look around while he went on with preparations for the festival. There were only two parts of the *terreiro* that were closed to us: the house of Exu, and the *bakisse*, or "room of the saints," which contains the altars dedicated to the *orixás*, and in which a senior female initiate was in seclusion. We joined Joãozinho in the *barracão*, and helped him and other members of the *terreiro* strip branches brought from the forest, and strew the leaves on the floor.

Later in the afternoon Marinalvo dug out his collection of newspaper clippings, which document his career as a father-of-saint. There were stories and photographs of festivals at his *terreiro*, and accounts of his New Year predictions. One of Salvador's newspapers asks a number of parents-of-saint to "throw the cowries" at the end of the year. Marinalvo said his predictions had always come true. He had, for example, predicted that Mário Kértesz would be elected as mayor of Salvador, and that there would be a fire in the Model Market (a large indoor bazaar in the Low City).

The festival finished late, and, like many of the other guests, we stayed overnight, since there were no more buses back to the city. Everyone, including Marinalvo, slept on the floor.

Marinalvo asked us to come back for another festival two weeks later, and told me to invite Xilton, which I did. Archipiado and I arrived early for the festival, and, for the first time, I met Taís, who was helping Marinalvo with the preparations. The festival was well under way when Xilton arrived with his chief *ogã* and with another father-of-saint who doubles as a lawyer. They spent the evening exchanging glances and remarks. Xilton could not understand why I was spending my time in Jaraci, when he had already introduced me to some of the most elite and "orthodox" *terreiros* in Salvador.

In the course of the festival Archipiado received an *arrepio*, or "shiver." This is a brief bodily spasm associated with the onset of trance. However, it does not develop into the vertiginous state called a *barravento*, nor into trance proper. Xilton made an ironic comment to him, and Archipiado walked out of the *barracão*.

Xilton drove us back to the city when the festival was over.

That night I had a dream in which a doctor told me I needed an operation that entailed the insertion of a needle through the top of my skull. I had a choice about whether or not to go ahead with it, but I agreed to the procedure. The doctor inserted the needle, and my body convulsed violently, as from an electric shock. I blacked out. When I recovered consciousness, the needle was still in my skull, with the syringe—the heavy, old-fashioned type made of glass—attached. I moved, and the syringe broke off, leaving the needle itself protruding from my head. I knew that I would need another operation to remove it. (During the initiation of a child-of-saint a cut, usually in the form of a cross, is made in the apex of the skull, to allow the *orixá* entry into the initiate's head.)

* * *

Archipiado and I were due to make a trip to Campinas, near São Paulo, for the annual meetings of ABA, the Brazilian Anthropology Association.

In the interim we continued to visit other *terreiros* and attended one more festival at Marinalvo's.

When we got back from the conference, the anthropologist in me knew it was time to start establishing closer ties with one particular *terreiro*. Or perhaps it was my *orixá* who was growing tired of being without a home. But I put off going to Jaraci for a couple of weeks, and Archipiado and I attended the coming-out ceremony at the *terreiro* of Gelson, and the *caboclo* festival at Sérgio's. Was it the anthropologist or the *orixá* who was taking time to make up my mind?

Finally I decided to visit Marinalvo, to ask him to "wash the beads" for Archipiado and me. This is a simple procedure that establishes a symbolic link with Candomblé, but not necessarily a formal affiliation with any particular *terreiro*. One leaves a set of beads of the color appropriate to one's *orixá* with a parent-of-saint, who places them in a herbal infusion. This is a preliminary move that does not entail any commitment, at least in principle.

It was mid-morning when we arrived unannounced at Marinalvo's. He was standing in the front yard, welcomed us in, and proceeded to bring us up to date on all the events we had missed during our absence. He had remodeled the *bakisse*, or "room of the saints," and the *roncó*, or "retreat room," with the help of a young man called Paulo, whom he intended to initiate as *ogã*. In the *roncó* a *barco* of new initiands was in seclusion. *Barco* means "boat," but in Candomblé refers to a group of children-of-saint who are initiated at the same time. There were three members of the *barco*, which meant that this initiation was an ambitious undertaking for a small *terreiro*. At the time we first met him, Marinalvo had only five children-of-saint.

The final *saida*, or coming-out ceremony, when the new initiates would call the names of their respective *orixás*, was due to take place in a couple of weeks. In the interim there was going to be a talk at the *terreiro* by a candidate for the forthcoming local mayoral election.

Marinalvo invited us into the kitchen. As we passed the *roncó* we could hear the babble of *erês*. Children-of-saint undergoing initiation spend almost the whole period of their seclusion "incorporated" by their *erês*, or child spirits. They come out of retreat once a week, on Friday, the day of Oxalá, to take the sun.

Various people were going about their business in the *terreiro*—Taís, Neuza, a woman called Angélica, who acted as Marinalvo's housekeeper, and Marinalvo's new boyfriend Delcir. The latter was a computer programmer Marinalvo had met during *carnaval*, who was the "little father" (sponsor) of one of the members of the *barco*.

Marinalvo poured us some beer, and shortly afterwards received another visitor, a father-of-saint called Almiro, whom I had noticed at the *caboclo* festival at Sérgio's. Almiro was visiting from Rio de Janeiro, though he was originally from Bahia. The next few hours of gossip revolved around the famous *terreiros* of Fernando Pessoa and Salvador. At one point Almiro and I were left alone talking. Outside, Marinalvo complained to Archipiado that I was paying too much attention to Almiro, and that the latter was not to be trusted.

Eventually I broached the subject of washing the beads. Marinalvo offered to throw the cowries for us immediately, so that he could establish the identities of our *orixás*. Archipiado and I had been told previously, by different parents-of-saint, that we were of Obaluaiê, also called Omolu, the *orixá* responsible for diseases and their cures. Marinalvo did not accept this.

He fetched a large, circular wickerwork tray containing his divination equipment, and he and Archipiado and I went into the *barracão*. Marinalvo sat on the throne of his *orixá* Iançã, placed the tray on his lap, and removed the cloth that covered it.

Three large necklaces formed a circle around the perimeter of the tray. One consisted of red and black beads, the other of red beads, and the third of paired cowries. In the middle of the circle were seventeen loose cowries, a small conch shell, a smooth black seed, and two coins, scattered randomly on top of eleven cards from the Tarot pack. The cards were all from the minor arcana—four from the suit of wands, three from the suit of coins, and two each from the suits of cups and swords.

Marinalvo asked which of us was to go first, and Archipiado said I was. Marinalvo rang a double bell (called *adjá*) above the tray, then proceeded to gather up the cowries in his hands and throw them down.

The cowries used in this divination procedure are prepared in a particular way, which entails removing the hump on the back of the shell. I had spent a morning at Xilton's learning how to do this, by cutting a small notch at the end of the hump, then inserting and twisting the point of a knife, which causes the hump to spring off. This creates a shell with two openings, one natural and one artificial. When the cowries are thrown, those that fall with the artificial opening upwards are considered to be "open," and those that fall with the natural opening upwards are considered to be "closed." The divination is based on a consideration of the number of cowries that fall in the open and closed positions on each throw, and their arrangement in relation to each other.

Different parents-of-saint have different methods for throwing and interpreting the cowries. Marinalvo made his throws so rapidly that it was impossible for me to ascertain which method he was using. The usual procedure is first to throw sixteen cowries, to determine the identity of the *orixá* who is speaking through them (Braga 1988:95), though a larger or smaller number may be used. The late Joãozinho da Goméia is reported to have used seventeen (Cossard-Binon 1970:49; Braga 1988:87). This reading is then confirmed or modified by throwing just four cowries. Subsequent throws are intended to answer particular questions related to the client's situation. (Some idea of the range of variation in the methods of throwing the cowries can be gleaned by comparing the definitive scholarly work on the subject, by Julio Braga [1988], with the popular manual used by many parents-of-saint, by José Ribeiro [1985].)

Marinalvo made a series of pronouncements. In the first place, he said, the owner of my head was the elder Oxalá, known as Oxalufã, father of the *orixás*. In the second place, I was suffering from the irradiation of an *egum*. This was the spirit of a person close to me, who had died. The *egum* was causing me harm, although intending to help me. He asked me to think who this person might be. I inquired whether the person had died recently, or a long time ago. He did not answer my question, but said my situation was dangerous, and needed to be dealt with as soon as possible, by means of a ritual called "cleansing of the body." He added that I should give food to Oxalá as soon as I could, because he wanted to eat, and also to my *exu*, called Boca de Fogo ("Mouth of Fire").

He asked if I had any other questions. I wanted to know about my other *orixás*. He told me my *juntó* was Omolu, and my "third" Iemanjá (goddess of the sea). I inquired whether I was capable of receiving saint, or whether I was the kind of person who becomes an *ogã*. He said I would probably receive at most a *barravento*, so it would be better to think in terms of being an *ogã*. I asked about the future. He said that I would have to travel, possibly before I expected.

Archipiado, who has a mischievous streak, proceeded to ask Marinalvo how it could be that his cowries had said that I was of Oxalá, whereas the cowries of two mothers-of-saint I had consulted previously (on my first trip to Brazil) had said I was of Omolu. Marinalvo replied that he had simply told us what the cowries said, and they do not lie. It looked as though Archipiado was going to proceed with this line of questioning, when Marinalvo began to rock back and forth on his chair, and received his *caboclo*, Sultão das Matas. The loud braying noise he made attracted other people into the *barracão*—Delcir, Almiro, and Angélica, who all embraced the *caboclo*. Angélica brought a cigar, and lit it for him.

Sultão das Matas confirmed all that Marinalvo had already told us, and emphasized that I needed to perform the prescribed rituals as soon as possible. Marinalvo had not got around to throwing the cowries for Archipiado, but Sultão das Matas provided the necessary information: Archipiado's owner of the head was Oxum, his *juntó* Oxosse, his "third" Iançã, his *exua* Padilha, and his *caboclo* Laje Grande. I asked about my own *caboclo*, which Marinalvo had not mentioned. Sultão das Matas said I did not have one. I was disappointed. Archipiado subsequently provided an interpretation: you acquire a *caboclo* by being born on Brazilian soil.

Someone fetched a bottle of beer, from which Sultão das Matas took a few swigs. He then passed it to Archipiado, holding it to the latter's mouth. Archipiado immediately received a *barravento*, which threw him back in his chair, with eyes glazed. Delcir laughed, and Archipiado struggled against the trance, but it overpowered him, at least for a minute or two. Then he came to, looking confused and embarrassed.

Sultão das Matas said we should come back to the *terreiro* later in the week, and that we should tell Marinalvo he was not to throw the cowries for us jointly again. He added that we were too trusting, and that we should not place our confidence in everyone we met. Then he departed, and Marinalvo regained consciousness.

We gave Marinalvo a report on what the *caboclo* had said. Archipiado, who is irrepressible, complained about being of Oxum, saying he would have preferred a saint who was more *macho*. Still, if he was to be of Oxum, he would insist on wearing a full skirt covered with little golden fishes. (The sons-of-saint in Marinalvo's *terreiro* do not wear skirts, because his mother-of-saint does not approve of this practice. They wear baggy pants instead.)

Marinalvo picked up his divination tray, then rang the *adjá* above Almiro's head, attempting to make him go into trance. Almiro protested. This was played as a game, but the rivalry between the two fathers-of-saint was unmistakable.

Before we left I asked Marinalvo when he could wash the beads for us. He said, "Any time," and told us the best place to buy them, and what colors we should get: amber for Oxum and white for Oxalá. Archipiado asked him how much we owed for the consultation. He said he would be satisfied with a red seven-day candle for Iançã.

We walked to the bus-stop with Almiro, who was also going to the city. Archipiado asked Almiro what he thought of the fact that Marinalvo's reading contradicted what we had been told by other parents-of-saint. Almiro said he could arrange for us to have another reading with a local father-of-saint who was a friend of his. (Subsequently we were told by Joãozinho that if there is any uncertainty over the identity of one's *orixá*, one may consult up to seven parents-of-saint, then accept the majority opinion.)

When we got home, Archipiado and I tried to prove to each other that we were cleverer than Marinalvo, with our combination of book learning and acquired scepticism. We offered each other suspicionist interpretations of the day's events. Archipiado said it was unusual for a parent-of-saint to receive a spirit in the course of a consultation, and that Marinalvo had done so as a way of convincing us all of the authenticity of his reading. His authority as a human father-of-saint could be doubted, but not the authority of the spirits. He noted also that Almiro, as a rival of Marinalvo's, would probably have criticized the results of the divination, in our private conversation with him, if these had been presented by Marinalvo alone. But he could not challenge the pronouncements of the *caboclo*, because to do so would be to *undermine the whole belief system of Candomblé*.

I, for my part, was thinking about the logistics of mounting an initiation for a *barco* of three children-of-saint in a poor *terreiro*. They had to be fed while they were in seclusion, and the series of three coming-out ceremonies would require animals for the sacrifices, costumes and other ritual paraphernalia for the new initiates, and hospitality for a large number of guests. I wondered what part I, as an axiomatically rich *gringo*, was destined to have in all of this.

I told Archipiado that I was going to play along with Marinalvo's game, because I needed to do so for my research. This gave me the reassuring sense that I was the one in control.

* * *

I finished writing these words five days short of a year after the events they describe. The same day I received a letter from Archipiado. I had asked him, in previous correspondence, if he would mind if I wrote about what happened to him at the *caboclo* festival at Gelson's. He replies:

I give you complete authorization to write about that episode that happened in the house of [Gelson]. After a long talk with N. [Argentinian ethnographer and poet living in São Paulo] I regret deeply not having given myself the luxury of letting myself be carried away by the will of the *orixás*, or rather, of having blocked, by means of my consciousness, penetration into the world of madness, which is trance. I lost a great opportunity to know this other side of the psyche . . .

This week I met with that [other] father-of-saint from the house of [Gelson], who reminded me of this fact of *having fallen* in a *terreiro* near my natural habitat [Archipiado's home is not far from Lobito] . . . and in a "humble" location—recalling my membership in a lower social stratum (economically speaking, I think). He said that he too was from the "lower class" (his name is C., and he was born in an old zone of prostitution in Salvador. Do you remember him?). Among other things we spoke about why, for example, people, when kissing the feet of Oxum—who may be dressed in gold, but is barefoot, to show the simplicity of Candomblé—are unconsciously denying the riches of life and adoring the earth, from which she comes and to which she returns (according to C.), and that this act represents the recognition of such a simplicity in our lives . . .

I saw [Marinalvo] this week as well. I was in São Paulo when the festival of his saint took place, which, they say, was a success. It even came out in *A Tarde*! [the more conservative of Salvador's two daily newspapers]. He complained about my not having gone, and invited me to a confirmation. . . . I told him you wanted to give an "obligation of one year" for your confirmation as *ogã*, and he promised to let me know what would be necessary.

* * *

I sometimes feel a certain nostalgia for the lost paradise of anthropology, when it was possible to distinguish twitches from winks, and real winks from burlesqued ones (Geertz 1973:16). How cheering it would be if there really did exist some transcendent epistemological realm, beyond all ambiguity, from the security of which one could contemplate other cultures, one's own culture, and one's own practice, and say, "Yes, this was a twitch and that was a wink; this wink was real and that one was mimicked."

III

Orixá

Glória a ti nesse dia de glória!
Glória a ti, Redentor, que há cem anos
Nossos pais conduziste à vitória
Pelos mares e campos baianos.

Dessa Sagrada Colina,
Mansão da misericórdia,
{Dai-nos a graça divina,
{Dai justiça e dai concórdia! [bis]

Glória a ti nessa altura sagrada,
És o Eterno Farol, és o Guia!
És Senhor, Sentinela Avançada!
És a Guarda Imortal da Bahia!

Glory to Thee on this day of glory!
Glory to Thee, Redeemer, who, a hundred years ago
Led'st our fathers to victory
Through the seas and fields of Bahia.

[Chorus]
From this Sacred Hill,
Abode of mercy,
{Give us divine grace!
{Give justice and give concord! [twice]

Glory to Thee on this sacred height,
Thou art the Eternal Beacon, Thou art the Guide!
Thou art the Lord, Advance Sentinel!
Thou art the Eternal Guardian of Bahia!

"Hymn to Our Lord of Bomfim."

(In Bahia this hymn, sung by Caetano Veloso, is played on the radio every noon. The Sacred Hill on which the Church of Bomfim stands is likened, in Candomblé, to the first piece of earth created by Oxalá.)

7. Child Spirits

Ants. And the cloying sweet odor of decay. The ants are proceeding in an orderly column to the offerings, and out again, under the locked door of the *bakisse*. They are not paying much attention to the little cooked carcass of the dove.

I am not permitted to kill any living thing while I am here in seclusion, in the room of the saints.

The offerings have been here less than twenty-four hours, but, because of the heat in this little cell, the African dishes are already beginning to decompose: *molocum*—beans, shrimp, and onion, decorated with boiled eggs, food of Oxum; *opetê*—shrimp and onion; *acaçá*—cakes of fine corn meal; *ebô*—boiled white corn, prepared with oil and honey, food of Oxalá.

From the front of the mound of white corn protrudes the head of the dove. Its eyes are open, but have glazed over, and blood has congealed around its neck. Its wing feathers have been arranged vertically on either side of the plate of corn. A bunch of feathers at the back represents its tail.

The offerings include also a bowl of fruit and a plate containing cake, leaves, part of a cola nut, and seven coins. With the food offerings stands a vase of white flowers—gladioli, chrysanthemums, *angélica*. They are beginning to wilt. There is also an enamel basin filled with the herbal infusion called *amaci*.

The candles that were lit last night have burned themselves out. The clay pot that contains my drinking water is, like all the offerings, spattered with congealed blood and feathers. The pot will remain here, with the ritual objects, when my seclusion is over.

I am starting to itch. I have been using only herbal infusions for bathing. I cannot scratch my head, which is caked with blood and feathers, because it is covered with a white lace prayer-cap and bound with a turban. The narrow cords of plaited raffia called *contra-egum* ("against the spirits of the dead") are hurting my upper arms, around which they are bound.

A bell is tied to my right ankle, and the string is irritating my skin. The bell is of the small spherical type I associate with the jester's cap, and thus with the Fool of the Tarot pack. However, in Candomblé it indicates the initiand's prisoner-like status. The bell gives a warning signal if the initiand tries to flee.

I am dressed in a white T-shirt and loose white trousers with lace sewn to the cuffs. They are drenched with blood. Around my neck I have a raffia necklace and a string of small white beads.

I think it is mid-afternoon. A few minutes ago Marinalvo came in with Sebastião, his chief *ogã*, to fetch something. The *bakisse* serves as a storeroom for ritual paraphernalia, as well as housing the *assentamentos* ("seats") of the *orixás*. I was sleeping so deeply, in spite of being separated from the floor by only a straw mat and a sheet, that when I awoke I did not know where I was.

I am strangely calm, in spite of the trouble going on outside in connection with my initiation. In the early hours of this morning I almost fled. Shortly afterwards Archipiado was at the closed door of the *bakisse*, weeping.

This afternoon I feel like a child. People bring me my food, remove my chamber pot, wash me. I am helpless, and therefore tempted to feel innocent. But when I look at myself in terms of the events of the last few days, I see just another member of a species that is unique in its rapacity, its cunning, and its capacity for self-deception.

Perhaps I could use the remainder of my period of seclusion as a kind of Zen retreat. But I would need a *koan* to break my head over. Let me formulate one . . . : Is it better to delude oneself that it is possible to be free of illusions, or rather to choose one's illusions with open eyes (in the manner of duelists choosing their weapons)?

I wonder what is happening with the three *erês* on the other side of the wall, in the *roncó*? They are, according to Archipiado, who has been passing me forbidden cigarettes and chocolate bars under the locked door of the *bakisse*, encircled by offerings similar to the ones that surround me here.

* * *

Three days ago the *erês*—the "child spirits" of those in seclusion in the *roncó*—had to "seek the name in the waters." Every *orixá* has a variety of what are called *marcas* ("brands," "types," "qualities"), and each *marca* has his or her own individual name, which, in the Angola nation, is called the *dijina*. Those undergoing initiation as children-of-saint have to discover the *dijina* of the *marca* of their *orixá* in a dream.

They dream of waters, of peace, of good things. According to Joãozinho these waters are called "the waters of Oxalá." Because Oxalá is father of the *orixás*, who all live in his land, he has the privilege of bestowing on them their names. Joãozinho connected the waters also with a festival called "the waters of Oxalá," which takes place on the twenty-eighth of January. Water is fetched from a spring, and the *orixás* bathe Oxalá, who is seated in a basin in the *barracão*. This commemorates a similar bathing that took place in mythical times, when Oxalá had his white clothes repeatedly soiled by Exu.

The waters also have other symbolic associations in Candomblé, principally with the *iabás*, or female *orixás*. Oxum is linked with fresh waters, Iemanjá with the waters of the sea, and Nanã with the rain that penetrates the soil to make mud (cf. Cacciatore 1977:138).

Joãozinho tells me that the offerings here in the *bakisse* and also those in the *roncó* will be disposed of, after the initiations are over, in a nearby creek. Their dispersal in running water will bring good luck to those who have been initiated, and also to the *terreiro*. This may be why the offerings include the food of Oxum, *orixá* of fresh and running waters. Marinalvo said that the oblations to Oxalá and Oxum would bring me peace. (I recall also that when a parent-of-saint dies, the pots and plates belonging to the *assentamentos* of his or her various spirits are broken up and sunk in the waters.)

Tonight, at the last of the three coming-out ceremonies, visiting parents-of-saint or senior initiates will ask each of the three new children-of-saint for the *dijina*. When the name is called, the *orixá* descends, displacing the *erê* who has been materialized in the initiand for most of the period of seclusion. The *orixá* is then dressed in his or her costume, and dances.

It is a matter of some shame—for the initiand, the *terreiro*, and its parent-of-saint—if the initiand is not able to call the name. Marinalvo's elderly mother-of-saint, Dona Clara, once told me the story of her own initiation, which had taken place fifty-six years earlier. She spent the last period of her six-month seclusion crying, because she was so worried that she would not be able to find the name in time.

To avoid the possibility of a public loss of face, it is apparently a common practice for the parent-of-saint of the *terreiro* to ask the initiand for the name on the morning before the ceremony, and to throw the cowries to make sure the name is correct. He repeats the question before the festival starts. Some sceptics say that parents-of-saint in fact tell the initiands the name. I have no way of knowing whether this ever actually occurs.

While the initiands are in seclusion, their *erês* are taught the songs and dances associated with their *orixás*. They also learn the African vocabulary used in *sotaques* ("banter"), so that when they visit other *terreiros* where *sotaques* are directed at them, they know how to respond. In addition, they are instructed in inter-*terreiro* politics. They find out which *terreiros* stand in a relationship of enmity to their own. Being in trance seems to make these complex teachings easier to assimilate.

There are reports that the herbal infusions which the initiands drink and in which they bathe have hallucinogenic properties (e.g., Fichte 1976:323–52). However, I do not believe that trance is in any way dependent on these substances. Otherwise it could not occur, as it often does, among casual visitors to a *terreiro*. The infusions seem to be an adjunct, which perhaps prolongs the trance or makes it more profound.

* * *

Erê is the term used for the child form of an *orixá*. (A female *erê* is called an *erea*.) Some *erês* have names that link them to particular attributes or symbols of their respective *orixás*. An *erê* of Oxalá, for example, may be called Ebozinho ("Little Ebô"), Pachorô ("Scepter"), or Pombinho ("Little Dove"). (*Ebô*, as I have mentioned, is a ceremonial dish of boiled white corn. The *pachorô* is a kind of scepter of silver-colored metal, usually surmounted by a crown or globe and a dove. Oxalá, who is old and frail, uses the *pachorô* as a walking stick.) An *erê* of Oxosse may be called Caçadorzinho ("Little Hunter"), and an *erea* of Oxum, Conchinha ("Little Shell").

Another favorite source of names for *erês* is the domain of flowers: Lírio ("Lily"), Margarida ("Daisy"), Rosa da Noite ("Rose of the Night"), Flor do Dia ("Flower of the Day"), Cravo ("Carnation"), Capuchinha ("Nasturtium").

The *erê* of an *exu* is called an *exu-mirim*. (Brazilian Portuguese has borrowed the term *mirim*, meaning "little," from Tupi [Ferreira 1975:928].) However, people receive an *exu-mirim* only in those rare cases where they have Exu as owner of their head. These little *exus* are said by some to be the spirits of children who live in the *brega* and die young.

Erê is one of the items of Candomblé vocabulary that have spread beyond the religious sphere to other contexts in Brazilian society. Perlongher notes that the term is used in the street world of São Paulo to denote a young male prostitute (1987:147).

Various African languages have contributed to the small core of Candomblé words that have achieved such an extended distribution, but Castro notes that most of these words come from Yoruba (1983:103–4). (By contrast, the majority of "secular" African loan-words that have come into Brazilian Portuguese are from the Bantu languages.)

Even within Candomblé, Yoruba religious terminology predominates. For example in Marinalvo's *terreiro*, which belongs to the Angola "nation," the Yoruba-derived terms *orixá* and *erê* are generally used rather than the corresponding "Angola" (Bantu-derived) terms *inquice* and *vunje*. Moreover, the *orixás* themselves are most often referred to by their Yoruba-derived names.

There are some Angola *terreiros* (such as Tanuri Junçara, in Engenho Velho da Federação) that pride themselves on their use of "Angola" vocabulary. But at Marinalvo's there are only a few contexts where "Angola" terms are obligatory. One of these is the selection of *dijinas*. The name that the new initiate calls at the final coming-out ceremony must be an "Angola" name. (At Marinalvo's these names generally end in *-zambe*, the "Angola" word for "God.") Also there is a core group of Angola songs that is sung in the rituals at Marinalvo's. These songs are used along with others in which the vocabulary derives from Yoruba. This kind of linguistic mixture seems to be common in Angola *terreiros* (cf. Binon Cossard 1970:15).

Some people call the *erês* by the term *bejes* or *ibejes*. Xilton told me this usage is incorrect, because in Africa the term *ibeji* refers only to the spirits of twins. However, the connection between the *erês* and the *bejes* seems to be deeply rooted in Candomblé, perhaps mediated by the close association between the *bejes* and São Cosme e Damião (Saints Cosmos and Damian).

In Portuguese the title of these saints (São) is almost always singular, as though Cosme and Damião were a single entity. They are always pictured together, and in the popular imagination they are twins (although according to official Catholic doctrine they were merely brothers). They are the patron saints of children, and associated with purity of heart and tranquillity of conscience (Scopel 1983:122). Statues or portraits of São Cosme e Damião are often to be found in association with the *assentamentos* of the *erês*.

According to Joãozinho, if an initiate, in consultation with a parent-of-saint, decides to "seat" his or her *erês*—a procedure that is optional—only one *assentamento* is required. The ritual objects dedicated to the *erê* of the *orixá* who is the initiate's owner of the head serve for the *erês* of all the initiate's other *orixás* as well.

Similarly, only one strand of beads is worn for the *erês*, whereas each of the initiate's *orixás* requires a separate set of beads. The beads of the *erês* are multicolored, unlike those of an *orixá*, which are usually of one or two colors only. It may be noted in passing that people do not usually wear beads for their *exus* and *caboclos*.

* * *

Joãozinho said that all the *erês*, including Cosme and Damião, are the children of the *orixá* Iançã, but that she did not raise them. They were brought up by Oxum, who, according to one account, is a virgin, and has no children of her own (cf. Augras 1983:152, 154).

I find it difficult, in fact impossible, to reconcile all the different stories I heard about the genealogy of the *orixás* and other spirit entities of Candomblé.

Sometimes people say that Oxalá is the parent of all the *orixás*. From this perspective Oxalá is sexless. He created the world by making a *mingau* (a kind of pudding). Some *assentamentos* of Oxalá (for example, that of Joãozinho) include spoons, which are symbolically connected with this event.

Another version, recounted by Joãozinho, is that Oxalá had two wives. His first wife was Nanã, and their children were Obaluaiê (who is also called Omolu) and Oxumaré. His second wife was Iemanjá, and from their union were born the other *orixás* (cf. Augras 1983:168).

At other times people say that Nanã is the grandmother of Oxalá and the mother of Obaluaiê and Iemanjá. Iemanjá is both mother and wife of Oxalá, and Obaluaiê is his uncle. This version may have been influenced by Christian hagiography, since Nanã is linked iconographically with St. Anne, who is God's grandmother and the Virgin Mary's mother; Iemanjá with Our Lady of the Immaculate Conception; and Oxalá with Jesus, in the form of Our Lord of Bomfim.

There are other candidates for the title of oldest *orixá*, apart from Oxalá and Nanã. Some people say that Obaluaiê is the oldest, because one of his names is O Velho ("The Old One"). Some say that Tempo has to be the oldest, because "*tempo* ['time,' 'the weather'] is everything." Others say that Oxumaré, the *orixá* who is both serpent and rainbow, is even older than Tempo, because "the rainbow encircles *tempo* ['the weather']."

The relationship between Oxalá, Obaluaiê, and Tempo may be another case where Candomblé has been influenced by Christian doctrine, since this triad seems to bear some resemblance to the Trinity. Obaluaiê is "The

Old One," Oxalá is associated with Jesus, and Tempo is sometimes likened to the Holy Spirit. People occasionally say that Tempo has "a part which is Obaluaiê and a part which is Oxalá," though I have not heard the Trinitarian implications of the relationship among these three *orixás* made more explicit than this.

The idea of Oxalá as father of the *orixás* is complicated even further by a "rule" someone once enunciated for my benefit: whereas among the *exus* and *caboclos* relationships occur between brothers and sisters, among the *orixás* they are only possible between parents and children. If this rule (which is contradicted by certain myths about brother-sister relationships between the *orixás*, for example, between Ogum and Iançã) is applied, it is evident that Oxalá must be grandfather rather than father of some of the *orixás*, in order for his children to be able to have relationships with their own children. To give some examples: Xangô is sometimes said to be both father and partner of Iançã; Oxum is sometimes said to be both mother and partner of Oxosse.

The relationship between the "senior" *orixás* is complicated by the same rule. Nanã is sometimes said to be mother and partner of Obaluaiê. In addition, there is an aspect of Oxalá himself called Oguiã (or Oxaguiã), who is sometimes said to be the father and partner of Iemanjá (thus contradicting the version according to which Iemanjá is the mother of Oxalá). Oguiã is the young, vigorous Oxalá, as distinct from Oxalufã, who is the old, frail Oxalá.

The *erês* have a particular conception of the genealogy of the *orixás* which, while no more definitive than any of the versions I have adumbrated above, at least has the advantage of simplicity. This genealogy is reflected in the names that the *erês* use to refer to the *orixás*:

Usual name of ***orixá***	***Erê*** *name for* ***orixá***
Obaluaiê	Vovô ("Grandpa")
Nanã	Vovó ("Grandma")
Oxalá	Papai ("Daddy")
Iemanjá	Mãe ("Mother")
Ogum	Guerreiro ("Warrior")
Oxosse	Caçador ("Hunter")
Xangô	Machadinha ("Little Ax")
Iancã	Alvoroçada ("She who is Restless [for war]")
Oxum	Abebé ("Mirror")

(*Abebé* is an African loan-word that is usually translated as "fan." Other *orixás* apart from Oxum also carry fans, but the fan of Oxum is distinctive in that it has a mirror at the center. People in Jaraci also seemed to use the word *abebé* to mean "mirror" rather than "fan.")

The terms used by the *erês* are sociocentric rather than egocentric. In other words, all the *erês* use the same terms, no matter what their own relationship to a particular *orixá* may be. Joãozinho, when he gave me these terms, did not specify that Ogum, Oxosse, Xangô, Iançã, and Oxum were brothers and sisters, but this would not be an unreasonable extrapolation.

It is interesting that all the names for the junior *orixás* have some connection with weaponry—even the mirror of Oxum was used, as I have mentioned earlier, as the ultimate weapon in the *orixás*' battle with the *exus*, when conventional arms had failed. Perhaps this reflects the rivalry between the *orixás*, who, in the everyday world of Candomblé, are often at war with each other. They may be doing battle over possession of the head of a particular individual (which is why sometimes the cowrie divination gives an incorrect result. It is then said that a rival *orixá* "came in front" of the individual's true *orixá*.) Or they may be at war with each other on behalf of different individuals, or of different *terreiros* (cf. Velho 1977).

In this connection it is worth noting Durand's hypothesis that the imagery of weapons is typically associated with dichotomization and ascent (1962:Book 1, Part 2). On the one hand, weapons are the symbolic means of dividing light from darkness, the upper from the lower, spirit from matter, good from evil; on the other, they make possible a battle against the negative terms, and an ascent towards the positive ones.

It seems that even in the realm inhabited by the *orixás*, at the top of the spirit-matter continuum, this battle does not cease. If anything, it is intensified. The pursuit of transcendence does not result in peace, but in a constant dualist polemic, or a state of surveillance and preparedness for battle (Durand 1962:219. This is why, as Durand drily notes, quoting Alain, " 'you get tired of being a Platonist.' ")

The peaceful waters of Oxalá, in which the *erês* find their names, have a paradoxical relationship to the martial realm of spirit. One way of approaching this paradox would be to consider it in terms of the notion of "liminal spaces" in Candomblé.

I have mentioned earlier that offerings to the spirits, after they have served their ritual function, are taken to a liminal space—a crossroad, a forest, or a body of water. Each of these locations has an especially close link with a particular spirit realm: the crossroad with the world of the *exus*, the forest with the world of the *caboclos*, and the waters with the world of the *orixás*. Each represents, as it were, the aspect of liminality, or lack of differentiation, that is most salient in that particular realm.

The liminality of the crossroad is antisocial and dangerous. The crossroad lies at a place where territorial boundaries begin to dissolve into each other, and is, perhaps for this reason, associated with disintegration of body and soul, thought to be caused by the spirits who gravitate there. People avoid passing through a crossroad at those hours of the day which together form what we could think of as the "crossroad of the daily cycle"—6:00 a.m., midday, 6:00 p.m., and midnight. If they are obliged to traverse a crossroad on their way to a Candomblé festival, they should bathe before participating in the ritual, in order to remove "negative influences."

The forest represents a rather different way of conceptualizing liminality. The goal of a *caboclo* festival, for example, seems to be to recreate a forest community in which individual egos lose their sense of separateness in a culminating spirit of effervescence. Lack of differentiation, in this case, is not antisocial, but eminently social.

The symbolism of the waters is virtually the inverse of the symbolism of the forest. If the movement of a *caboclo* festival is from individuation to undifferentiation, the movement of initiation into the world of the *orixás* is from undifferentiation (represented by the waters) to individuation.

During the period of seclusion initiands lose their previous identity and become, not only socially but also psychologically, like children. When they enter the waters to seek the name, the dissolution of their prior selves is complete. But this is only a preliminary step in the initiation process. The culmination occurs when, at a public ceremony, the initiand calls the name discovered in the waters, thereby establishing a new identity. The infantile *erê* has become an adult *orixá*, a new warrior on the battlefield of spirit.

When Joãozinho gave me the names used by the *erês* to refer to the *orixás*, he omitted three major entities, namely Oxumaré, Ossãe, and Tempo. This may be significant, in that all three have an ambiguous relationship to the world of spirit. Oxumaré and Ossãe are denizens of the forest (and also *metá-metá*). Tempo is simultaneously an *orixá* and a kind of *exu*.

* * *

Here in the *bakisse* I lie facing the *assentamentos* of the members of Marinalvo's *terreiro*, which are arranged on a kind of multi-level altar at the end of the room, behind the pond of Oxum. (This is a square, tiled pool, about eighteen inches wide and nine inches high, in the middle of which sits Oxum in the form of a mermaid, on a little pedestal surrounded by water.)

Each *assentamento* ("seat") is a collection of ritual objects associated with a particular *orixá*. What these *assentamentos* have in common is that they all include a basin, in some cases enamel, in other cases earthenware, which sits on top of an earthenware pitcher. The other objects vary. Many of the *assentamentos* have china plates inside the basins; a number have smaller earthenware pots standing next to the large pitchers; a few include small metal sculptures called *ferramentas*, which represent the implements used by the particular *orixá*; one incorporates a statue of the Christian saint associated with the *orixá*; several are decorated with parts of the costume worn by the *orixá* during rituals—a crown, a sword, a helmet, a flywhisk. Beads, *mocãs* (raffia necklaces), and *contra-eguns* (raffia arm-bands) hang from some of the objects. The skulls of chickens and goats stare blindly from some of the assemblages. The altar is adorned with ribbons, colored lights, and vases of flowers.

From where I am lying I cannot see the stones called *otá*, but I am told they are contained in the basins that are the central items of the *assentamentos*. An *otá* is the head of an *orixá*, the physical link between the *orixá* and his or her human vehicle. When a member of the *terreiro* is in seclusion, the offerings that he or she consumes materially are consumed spiritually by the *otá*. After the period of retreat, the plates and pitchers used for these offerings are left with the *otá*, to form part of the *assentamento*. When an initiate's head receives blood sacrifices, so does the *otá*. If a parent-of-saint wants to take revenge on some member of the *terreiro* who has caused offense, he or she may pour mercury over the *otá*. This causes a burning sensation in the head of the offender, who ends up going crazy.

On the top level of the altar are the *assentamentos* of Marinalvo's *orixás*: in the center, on a raised pedestal, the *assentamento* of Iançã, the owner of his head, with a statue of St. Barbara; to the right, the *assentamento* of Oxosse, his *juntó*, which includes *ferramentas* (metal sculptures) in the form of miniature bows and arrows; to the left, that of Oxum, his *adjuntó*, which includes a golden crown.

The second level bears the *assentamentos* of the *orixás* of the *terreiro*'s two *ogãs*, Sebastião and Dudu. Sebastião is the *axogum*—the *ogã* responsible for the sacrifice of animals. Dudu is the *alabê*—the head drummer, responsible for leading the music in rituals. For Sebastião there is an *assentamento* of Oxosse, and for Dudu, *assentamentos* of Ogum and Xangô.

Arranged along the third step are the *assentamentos* of Oxum, Ogum, and two Ianças. This Oxum is owner of the head of a son-of-saint called Gilberto; the Ogum is *juntó* of the *equede* Zita, and one of the Ianças is Zita's owner of the head; the other Iançã is owner of the head of Marta, the *terreiro*'s "little mother." (In this context the terms "little mother" and "little father" refer to senior initiates who are the deputies of the parent-of-saint, and may perform many of the same functions as the latter. These terms may also be used in another sense. The "little mother" and "little father" of an initiand are his or her sponsors and instructors.)

The *assentamentos* on the bottom step are those of Oxum, Oxalá, Iemanjá, Obaluaiê, and another Iançã. All of these are *orixás* of Marinalvo's children-of-saint. Oxum is the *juntó* of Joãozinho, and Oxalá his owner of the head; Iemanjá is owner of the head of a young woman called Joana; Obaluaiê the owner of the head of another young woman called Luisa; and Iançã the owner of the head of an elderly daughter-of-saint called Rosilene.

Marinalvo has mentioned, in passing, other people he refers to as his *ogãs*, *equedes*, and children-of-saint, but they do not have *assentamentos* here in the *bakisse*. In some cases they are people who have left the *terreiro*. In other cases their initiation entailed only a *bori*—the ceremony of offering sacrifices to the head (cf. Verger 1981)—and not a removal of hair. It is only when hair is removed that an *assentamento* is set up for an individual's *orixá*.

There are two processes for ritually removing hair, called *raspagem* ("shaving") and *catulagem* ("clipping"). *Raspagem* entails shaving all the hair from the head. There are different forms of *catulagem*, but they all involve, essentially, cutting hair away from the parts of the head where ritual incisions are made. "Clipping" is regarded as a lower form of initiation than "shaving."

All of Marinalvo's children-of-saint have been "shaved," as well as the *ogã* Sebastião and the *equede* Zita. Dudu, the head drummer, has been "clipped." *Ogãs* and *equedes* whose hair has been removed during initiation may, if they perform all the necessary obligations over a period of years, and have the requisite knowledge, become parents-of-saint in their own right, even though they do not go into trance. This enables them to initiate their own children-of-saint.

There is a continuing debate among the intellectuals of Candomblé about whether *ogãs* and *equedes* can be considered to have the same sacerdotal initiation as children-of-saint. Some *terreiros* do not countenance the possibility of *ogãs* and *equedes* becoming parents-of-saint, and therefore do not shave their heads. But there have been several well-known parents-of-saint who began their careers as *ogãs* or *equedes*—including, apparently, the late Menininha of Gantois, who was perhaps the most celebrated mother-of-saint of all time.

People who have been "clipped" and not subsequently "shaved" are at a certain disadvantage if they envisage becoming parents-of-saint. Because you cannot perform on others a type of initiation higher than you have received yourself, they are only able to "clip" their own children-of-saint.

Some people have told me that part of the hair that is removed during initiation is kept, in a small package, with the other objects of the *assentamento*. Others say that part of the hair is placed in the *terreiro*'s "foundation"—the tile-covered hole at the center of the *barracão*, which is periodically opened so that it may be "fed."

There are no sacred objects for the *erês* here in the *bakisse*. According to Joãozinho, children-of-saint who want to set up an *assentamento* for their *erês* do so in their own homes. (This may depend on the particular *terreiro*. Lody writes that the *assentamentos* of the *erês* are located in the rooms of the saints, and consist of objects similar to those found in the *assentamentos* of the *orixás*, but in miniature [Lody 1975:78].)

* * *

One of the first *erês* I ever met was Joãozinho's Cravo ("Carnation"). It was during my first visit to Marinalvo's *terreiro*. Joãozinho had gone into the *bakisse* to pay his respects to the *terreiro*'s little mother, who was in seclusion. When he came back out into the yard he had with him a long switch, and used it to taunt various women who were in the vicinity.

Joãozinho is habitually high-spirited and playful, so this behavior did not strike me as being out of character. However, when he hit Marinalvo's mother across the legs and kicked over a basin in which laundry was soaking, I realized it was not Joãozinho, but his *erê*. The women complained, but not too much. *Erês* seem to be treated with a certain indulgence.

At the time, Dona Laura was staying in the *roncó*. Dona Laura is the little mother of the *terreiro* of Marinalvo's mother-of-saint, and often came to help Marinalvo with his festivals. She is elderly and somewhat frail, and had been given the *terreiro*'s only bed. While she was out of the *roncó*, Cravo ran in and rummaged among her things under the bed. He found a bottle of honey, consumed most of it, tipped the rest on the floor, and proceeded to doodle in the sticky little puddle he had made.

Later the *ogã* Sebastião approached him, and Cravo fell over backwards, as though fainting from shock. Someone told me this was because Sebastião was wearing leather sandals, which *erês* take to be alligators.

In the meantime some other members of the *terreiro* had received their *erês*. Two of them rushed into the kitchen, stole some food that had been prepared for the festival due to take place that evening, and came back stuffing it into their mouths. Another *erê* was performing the acrobatic dance called *capoeira* inside the *barracão*. Joãozinho found a hen's egg and began to play with it.

Some of the *erês* asked us for candy and soft drink. At the time I found their speech completely incomprehensible. Archipiado, however, made some sense of what they were saying, and gave them money. They looked at it uncomprehendingly. Not all *erês*, however, are so naive. At a *terreiro* we had visited previously, the *erês* not only knew what money was, but went around collecting it.

Eventually Dona Laura must have got tired of their antics, because she took a white cloth, placed it over Cravo's head, then whipped it away, which brought Joãozinho out of trance. She repeated the procedure with the other *erês*.

Cravo had been sucking a pacifier, which had periodically fallen in the dirt. Now Joãozinho spent some time spitting out sand. The *erês* are not very discriminating about what they put in their mouths. I have seen Marinalvo's *erê* attempt to eat nasal mucus (he was stopped by horrified onlookers), and heard of an *erê* who eats cockroaches.

There are other matters, however, about which they are not so undiscriminating. Their attitudes about sexuality, for example, are more complex. They are very interested in other people's sexuality, but hate any reference to their own. One *ogã* I know made the mistake of admiring the breasts of an *erea*. She elbowed him in the chest, then burst into tears.

Much *erê* behavior consists of sexual teasing of other people. Two *erê* songs I recorded illustrate the point. (The first of these was reproduced for me without the phonetic substitutions characteristic of *erê* language.)

Ocánia ficou sentado,
Apanijé mandou entrar.
Ocánia ficou cansado,
Apanijé mandou sentar.

Seu cu como, como,
Seu cu como.

Cock was sitting down,
Cunt told him to come in.
Cock got tired,
Cunt told him to sit down.
I fuck, fuck your ass,
I fuck your ass.

(*Ocánia* and *apanijé* are terms from the African vocabulary of Candomblé.)

Ai, ai, ai Bombanai,
Condo fua da mãe
Ena mofa, Bombanai,
Vagamume fabe maif.
Agona que ena é pupa, Bombanai,
O vagamume cone atai.

In standard Portuguese this would read:

Ai, ai, ai Bombalai,
Quando sua mãe
Era moça, Bombalai,
Vagalume sabe mais.
Agora que ela é puta, Bombalai,
O vagalume corre atrás.

Oh, oh, oh Bombalai,
When your mother
Was a virgin, Bombalai,
The firefly knows best.
Now that she is a whore, Bombalai,
The firefly runs behind [to light up her backside].

The *erês* also have an interest in, and uncanny knowledge of, a *terreiro*'s sexual secrets. People who are curious about these secrets sometimes take advantage of the *erês*' notorious lack of discretion. For example, a member of Marinalvo's *terreiro* suspected that her son was having a clandestine relationship with a particular woman. She invited an *erê* to visit her, promising an *erê* feast of candy, cake, and soft drink, and the *erê* obligingly provided her with all the details she required about the affair. The woman who was the subject of this interchange subsequently confronted the *erê*'s human vehicle about this indiscretion. He replied that if she had any fight to pick, it would have to be with the *erê*, not with him.

The *erês* seem to be allowed to take liberties that would not be permitted from any other spirit—but only after the calling of the name. During the period of seclusion that precedes initiation they are fairly strictly disciplined. They are kept locked up most of the time, and in some *terreiros* there is a special stick that is used for punishing their misdemeanors. Marinalvo does not physically castigate his *erês*. His mother, however, claims that he should—it is the only way to socialize them properly.

The *orixás* also administer punishment, but in a different way. If an *erê* does something that merits chastisement, the *orixá* descends and causes the corporeal vehicle to inflict an injury on itself, for example, by throwing itself against a wall, or by striking a body part against something sharp.

There is a paradox here, in that spirit entities are not supposed to feel pain. I have even known people to receive their *erês* in order to obtain relief from some acute physical discomfort. The explanation I have been given for this paradox is that the spirits can take away pain or inflict it, even during the trance state, according to their pleasure or displeasure.

There is a term used in this context that at first caused me a little confusion. I have mentioned earlier that *apanhar* ("to get," "to grasp," "to catch," etc.) can be used transitively, with a spirit as subject and a human being as object. A phrase of this kind is used when a spirit causes trance in a person, and has nothing to do with punishment. However, *apanhar* can also be used intransitively, with a human being or, in some cases, a spirit, such as an *erê*, as subject. In this sense *apanhar* could be translated by the slang expression that exists in some dialects of English, "to collect it"—that is, to receive some kind of physical ill treatment (in the present context, from a spirit that has authority to punish the entity in question). There are two other expressions in Bahian Portuguese that are used in the same context and with the same significance, namely *levar/tomar uma surra*, and *levar/tomar porrada*, which mean roughly "to take a beating."

Even after the period of seclusion the *erês*' liberty is not without its limits. They are still under the authority of the parent-of-saint and other senior members of the *terreiro*, and may be required to perform domestic duties, such as cleaning, cooking, washing, and ironing.

While in seclusion the initiand, as human entity, is usually referred to as a *iaô*, a term derived from a Yoruba word meaning "youngest wife" or "recently married woman" (Cacciatore 1977:140). In Jaraci this term is sometimes also applied to *ogãs* and *equedes* during their initiation, or to any member of the *terreiro* who is in seclusion during an "obligation."

This usage, which connects the term *iaô* with the period of seclusion, cuts across another that is encountered more frequently in the literature. According to this second usage, *iaô* is interpreted to mean "bride of an *orixá*," and refers only to initiates who go into trance (cf. Binon Cossard 1970:178).

To complicate matters even further, *iaô* can be used to refer to members of a specific subset of those who go into trance, namely junior initiates, who are also called "children-of-saint." In this sense the term is contrasted with the terms used for such senior initiates as parents-of-saint, little fathers and little mothers, and *ebames* (those who have been initiated for seven years or more). People in Jaraci used the term *iaô* in all these senses.

Technically speaking, *iaô* always refers to a human rather than a spirit entity. However, it is common practice to refer to initiands in seclusion as *iaôs*, even though they spend most of the period of their seclusion incorporated by their *erês*.

* * *

I came here to attend the first of the three coming-out rituals of the new initiates last Tuesday, five days ago. It was a small ceremony, with only about a dozen guests, mostly family and friends of the *iaôs*.

The music for the despatch of Exu was performed with only two drummers. A young woman played the *agogô* (two cones of metal, struck with a metal rod). Later the same woman began to drum. I mention this because it is an indication of a certain flexibility of gender roles in Marinalvo's *terreiro*. Elsewhere I had been told that women could never drum in Candomblé rituals. However, Marinalvo's is not the only *terreiro* in which I have seen them do so.

Marinalvo entered, and the first *roda* began. The other dancers included the *ogã* Sebastião, the *equede* Zita, two children-of-saint, and a young man called Celso, who was hoping to be confirmed as "little father" of the *terreiro*. They performed the usual ritual greetings, to the front door of the *barracão*, to the tile in the center, beneath which lies the "foundation" (also called *entoto*), to the drums, and to each other.

Periodically Marinalvo went over and bent down to peer through a spyhole behind the thrones, which stand next to the drums. This hole had been bored through the wall that divides the *barracão* from the *roncó*, and gave Marinalvo a view of what was happening to the *iaôs* who were in seclusion.

The *iaôs* entered the *barracão* twice, but there were only two of them—the *iaô* of Ogum and the *iaô* of Obaluaiê. Both were in the trance of *erês*.

Their heads were shaved. The crown of the *iaô* of Ogum was painted blue, and that of the *iaô* of Obaluaiê, blue-green. Each wore a black and white speckled feather of a guinea fowl in the middle of the forehead, and an *adoxu* on top of the head. The *adoxu* is a small cone made of herbs, cola nut, the magical powder called *pemba*, and other substances (cf. Binon Cossard 1970:178), which protects the spot through which the *orixá* enters the head.

They wore white, their bodies were covered with white spots, and they had a white cross on the top of each foot. Each carried a long switch in one hand, and in the other a sword-like leaf. They made three prostrations—to the front door, the drums, and the *entoto*—then exited.

There was an interval, during which the guests speculated about what had happened to the *iaô* of Oxumaré, who was also supposed to have participated in the ceremony. It was assumed that those responsible for the initiation had not been able to "call" her *orixá*.

The two *iaôs* entered again. This time the spots on their bodies were multi-colored. They circled the *barracão* twice, then exited. The other members of the *terreiro* danced, and the ceremony finished early. (I have not given a detailed account of this or the two subsequent coming-out ceremonies, because they have been described at length by other writers, e.g., Binon Cossard [1970:157–217], whose field work was also carried out in an Angola *terreiro*.)

I stayed at Marinalvo's overnight, rather than returning to the city. The evening and the next morning were filled with stories, some of them fantastic, others having a more obvious relationship to the everyday world of Jaraci.

Joãozinho, who for some reason was disgruntled with Marinalvo, had not attended the evening's ceremony. He had been on his way to visit friends in another district of Fernando Pessoa called Fazendão, when his *erê* had descended and brought him to the *terreiro*, after the *saida* (coming-out ceremony) was over. He was sitting in the kitchen with Marinalvo's mother when I encountered him, and his *erê* had apparently departed. But the series of stories he told left me uncertain exactly what kind of entity was talking.

One of the stories concerned the circumstances of his birth. He said his mother had borne him at exactly midnight on the twenty-fourth of December, in the middle of a crossroad. He had been crying in the womb, because his twin had aborted at three months. There followed a discussion of astrological signs, and their connection with the *orixás*.

Joãozinho seemed penitent about whatever the problem had been between him and Marinalvo. He talked about the spiritual protection Marinalvo gives his children-of-saint. He had once been walking in the middle of a road and was nearly run over by a car, but Marinalvo was telepathically aware of the danger, and had moved him out of the way just in time.

I spent the night in the *barracão*, where those members of the *terreiro* not involved in the continuing ritual business in the *roncó* had made themselves beds on straw mats, pieces of foam, or strips of cardboard. Periodically they would get up to peer through the spy-hole behind the thrones, to see what was happening to the *iaôs*.

The stories continued. Someone talked about the *terreiro*'s dog Chela, which is considered almost an initiate—even though it has never been "shaved"—because it has spent time in seclusion with two different *barcos* of *iaôs*. This inspired someone else to talk about a *terreiro* in Recife that has a large snake. The snake dances in the *roda*, and receives saint.

Some of the stories concerned Marinalvo. From these, and from conversations with Marinalvo's mother the next day, I have been able to piece together the following account.

Marinalvo's father was from a landed family with a branch in Ceará, and his paternal grandmother was Jewish. When Marinalvo and his five brothers and four sisters were still relatively young, their father left to go and look after the family property in Fortaleza, and did not return. Their mother, Neuza, went to work in the main bus station in Salvador, and she and the children lived in an invasion on the bank of the river that runs through Fernando Pessoa.

From an early age Marinalvo had been attracted by Candomblé. As a child he had set up *assentamentos* of Tempo and Exu in the yard, to the chagrin of his mother—he tore up a bed sheet to make the ribbons with which Tempo's tree is decorated, and borrowed household utensils to create the ritual objects of Exu. He and one of his sisters would sometimes walk down the street dressed as *orixás*.

He began to visit the *terreiro* of a famous mother-of-saint in Fazendão, and was considering being initiated there, but then discovered the *terreiro* of Mané, in another district of Fernando Pessoa called Matungo. His mother was not at all pleased, because this particular father-of-saint had the reputation of liking other men.

Neuza must already have had some inkling of the direction in which Marinalvo's life was heading. Apart from other clues, he had once attended *carnaval* dressed in the skirts of a Baiana. Nonetheless, she tried to discourage his association with Mané, by taking him to *terreiros* she considered more suitable. The parents-of-saint of these *terreiros* threw the cowries to find out whether they could initiate Marinalvo, but told his mother he was destined to join the house of Mané.

There was a problem, however, in that Mané is an *abicu*—a person whose head cannot be shaved. Mané had only been *catulado* ("clipped") during his initiation, so this was the only form of initiation he was able to perform on his children-of-saint. After a time as member of Mané's *terreiro*, Marinalvo began to think of opening his own house, and wanted to be able to perform the full initiation.

So he left the *terreiro* of Mané—thus making a permanent enemy of the latter—and sought out Dona Clara, an elderly mother-of-saint in Fazendão, of an impeccable Angola lineage, who was prepared to shave his head and to give him the *decá*, which would enable him to open his own *terreiro*.

Apparently, when he received the *decá* he had not been initiated for the full seven years that are usually considered necessary for an initiate to become a parent-of-saint. However FEBACAB (the Bahian Federation of the Afro-Brazilian Cult), with which all new parents-of-saint are supposed to be registered, was prepared to accept the highly respected Dona Clara's guarantees of his competence. It was understood that she and Dona Laura, the little mother of her *terreiro*, would continue to oversee Marinalvo for a period, to ensure that things were done properly.

Marinalvo initiated his first child-of-saint, Joana, while he was living by the river, six years ago. At that time he practiced his profession in the house he shared with his mother and siblings, a situation that was difficult for all concerned. Within the same year, however, the council of Fernando Pessoa decided to put a road through the invasion, and offered the residents title to land in Jaraci, as well as materials to construct new homes. Thus many of the people who were neighbors in the community by the river continued to live in proximity to each other in Jaraci.

Marinalvo took advantage of the opportunity to establish his own premises, though it is unclear to me why he was given a larger block than most of the others affected by the move, and a supply of building materials sufficient to construct a relatively large *terreiro*. There are rumors of a liaison between Marinalvo and the mayor, of vote-buying, of the influence of Marinalvo's father's brother, who is a minor official in Fernando Pessoa. Whatever the truth of the matter, it is clear that Marinalvo pressed his claims more vigorously and more effectively than the others who moved to the same street on the edge of Jaraci.

Marinalvo's material advantages, his ambition, and a certain aloofness in his makeup, have set him apart from the other fathers-of-saint in Jaraci. He is also the only one with the *decá*, and the only one whose *terreiro* is registered with FEBACAB. Technically, every *terreiro* is supposed to be registered. If it is not, the Federation is legally empowered to close it down and to confiscate its drums. But Fernando Pessoa is perhaps too remote from the political machinations of the capital for the other parents-of-saint in Jaraci to be worried about interference from the Federation. Registration also has certain disadvantages. Every new initiate in a *terreiro*, whether child-of-saint, *ogã* or *equede*, is supposed to be certified by the Federation, and every public festival is supposed to receive a clearance. All of this paperwork requires, of course, the payment of a fee.

Marinalvo is always cordial towards the other fathers-of-saint. They have standing invitations to his festivals, which they often attend. Occasionally, after a large sacrifice, he sends them gifts of meat. However, he rarely takes part in their ritual activities.

There is greater solidarity among four of the other fathers-of-saint. Edivaldo, Biju, Luiz, and Oswaldo are regular visitors to each other's houses, and give each other support in the mounting of festivals.

The sixth father-of-saint in Jaraci, Seu Antônio, who operates a bar at the bottom of Marinalvo's street, is not considered part of the same network as the others. To begin with, his is a *terreiro* of Umbanda, while the other five belong to Candomblé. His ceremonies are also private affairs, with attendance restricted to members of the house. In addition, Seu Antônio is considerably older than the other five fathers-of-saint, who are all in their twenties, and is the only one who is married.

The stories went on into the night. Next morning I went looking for Joãozinho. I thought he had gone to visit Marinalvo's mother, and sought him out there.

Neuza was outside painting her nails and chatting with Marinalvo's elderly daughter-of-saint Rosilene, who is her neighbor. Joãozinho was not there, but Neuza asked me to sit down, and proceeded to tell me about the *terreiro's* internal conflicts. In most cases the cleavages were due to love affairs that were in some way problematic—some people had stolen other people's partners, some members of the *terreiro* were involved with other members, thus infringing the rule of *terreiro* exogamy. The conversation also ranged over other residents of Jaraci. Neuza described one of the other fathers-of-saint as a *giletão*—a person who has sexual relations with both sexes. (The term is derived from the brand name "Gillette," because this type of razor blade cuts on both sides. It is worth noting that the term can also be applied to persons who are both active and passive in relations with the same sex.) "Why would a woman want a *viado*?" she added, rhetorically.

In the course of the day various members of the *terreiro* took me aside to give me their versions of the stories Neuza had told me. My integration into the gossip network of Jaraci would probably have happened more gradually, had it not been for a particular coincidence.

On a previous visit to the *terreiro*, when I was making inquiries about accommodation in the district, a young man whom Marinalvo at that time intended to make an *ogã* had offered to sell me his house in the invasion.

When I mentioned this to Neuza, she was horrified, partly because she considered the invasion unsafe, and partly because the young man was currently at the center of a major furor. According to Neuza he was suspected of maintaining a liaison with one of the *iaôs* who were in seclusion. This was doubly scandalous. On the one hand, it violated the rule of *terreiro* exogamy; on the other, it breached the sexual prohibition that is operative during any period of seclusion.

Later in the day I met the young man in question, whom I found agreeable company, and went with him to look at his house. When I got back to the *terreiro*, our little walk seemed to be common knowledge. Marinalvo and Zita took me aside and asked me what the young man had said. I replied that he had been discreet.

* * *

Before the evening's ceremony Marinalvo received his *caboclo*, who gave various instructions, including some that referred to my own "obligation." It would begin with a "cleansing of the body" the following evening. I would then go into seclusion, prior to the offering of food to my *orixá*. He gave a list of items required for these ceremonies, which I would need to purchase in the city.

That evening the second *saida* took place. The audience was smaller, but this time all three *iaôs* came out, including the *iaô* of Oxumaré, beneath a canopy of white cloth held up by members of the *terreiro*. Again their bodies were painted with white spots for their first appearance, during which they prostrated themselves three times. They made two more entrances, this time painted with multi-colored spots, during each of which they circled the *barracão* twice.

After the ceremony several people received their *caboclos*. These did not stay long, except for the Boiadeiro of Celso (the young man who hoped to become little father of the *terreiro*), who proceeded to deliver a harangue that lasted well into the night.

There were a couple of things on his mind. One was the current state of internal dissension within the *terreiro*, which had been reflected in the evening's ceremony: the chief drummer had not attended, and the audience was very small. Boiadeiro said that Marinalvo, whom he called "father of others," should make offerings of boiled white corn (food of Oxalá) at all the important locations in the *terreiro*: the room of the saints, the house of Exu, the compound of Tempo, the altar of Ogum that stands just inside the front door, the four corners of the *barracão*, and the *cumeeira*. (The *cumeeira* is the central roof-tree of the *barracão*, which is positioned directly above the *entoto*, or "foundation." Generally there is an *assentamento* there. I have been told, on the one hand, that this *assentamento* is for the *orixá* of the *terreiro*'s second in command, and, on the other, that it is for the *juntó* of the parent-of-saint. At Marinalvo's these explanations are not contradictory, because Oxosse is the owner of the head of the *ogã* Sebastião and also Marinalvo's *juntó*.)

Boiadeiro said these offerings should be made to bring peace to the *terreiro* before the major festival, the ceremony of the name, on Saturday night.

He also delivered a tirade against his own "horse," Celso. Celso had been involved in a loud argument earlier in the evening, when someone accused him of drinking alcohol before the ceremony, which was incompatible with the ritual purity required of him as little father of one of the three *iaôs* (the *iaô* of Oxumaré). Boiadeiro recited a litany of Celso's defects, and, as in the case of his commentary on the *terreiro*'s internal conflicts, kept repeating the phrase "*Tudo com o tempo tem tempo*" ("With time there is time for everything"). I think the implication of this proverbial expression is that everyone, in the long run, gets his or her just deserts.

The members of the *terreiro* and a few visitors had already bedded down in the *barracão*, and eventually someone told Boiadeiro that we wanted to get some sleep. Visibly offended, he took himself outside to the hut of the *caboclos*, and left us in peace.

* * *

The next morning Marinalvo and Sebastião went with me to the São Joaquim market to buy the items necessary for my obligation and for the coming major festival. They took the purchases with them on the bus back to Fernando Pessoa, leaving me with a list of things still to be procured. I returned to the city, bought the additional items, and met Archipiado. He was hesitant about coming with me to Jaraci, and anxious about the uncertainty surrounding his proposed trip to the United States. However, in the evening we set out for Jaraci together.

Marinalvo had arranged for Celso to perform my "cleansing of the body"—the rite intended to remove the *egum* that was troubling me. Soon after our arrival Celso took me to the front yard and asked me to stand barefoot on a large plastic bag he had placed in front of the compound of the *orixá* Tempo. He lit a candle at the entrance to the enclosure. It went out, and he told me not to re-light it.

He sang as he proceeded to pass over my body the elements of the cleansing rite: black beans, brown beans, white corn, balls of manioc flour, yellow corn, dry manioc flour, six boiled eggs, four raw eggs, chopped raw vegetables, popcorn, manioc flour toasted in palm oil, and three candles. They tumbled onto the bag after they had purified me. He then took some leaves, wiped my body down with them, ending at the feet, and transferred them to the enclosure of Tempo. He brought back a plate of boiled white corn, which he also passed over my body.

He performed two kinds of divination, to ascertain whether the rite had been successful. For the first, he went to the entrance of the compound of Tempo and cut a pear in half. He dropped the two halves onto the floor of the enclosure a couple of times. I could not see which way they landed. He then took a handful of grains and threw them onto the ground. He was apparently able to read something into the pattern in which they fell. After this he drew, with four fingers, a series of wavy lines in the ground around the bag.

I had left my thongs next to the bag. Now I was instructed to step into them, without touching the ground, and to stand a short distance from the bag. Celso took gunpowder from a small cylindrical container and made four crosses with it on the ground—to my left, behind me, to my right, and in front of me.

Before going on, he asked me to make an offering of money "for the one who takes the *ebó*." I did not know what this meant. I had seen coins and notes of small denominations among the components of the "works" that one encounters at crossroads in Salvador, and assumed it was a spirit who took the *ebó*. I gave Celso a small note, thinking of it as a token, which would be left to rot with the other elements of the rite.

Celso looked dismayed, but concluded the cleansing, which entailed igniting the four crosses of gunpowder, in the same sequence in which he had laid them out.

He told me to walk in my thongs to the shower, take a bath using the herbal infusion called *abô*, and put on white clothes.

The shower is a concrete block behind the kitchen, surrounded by low walls of scrap sheets of corrugated asbestos, with a tap at about shoulder level.

Afterwards I went and sat in the kitchen, where Archipiado was talking to Zita. Celso was also there, tying up the bag that contained the ingredients of my cleansing rite. Zita asked him if the bag was heavy. He grinned wrily and said, "No, not very."

Zita explained that he was going to take the bag to the forest, and that it feels heavy if there is a lot of evil affecting the person undergoing the rite. So I realized that Celso was in fact the one who would "take the *ebó*," and wondered whether the "heaviness" of the bag might also have something to do with the amount of money in it.

Celso left, and Marinalvo came in to tell me the procedure for the rest of my obligation. I was to sleep alone in the kitchen that night, and the next day I would go to the *bakisse* to start my formal period of seclusion.

Archipiado said he did not want to sleep in the *barracão*, and asked if he could not stay with me in the kitchen. Marinalvo agreed to this, provided Archipiado and I did not touch each other, since this would "break the precept." He added that we would have to sleep with our bodies in opposite directions, our heads towards each other's feet.

I asked if I could smoke during the seclusion. Marinalvo replied that he had no objections, but I would have to take care not to be caught smoking by Dona Laura. Dona Laura is supervising all the current ritual activities, and is, according to Marinalvo, very strict about these things. Zita added that she herself always smokes when in seclusion, but gets rid of the evidence by throwing the butts out through the crack under the door of the *bakisse*.

Marinalvo and Zita left, and Archipiado and I rolled out our straw mat on the floor. Archipiado was peeved that I, with my strange notions about what constitutes good faith, insisted on following Marinalvo's instructions concerning our sleeping arrangements. He said that if Marinalvo had really meant us to take them seriously, he would not have left us alone together in the kitchen.

Archipiado was probably right. The next morning Zita roused us early so that the kitchen could be used for making breakfast, and I thought I detected a certain sly tone in her voice when she asked us if we had slept well. In fact, even after Archipiado resigned himself to my intransigence, we had had a very disturbed night.

* * *

Later in the morning I bathed in fresh water, then in the herbal infusion, and was led to the *bakisse* by Zita, who showed me how to enter with the right foot, touching the floor with it three times. The same procedure had to be repeated when I stepped onto the straw mat where I was to spend the rest of my seclusion. Zita placed my white beads and a *mocã* around my neck, and tied *contra-eguns* to my upper arms, and a bell to my right ankle. I made three obeisances to her, then she left, saying that no one else could enter the *bakisse* during my obligation.

Shortly afterwards Archipiado opened the door, which Zita had not locked, in order to leave my camera with me for safe-keeping. (Marinalvo had asked us to take photographs whenever we attended public festivals at his *terreiro*. Generally Archipiado did this, since it was a task he enjoyed and I did not.) I told him about the ban on entering, mainly to avoid trouble if someone came by and saw him there. He left in a huff.

In the course of the day other people did enter the *bakisse*, but they were officials of the *terreiro*—Marinalvo and Sebastião—who came to fetch things that were stored there. At one point, when the door was open, Joãozinho came and sat outside, to chat with me. He explained who the various *assentamentos* in the *bakisse* belonged to, and recounted some stories of the *orixás*. He also told me a little of what was happening to the *iaôs*. It was their day off, and they spent it in their human state of consciousness. He talked about the places where cuts are made on the bodies of the *iaôs* during their initiation: in the top of the head, the tip of the tongue, the back, the upper arms, and the soles of the feet. Some parents-of-saint cut in other places as well, for example, on the thighs and the buttocks. "Cures" prepared from herbs and leaves are placed in the cuts, which helps them to heal. The cuts leave cicatrices, but Marinalvo is said to cut "lightly."

* * *

I spent the periods when I was alone catching up on my field notes, sleeping, and thinking about the viability of a house of Candomblé as a putative "family."

The troubles that are currently besetting Marinalvo's *terreiro*, which include rumors that several members are planning to leave, are by no means unique. I have been told by several senior initiates who would be in a position to open their own *terreiros* that they never wished to do so. The problem they all mentioned was the trouble and expense of initiating people who are likely to be ungrateful and eventually to leave the *terreiro*.

A certain instability of membership seems to be typical of Candomblé *terreiros*. Three of the four Jaracian fathers-of-saint to whom I have talked about their sacerdotal careers transferred their loyalty to a different *terreiro* after their initiation. No doubt this makes them keenly aware of the fragility of the allegiance of their own children-of-saint.

In some cases the defections are due to ambition, or personality conflicts, or the desire for independence. In some cases they are attributed to the will of an *orixá*. But there are also structural factors that seem to exacerbate the personal tensions. There is one such factor that merits particular consideration. It is what some previous writers have referred to as the question of "gender" in Candomblé.

Patrícia Birman has made some very astute observations on this issue. She argues that what serves to distinguish between genders in Candomblé is trance. Those who do not—in fact, are not permitted to—go into trance, namely the *ogãs* and *equedes*, are associated with the masculine pole, and those who do go into trance, namely the children-of-saint, with the feminine pole (Birman 1988:172).

We could take Birman's argument a step further by looking at the ambiguous gender of the parent-of-saint. It seems that once people receive the *decá*, they transcend their prior status as *ogãs*, *equedes*, or *iaôs*, and thus also the gender distinction that separates the former two categories from the latter. There is no terminological distinction between parents-of-saint who were initiated as *iaôs* and those who were initiated as *ogãs* or *equedes*. Their position and functions within a *terreiro* are also the same.

There is an interesting connection with Birman's argument in that *iaôs* who become parents-of-saint are said to be able to control their trance states. Conversely, I have been told that *ogãs* and *equedes* who become parents-of-saint sometimes begin to go into trance. I have not been able to verify either of these assertions, but the fact that such possibilities are even discussed indicates that a parent-of-saint's relationship to trance, and thus also his or her gender, are ambiguous.

So there are, from this perspective, three genders in Candomblé: the "masculine" category, constituted by *ogãs* and *equedes*; the "feminine" category, constituted by children-of-saint; and what we might call the "androgynous" category, constituted by parents-of-saint.

Terminologically, the kinship system of Candomblé is conceptualized in terms of relationships between consanguines. Children-of-saint call the head of the *terreiro* and the *ogãs* and *equedes* "father" or "mother," and each other "brother" or "sister"; the parent-of-saint and the *ogãs* and *equedes* call each other "father" or "mother," and the children-of-saint "son" or "daughter." (A more detailed analysis of Candomblé kinship terminology is contained in the excellent study by Lima 1977.)

The distinction between masculine and feminine terms is based on the biological sex of the individual involved, rather than on his or her membership in one of the gender categories recognized by Birman. But what would the kinship structure of a *terreiro* look like if we tried to conceptualize it in terms of these gender categories?

The literature provides us with some clues. When parents-of-saint perform an initiation, whether of *iaô*, *ogã*, or *equede*, they "put their hand" on the head of the initiand.[1] After their death, those they have initiated have to find another parent-of-saint to "remove the hand" of the deceased.

According to René Ribeiro (1952:132), the expression "to remove the hand of the dead" is used, in the Afro-Brazilian religions of Recife, in relation to the "spouses and concubines" of the one who has died. (Whether it is also used in relation to persons initiated by the deceased is not mentioned.) In most other respects the Afro-Brazilian religions of Recife (often referred to as Xangô) are very similar to those of Bahia (cf. Carvalho 1984, Segato 1984). This justifies, I think, a little extrapolation.

Ribeiro's remark suggests that the gesture of "putting a hand" on the head of an initiand establishes a symbolically matrimonial relationship between the parent-of-saint and the person being initiated, in addition to the terminologically consanguineal relationship I have already mentioned. There is some support for this conjecture in the fact that, as I have said earlier, the word *iaô* derives from a Yoruba term meaning "youngest wife" or "recently married woman."

But, as we have seen, the parent-of-saint initiates people who are of two different genders. If the kinship structure of a *terreiro* is conceptualized in terms of these genders, it appears to be a simultaneously polygynous and polyandrous but (officially) platonic partnership between an androgynous head of the household and his or her "wives" (the *iaôs*) and "husbands" (the *ogãs* and *equedes*).

All the current tensions in Marinalvo's *terreiro* have to do with the sexual relationships of the members of the household. What I have called the "rule of *terreiro* exogamy" explains why Marinalvo is upset about some of these relationships, for example between *ogãs* and *iaôs* on whom he has "put a hand." (Strictly speaking, the prohibition on relations between members of the same *terreiro* applies only to those who have been initiated by the same person, because this person has "put a hand" on them. This is a convenient loophole that allows some couples to belong to the same *terreiro*: the parent-of-saint puts his or her hand on one member of the couple, and delegates another authorized person to initiate the other.)

But the *terreiro* exogamy rule does not explain why Marinalvo sometimes attempts to break up relationships between *terreiro* members and *outsiders*. To give just one example: he told the husband of an *equede* that the latter "rubs"—a term used to refer to the supposed sexual activity that occurs between women. This caused an argument that led, eventually, to the couple's separation.

Marinalvo's behavior may be more comprehensible if seen in the light of my conjecture that all the members of the *terreiro* are symbolic spouses of the parent-of-saint. Obviously relationships between these spouses cannot be tolerated, because they are "married" to the parent-of-saint, not to each other. But relationships between these spouses and outsiders also threaten the primary loyalty that the spouses owe to the head of the household.

This attitude is not, I think, primarily a matter of sexual jealousy. Marinalvo is tolerant of *affairs* between members of his household and outsiders—even sometimes encourages them—but only as long as the relationships do not show signs of becoming too serious. What is at issue is his "spouses' " allegiance.

This helps, I think, to understand why so many *terreiros* of Candomblé are riven with internal tensions, and why defections are so common. It does not take much imagination to see that this kind of multiple marriage is a hard trick to pull off.

* * *

After sunset Zita covered my head with a white cloth and led me to the shower, where I bathed in a herbal infusion, under her sporadic observation. Modesty is somewhat relaxed between members of a *terreiro*, because they belong to the same "family." I changed out of the clothes I had been wearing and put on a white T-shirt and loose white pants with lace cuffs.

When it was dark Dona Laura came to the *bakisse*. Zita told me how to prostrate myself in front of Dona Laura, and to clap my hands in a rhythm that begins slowly and gradually increases in tempo—a gesture called *bater paó*, which I repeated three times. Then I was instructed in asking the blessing. This custom is one that many Bahians acquire as children, when they are taught to ask the blessing of their parents. I said, "*A bença, minha mãe*" ("The blessing, mother"), took Dona Laura's hands, brought them to my forehead, my chest, my right shoulder, my left shoulder, and the back of my neck, then kissed them.

Dona Laura removed the colored sheet that covered the mat on which I had been sleeping and replaced it with a white one. She also put a white pillow on the sheet, where I was eventually to lay my head that night. Zita brought in the offerings, arranged them around the end of the mat near the door, and lit candles there and on the altar.

While we were waiting for Marinalvo, Dona Laura sat on a chair that had been brought for her. She was dressed in a long white skirt and a top of very fine white lace. She and I talked about the names of the offerings, and what they were made of. She seemed concerned to put me at ease.

Marinalvo arrived, and left the door open. Members of the *terreiro* gathered outside. Archipiado was also there.

Dona Laura censed the room with a makeshift thurible, constructed from the bottom half of a tin can, and blackened with use. She used aromatic herbs, but said she preferred incense. She rang the double bell called *adjá* over the various elements of the rite, and spoke some ritual phrases, to which Marinalvo and those outside responded.

She placed a white sheet around my neck, and performed a series of operations on my head. First she placed one hand on my crown and the other on my forehead, then bathed my head in a special infusion called *amaci*, which contained herbs pertaining to my *orixá*. She wiped my head with a white towel, then made a series of crosses on it, using three different substances. She drew the crosses on the top of my head, the forehead, the back, the right side, and the left side. The first time she used *amaci*; the second time, a black soap, imported from Africa, called *sabão da costa*; and the third time, a kind of white butter called *ori*.

Marinalvo fetched the dove. Dona Laura censed it and rang the *adjá* over it. I stood. Dona Laura took the dove, swept it up and down my body, then held it while Marinalvo slit its throat. She complained about Marinalvo's using a knife on the bird of Oxalá. I sat, and Marinalvo let blood drip over the offerings, then over my head. After Marinalvo decapitated the bird, Dona Laura applied the bleeding stump of its neck to various parts of my body: to the same five places on my head, to the back of my neck, the palms and backs of my hands, and the tops of my feet. She then removed bunches of feathers and stuck them on the smears of blood.

I think I had expected to get a mild thrill of moral indignation or disgust from this experience. What shocked me instead was that I found it so sensuous. The contact with the warm downy body of the little bird evoked memories of nuzzling the intimate parts of a lover, or of my mother; images of Leda and the swan, of the eagle and Ganymede; perhaps traces of my long forgotten experience of being born. It violated all the boundaries that made me separate from the rest of creation, and, like creation, it was beautiful in its profligacy. A god had just been dismembered, as a sacrifice to itself. A universe had died. The universe continued.

Marinalvo cut into four pieces the cola nut that was among the offerings, and dribbled some blood on them. He then threw them. Apparently Oxalá had accepted the sacrifice, because everyone clapped *paó*, and Dona Laura rang the *adjá*. She proceeded to chew a piece of cola nut, and rubbed it on my crown. I was given another piece to eat. Boiled white corn and the leaves called *folha da costa* were sprinkled over my head.

Dona Laura placed a white lace prayer-cap on my head, and bound it with a white turban. She told me to lie down, on my left side, and not to get up for twenty-four hours.

Marinalvo proceeded to cut up the dove, and to arrange its various extremities in the plate of *ebô*, in such a way that the mound of white corn took the place of the bird's body.

He left, and the onlookers dispersed. Dona Laura sat with me, while her bed was being prepared in the *roncó*. She talked about her health, and about how difficult it is doing everything on her own, not just because of her age, but also because of her swollen legs. She has raised three girls, but the youngest one, fourteen years old, "only wants to spend her time in the street."

After she left I tried to get some sleep.

* * *

I was roused a few hours later by a knock on the door from Archipiado. He had not wanted to go to bed, so had been delegated to wake the members of the *terreiro* at 3:00 a.m. He returned at intervals to tell me, through the locked door, what was happening in the *roncó*, where Dona Laura was in the company of the three *iaôs*.

Marinalvo entered the *roncó*, with Zita, Sebastião, Marta, Celso, and Delcir, then shut the door. Previously the animals for the sacrifice had been washed: three goats, three guinea fowl, three ducks, and fourteen chickens. Outside the *roncó* the other members of the *terreiro*, along with Marinalvo's mother and Archipiado, played drums and *agogô* and clapped.

During the sacrifice they sang a chant, over and over, that seemed to last for hours. Its melodic simplicity and rhythmic complexity haunted me, perhaps because I kept slipping between waking and dreaming.

Congo de abandá
Meu sinhô
Congo de abandá
Minha sinhá
Bé bé bé-é
Congo de abandá
Congo de abandá gudiá . . .

The animals were taken, one by one, into the *roncó*. Every time the door was opened Archipiado was able to see inside. Each animal was slaughtered over the head of a *iaô*, so that by the end of the rite the initiands were completely bathed in blood and covered with feathers.

Marinalvo placed all the dead beasts outside the door of the *roncó* and put a straw mat in front of them. Several members of the *terreiro* prostrated themselves before the animals, received saint, trembled and brayed, then went to do reverence to the three *iaôs*.

Before dawn Marinalvo and Zita came to tell me about the next rite that was to be performed on my behalf. There would be another sacrifice, and

I would have to leave a sum of money, which Marinalvo specified, on the ground. Zita mentioned that a journalist and photographer from one of Brazil's weekly magazines had been invited to cover the installation of the "*ogã* from Australia" at the ceremony due to take place in the evening.

I was confused and angry. Up until a few days ago I thought that I was going into seclusion only for the purposes of a *bori*—the rite Dona Laura performed last night. Then gradually, from hints and rumors, I gathered that Marinalvo intended to install me as *ogã*. I had no objection to the idea, but wished Marinalvo had been more explicit about what it entailed. Other people have complained to me about his habit of leaving things unexplained.

I had no desire to have my installation as *ogã* publicized. Also I could not afford the amount of money Marinalvo asked me to leave on the ground, and did not even have so much with me. I told him this. He accepted it with equanimity, and said to leave what I could afford.

My anger might have abated, except that Archipiado arrived shortly afterwards and told me, through the locked door, how my *bori* and forthcoming installation as *ogã* were being talked about in the *terreiro*.

Last night Neuza told Archipiado she was worried that after I was installed as *ogã* and Archipiado initiated as *iaô* in the *terreiro*, we would leave Brazil and cut our ties with Marinalvo. And during my *bori* there had been a lot of banter about the situation among the people outside, with interchanges such as this: "Well, mother, are you going home to Australia?" "No, I'm going home to Fazendão." After the *bori* Dona Laura said she thought Marinalvo was initiating me only for the sake of publicity.

Archipiado himself had been the object of repeated *sotaques*. Some of these made mocking reference to the fact that Marinalvo wanted to initiate Archipiado as *iaô*.

On previous occasions Marinalvo had sometimes jokingly talked about this possibility, but neither Archipiado nor I had any reason to take him seriously. Now it occurred to me that perhaps the reason Marinalvo had asked Dona Laura to perform my *bori* was so that he would be free to "put a hand" on Archipiado.

There was another incident as well. Marinalvo had suggested that Archipiado take advantage of my seclusion to visit the dunes with Sebastião.

I told Archipiado that I had had enough. As soon as the door to the *bakisse* was unlocked I was going to tear off the bell and the rest of my fool's garb and tell Marinalvo I was leaving.

Archipiado reasoned with me. Marinalvo knew that I was a foreigner and an anthropologist, so would have every reason to believe that my involvement with his *terreiro* was motivated more by self-interest than religious commitment. So I could hardly object if Marinalvo used my involvement to further his own self-interest. Besides, Marinalvo had been gracious enough to put on a good performance for me. It was now up to me to do the same for him. If, instead, I created a scandal, it would damage both the *terreiro* and my own research.

Archipiado is years younger than I. Yet there have been many times in our friendship when I felt that I was the child.

Shortly after sunrise Dona Laura came into the *bakisse* again, followed by the *axogum* Sebastião, his clothes stained with blood. Dona Laura removed my cap and turban, and two chickens were passed to her. She swept them up and down my body, then Sebastião slit their throats and dribbled blood over the offerings and on my head. After each chicken was decapitated, Dona Laura made a series of crosses on my body, in the same places as she had done with the dove, then stuck feathers onto the red blotches. She placed another prayer-cap on my head, and bound it with a fresh turban. The chickens were held over a tin cup, to collect their blood, which was then mixed with honey. Dona Laura put the cup to my lips, and I drank.

There was no mystical experience. Or perhaps it would be more accurate to say that my "mystical insights" were less lyrical, more ironic, than they had been the night before. I felt soiled, tired, dishonest, stupid, and sick at heart. I also regretted that three animals had suffered for the sake of my illusions.

There was a crowd outside, playing drums and *agogô*, clapping and chanting. I had to ask the blessing of Dona Laura and Marinalvo and other officials of the house. I got the movements mixed up. The *terreiro*'s children-of-saint came into the *bakisse* to ask Dona Laura's blessing. They clapped *paó*, and received saint on the last beat. Some of them asked my blessing, and kissed my hand. Others did not.

The crowd dispersed. Marinalvo said that when I returned to the United States I should send him and Dona Laura a present. She was horrified, and said they just wished me much peace for the journey. Marinalvo left, and Dona Laura stayed in her chair, to watch over me. She said I should try to sleep, but we talked for a while.

Marinalvo opened the door and told me that Archipiado was outside weeping. I asked if I could talk to him, but he was too upset to speak.

I went to sleep, on my left side, under the maternal eye of Dona Laura.

I have slept, on and off, for most of the day. At one point Archipiado came and explained why he had been crying. It was partly because he had been fighting with almost everyone in the *terreiro*, and partly because the sight of blood trickling down my face had reminded him of the crucifixion.

The dove was cooked in the kitchen, and brought to me on a plate. I was told I should eat it. To do so would bring me good fortune, since I would be eating the same food as the owner of my head; not to do so would give offense to my *orixá*.

So far I have not touched it. I am suffering from diarrhea, and have hardly eaten anything.

The smell of my shit mingles with the sweet odor of decay coming from the plates of food. Ants are proceeding in an orderly column towards the offerings, and out again under the locked door of the *bakisse*.

8. The Throne

The press did not show up for my installation as *ogã*.

After sunset Marinalvo removed my turban and cap. Dona Laura came, and I had to kneel three times in front of her. Then I was instructed in the procedure for coming out of seclusion. When I stepped off the mat I had to touch the floor three times with my left foot, then with my right foot. At the door I had to jump three times, look to the sky, the right, the left, and the ground, then exit left foot first. Dona Laura called to the four directions, the heavenly bodies, and other natural phenomena, to give them thanks and ask their blessing.

She led me, barefoot and with a white sheet over my head, to the shower, where she bathed me, head and body, first with fresh water and the black soap called *sabão da costa*, then with the herbal infusion called *abô*. I changed into the white clothes I had been wearing on the first day of my seclusion, which Archipiado had washed for me. Dona Laura led me back to the *bakisse*, where I stayed waiting to find out what the evening would bring.

Archipiado was in the *barracão* before the festival started, and wrote a series of notes on the events that led up to it. Each entry includes a precise annotation of the time. The entry for 9:35 reads, "The *terreiro* is in crisis. There are only four people in the *barracão* and no *ogãs* to play the drums. The people in the *barracão* are complaining about the delay." He goes on to record the gossip about the reasons for the crisis—certain key people were expected not to show up, because of Marinalvo's disapproval of their relationships. Probably their supporters would stay away as well. He adds the following comment: "As [Joãozinho] says, the only thing that is lacking is for the [new] *ogã* to flee before the *iaôs* give their names."

By ten o'clock, however, the mood had changed. The head drummer, who was at the center of one of the current scandals, arrived, apparently prepared to brazen it out. He came with one of the *terreiro*'s daughters-of-saint, and his two children by his former wife. Archipiado went to talk to them, and met the children.

Later Marinalvo's mother came up to the daughter-of-saint and whispered something that made her nervous. But other female members of the *terreiro* grouped around her, to show their solidarity.

By 10:30 all the drummers had arrived, and the children-of-saint were in the kitchen, changing into their white clothes. The festival began at 10:40, with the despatch of Exu. "Suddenly the house filled up, and at least fifty people attended the festival."

Sebastião distributed *pemba*, then the first *roda* began, with the children-of-saint dancing and performing ceremonial greetings. At 10:58 Marinalvo entered and received obeisances.

At this point Archipiado's notes switch from Portuguese to English. He did not want them to be read by the people sitting around him. His determination to keep on writing was no mere anthropological pose. He was trying to keep himself occupied and detached, to avoid falling into trance.

Celso said something to Marta about Archipiado, and they smiled at each other. Archipiado wrote, "I'm very nervous." Marinalvo started to dance, but avoided looking Archipiado in the eye.

By 11:11 the music had reached fever pitch. The head drummer "is singing as he never sang."

The audience was getting impatient, and some people left. But the coming-out ceremony was not due to start until after midnight. (In some *terreiros* it starts early, so that it can be completed before midnight. In both cases the reasoning is that the ceremony should not be in progress *at* midnight.)

Celso said to Marta, "Just a little while now," then looked at Archipiado and smiled. Archipiado wrote, "I can't understand what's happening."

There are four large throne-like chairs that sit next to the drums in Marinalvo's *barracão*. The one closest to the drums is the tallest, and the others decrease in size. The third one was covered with a long white cloth.

Archipiado went out to the front of the *barracão* to smoke a cigarette. There was a large crowd there, watching the festival through the door and the front window. He met the young man whose house I had visited in the invasion, and asked whether he would be drumming. "He said there's a gossip game against him and he doesn't know . . ."

At 12:01 the new initiates made their first entry. Dona Laura and Marinalvo were at the head of a group of six members of the *terreiro* who bore aloft a long piece of white cloth, under which the three *iaôs* came into the *barracão*, bent low. Their bodies were painted with white spots, but there was no *adoxu* on their shaved heads. Each one carried a switch. They made obeisances to the door, the drums, and the *entoto*, then exited.

At 12:20 they made a second appearance, circled the *barracão*, then left again.

Meanwhile, back in the *bakisse*, I had been told to get dressed in my *ogã*'s outfit: a white peaked cap, white shirt, white trousers, and white shoes.

I was led into the *barracão* under a length of white cloth. Archipiado took a photograph that shows Dona Laura walking backwards at the head of the procession, holding up a corner of the cloth with her left hand and ringing the *adjá* with her right. Marta, Sebastião and Celso can also be made out supporting the cloth. Underneath I am dancing awkwardly, with head bowed.

I was guided to the front door and the drums, but not to the *entoto*, to perform a salutation. Then I had to seat myself three times on the white throne. I was now an *ogã*.

I danced in a circle around the *barracão* with Dona Laura and Sebastião, attempting unsuccessfully to follow the smooth sliding movements of their feet and the coordinated motion of their arms, which they kept bent at the elbows.

I returned to the throne, and the head drummer made a speech. I was introduced as an Italian man who had come to Jaraci just so that I could make an obligation. "He doesn't know how to dance, but don't pay any attention to that." I think these remarks were charitably meant, but they seemed to lend a burlesque air to the subsequent interaction between me and the members of the *terreiro*, who came to greet me, to ask my blessing, and to congratulate me.

Then the three *iaôs* entered the *barracão* again. They were dressed in white, without any body paint. Each one wore a band of plaited straw around the head, and carried a switch.

Marinalvo asked for silence, and Celso made a brief speech in which he said, "Now we are going to prove that Marinalvo of Fernando Pessoa is a real father-of-saint."

Three visitors of senior rank were invited to step forward from the audience. Each in turn went up to one of the *iaôs* and asked the *orixá* to call the *dijina* out loud, so that all could hear. Each *iaô* called the name successfully, and simultaneously received the *orixá*, who performed a few joyful steps as the visitor rang the *adjá* and the drummers struck up a song connected with the particular entity. The first to give the name was Ogum, the second Obaluaiê, and the third Oxumaré.

Celso made another short speech, in which he said there had been gossip in Jaraci that the *iaô* of Oxumaré would "enter" (seclusion) but not "exit." However the *iaô*, of whom he was the little father, had come out, thus proving that he, Celso, had the capabilities of a father-of-saint.

The three *orixás* danced in their white clothes, then were led out to be dressed, for the first time, in their ritual costumes. When they came back, each one danced in sequence. Then came the turn of the *orixás* of the other children-of-saint. Marinalvo's Iançã cut them short so that she could dance, but exited after the arrival of Celso's Ogum. (Iançã and Ogum have a tense relationship, and often brandish their swords at each other if they descend at the same festival.) Ogum danced, then went around holding out his helmet for monetary contributions. He did not approach me.

Various members of the audience began to receive saint, and danced with Ogum. At this point Marinalvo told me to go back to the *bakisse* to get some sleep. I had a chance to speak briefly to Archipiado, who said that he did not want to stay at the *terreiro* another day.

So when Marinalvo came to put me to bed, I told him I had things to attend to back in the city. He said I could leave on the morrow, but would have to maintain the conditions of the obligation. This entailed continuing to wear my beads and the *contra-eguns*, keeping my head covered when out of doors, and abstaining from sex and alcohol.

* * *

When Archipiado knocked on the door the next morning, I asked him to get the key. He took a while to rouse Marinalvo, who came and removed the *mocã* (raffia necklace) I was wearing, but left on my beads and the *contra-eguns* (armbands). Marinalvo asked me for the money he had requested earlier, which was to pay the ritual assistants, and waved it above the offerings. Then he told me to put my cap on and go out to take a bath.

Archipiado had made tea in the kitchen. We sat drinking it while I waited for the shower to become available.

The *terreiro* was alive with gossip about the previous night's festival. In general, people seemed dissatisfied with it. One of the big disappointments was that Archipiado had not "rolled."

He himself said he thought arrangements had already been made for him to be taken into seclusion. After I had gone to bed, the drummers had played a rhythm that was supposed to make him go into trance. Everyone looked at him expectantly, but he occupied himself with writing notes, and had not experienced even a "shiver." The head drummer remarked that Archipiado was "strong."

There was some criticism of one of the new initiates—the one who was suspected of having broken the rule of abstinence from affairs of the heart that applies during the period of seclusion. The exact nature of her transgressions was never clear to me. One rumor was that she and her boyfriend had been passing each other love letters through the spy-hole behind the thrones. No one was indelicate enough to suggest that the spy-hole had been used for purposes other than this, but all were prepared to believe that, somehow or other, love had laughed at the locksmith.

In any case, there was disapproval of her costume, which was said not to move freely enough, and of her dancing, which was said to be incorrect for her particular *orixá*. This, of course, was an indirect but not exactly subtle reflection on her sponsors.

There were also stories of assignations made or attempted during the festival itself, and afterwards. The boyfriend of one of the daughters-of-saint had invited Archipiado to go swimming with him in the spring in the invasion. When the daughter-of-saint, overhearing the conversation, proposed going as well, the project was dropped.

It was said that Marinalvo's ex-father-of-saint, Mané, had arrived during the festival but not entered the *barracão*. It was claimed that he had left a "fetish" outside, to cause problems for the *terreiro*.

Certainly there were problems enough the next morning. People awoke to find four of the sacrificial chickens missing. In a community as poor as Jaraci, this was a serious matter. People count on eating well after a big Candomblé festival.

Part of the gossip apparently concerned me, but people were careful not to let me overhear too much of it. I gathered that the head drummer had put pressure on Celso's Ogum to ask me for money, but the latter had not wanted to approach me.

Celso was present during these discussions, but seemed not at all displeased with himself. Before the festival there had been much negative speculation about the *iaô* of Oxumaré, and about Celso's role as her little father, or sponsor. It was said that she had never "rolled," and in any case, how could a son of Ogum (that is, Celso) have a daughter who is of Oxumaré? But at the festival she had not only called the name, but also danced perfectly. No doubt Celso thought this enhanced his chances of being made little father of the *terreiro*. "Am I or am I not of the waters of M . . . K . . . ?" Celso asked, using the *terreiro*'s Angola name.

I had still not managed to bathe, because the three *iaôs* had got to the shower ahead of me. So Marinalvo asked me to go back to the *bakisse* with Marta, the *terreiro*'s little mother, for the final rites of my obligation.

I made an obeisance to the altar, then to the offerings. Marta prayed aloud in front of the altar, asking for peace and success in my life, and that I never speak badly of the *terreiro*. She lit a candle on the altar and put my earthenware drinking vessel, covered with blood and feathers, to one side of the base. We clapped *paó*, and Marta proceeded to put the remains of all the offerings in a basin, which she wrapped in a paper bag and a white towel. She folded my sheet, rolled up my straw mat, and put them in a corner.

When we emerged from the *bakisse*, Dona Laura was sitting in a chair in the yard, being served with coffee. I had to go and ask her blessing. Dona Laura told me to keep my *ogã*'s cap on, and not to expose my head to the sun. She said I could wear my cap in the street, even after the period of my obligation was over.

By the time Archipiado and I had bathed, it was after eleven o'clock. I took my leave of Dona Laura, asking her blessing once more, and of Marinalvo. He said I should observe the restrictions of the obligation for seven days. I could wear street clothes when I went out, but at home I should dress in white. He would remove the *contra-eguns*, which I was still wearing, at the end of the obligation. Then he said, "*Vai desculpando qualquer coisa.*"

This is a polite Bahianism used for departing guests, which means literally "Go excusing anything [that has been amiss]." I wished there were an equally elegant formula I could have used in response.

Archipiado and I headed for the bus stop, arriving at 12:03. Archipiado pointed out that we had probably walked through the crossroad near the bus stop at exactly midday. We had thus infringed a double taboo. It is considered dangerous to be on the street at noon, and especially perilous to pass through a crossroad at that hour.

* * *

During the journey back to the city we attempted to reconstruct the events of the past few days, which had been so complex and intense that they tended to blur together in my memory.

The conversation continued over lunch at our usual restaurant in the Pelourinho. We ordered beer. I was still uncertain whether Marinalvo intended me to take the rules of the obligation seriously, but I was not reluctant to accept Archipiado's view that they only applied when I was under the scrutiny of members of the *terreiro*.

I don't know if Archipiado has read Goffman, but his interpretation of recent events in Jaraci was very Goffmanian. If I may paraphrase the import of the conversation using Goffman's words, Archipiado thought that the only thing members of the *terreiro* were concerned about was "the individual performer maintaining a definition of the situation before an audience" (Goffman 1959:81, note 6). Archipiado believed that the *terreiro*'s performances had an essentially pecuniary motive, and was delighted that he and I, as a "performance team" (Goffman 1959:79), had successfully penetrated the backstage of the *terreiro*'s "team," thus getting what we wanted without letting them get too much of what they wanted from us.

This interpretation, of course, put us both in the role of "informers." "The informer is someone who pretends to the performers to be a member of the team, is allowed to come backstage and to acquire destructive information, and then openly or secretly sells out the show to the audience" (Goffman 1959:145).

Although the informer is usually regarded as discreditable, a Goffmanian interpretation would have allowed me to justify performing such a role, and provided me with a means of rationalizing the feelings of insincerity and self-deception that accompanied me through much of the performance. "The individual automatically becomes insincere when he adheres to the obligation of maintaining a working consensus and participates in different routines or performs a given part before different audiences. Self-deception can be seen as something that results when different roles, performer and audience, come to be compressed into the same individual" (Goffman 1959:81, note 6).

I was prepared to accept this interpretation for immediate practical purposes, such as deciding whether or not to drink beer with lunch, but it left me uneasy. This uneasiness was not, I think, due so much to feeling the presence of an "unseen audience" (Goffman 1959:81), whether social or supernatural, as rather to an apprehension that this explanation was too simple. It did not do justice to the "causal pluralism" of the situation, which I have tried to elaborate in my retelling. Nor did it take into account the complexity of the motivations of the persons involved (cf. Kendall 1982:201). It did not, for example, allow for the possibility of compassion and generosity on Marinalvo's part. (I should add that in other contexts, when I passed harsh judgements on Marinalvo, it was Archipiado who reminded me of this possibility.)

On reflection it has occurred to me that there is a problem with the whole "performance" metaphor, and thus with the particular ironic sociological perspective to which it is intrinsic (Burke 1962:511–17; Brown 1977:176). This metaphor divides social beings into "actors" and "audiences," but by doing so creates a kind of "meta-stage" on which both actors and audiences are performers. This makes the observer, and the readers with whom he or she presumes him- or herself to be in collusion, into a kind of "meta-audience," with a god's-eye view of what is happening on the meta-stage.

I could oppose to this trope the Bakhtinian metaphor of social life as carnival. "Carnival does not know footlights, in the sense that it does not acknowledge any distinction between actors and spectators. Footlights would destroy a carnival. . . . Carnival is not a spectacle seen by people; they live in it, and everyone participates because its very idea embraces all people" (Bakhtin 1984:7).

In the present ethnography I have tried to draw out the implications of Bakhtin's metaphor by avoiding the kinds of social scientific "staging devices" that permit the objectification of the modes of thought of "other cultures" (cf. Fabian 1983:107). I have attempted to treat my anthropological explanations as serviceable for restricted, localized purposes, but not as having any claim to an epistemological status that is different from the explanations and modes of thought of the people among whom I lived in Bahia. Making my own anthropological interpretations situational has enabled me to explore their interaction with other interpretations, whether offered by other participants in the situations in question, or generated by myself as immediate, unreflective, non-anthropological reactions to the same situations.

* * *

On the Friday following the "day of the name," the new initiates visited a number of churches and heard mass at the Church of Our Lord of Bomfim. (The number of churches that it is customary to visit on this occasion is seven.)

I had been to Marinalvo's once during that week, for an obligation of the *ogã* Sebastião. I found it hard to get used to the idea that, after my rapid ritual incorporation into the *terreiro*, I was now one of its dignitaries.

But I took Archipiado's view that it was all a matter of performance. Marinalvo told me to sit on my throne, alongside Sebastião and the *equede* Zita. I danced in the *roda*. A visiting father-of-saint from another *terreiro* in Jaraci even greeted me with the shoulder bow that parents-of-saint, *ogãs*, and *equedes* give each other. (This bow entails moving one shoulder, then the other, forward and slightly downward.) I responded appropriately.

I returned again on the Sunday after the day of the name, to attend the *quitanda*, or "market," that traditionally follows the making of new initiates. Archipiado and I took a bag of oranges.

I felt more comfortable dancing in the *roda*, and even performed a passable imitation of the steps. The thrones were a little crowded, because they had to be shared between the *terreiro*'s own dignitaries and two visiting fathers-of-saint from Ceará. We played an amicable game of musical chairs.

After the *roda* the *erês* of the three new initiates entered the *barracão*, carrying on their heads trays laden with fruit. Straw mats were spread out, on which the *erês* sat down and placed the trays. The musicians struck up a *quitanda* song, and the other children-of-saint received their *erês*, who danced merrily. This was the signal for the *quitanda* to begin.

All those who were not in trance participated in the game of buying or stealing fruit from the three *erês* in charge of the market. The other *erês* helped to protect the market from thieves. There was a general hubbub, and a great deal of mirth as people escaped with fruit they had stolen, or were thrashed by the *erês* with switches if they were caught *in flagrante*.

As a "dignitary," I thought it was my duty to offer exorbitant sums for the several pieces of fruit I bought. But the *erês* were not at all interested in prices. As far as they were concerned, the transaction simply consisted of receiving a piece of paper in exchange for a piece of fruit. They seemed to derive much more pleasure from dealing with the covert strategies of thieves than with the transactions of honest customers. So I tried a couple of times to steal some fruit, and received several solid blows, to the delight of the other participants.

My back smarted, but I was laughing.

I had been told that on the Monday after the *quitanda* there would be a ceremony called "flowers of the Old One," to close the festivities associated with the initiation of the three new children-of-saint. Chants would be sung to Oxalá, and "flowers," which in fact are popcorn, offered to Obaluaiê, the Old One.

I did not attend this ceremony, and do not know if it eventuated. But I did become a regular visitor to Jaraci, and eventually found a place to live that was a short walk from the *roça*. (This word means "small farm," but is regularly used by the people of Candomblé to refer to their own *terreiro*.) My presence in Jaraci began to seem less remarkable, both to me and to the residents.

Some people thought I was there because I wanted to become a father-of-saint. Others knew that I intended to write something about Candomblé. Some were suspicious of me, but most were prepared to act as though it was simply my fate to be there.

I got to know more people and more spirits. With some my relationship was close, with others, more distant. My friendships with members of other *terreiros*, in particular with Taís and Biju, involved certain conflicts with my role as an official at the *roça* of Marinalvo.

Taís, and others, told me that the purification of the body and the *bori* that had been performed for me were incorrect, that they were intended to cause me harm, and that Marinalvo wanted to cause trouble between Archipiado and me. Taís suggested that I get Biju to "look in the cowries" for me, to see how he, as a father-of-saint, could repair the damage. This would obviously mean a closer relationship with Biju's *terreiro*.

I did not take this critique very seriously, because one of the most common things you hear members of any *terreiro* say about other *terreiros* is that their practices are "incorrect." Still, I was tempted by Taís's proposed solution, because I liked Biju.

I was not the only one. Taís once said, "Everyone loves Biju."

Biju was probably the poorest of the fathers-of-saint in Jaraci. He kept to himself, hated gossip, and slept with a teddy-bear; but his *caboclo*, whom I met, and his *exu*, were known for their dash. He had a masculine demeanor; but in the summer he donned the skirts and turban of a Baiana and set up a street-stall in one of the beach-side suburbs, where he sold African food he prepared himself.

In the end I decided not to take Taís's advice. It seemed preferable to maintain my friendships with Taís and Biju without destroying my relationship with Marinalvo. This resolution caused occasional conflicts of loyalty; but such conflicts seemed to be the stuff of life in Jaraci.

The scandals that had surfaced during the initiation cycle ran their course. The *iaô* who was suspected of breaking the rules of the seclusion left the *terreiro* and went to live with her boyfriend in the invasion. This caused so much outrage that her ritual objects, except for the expensive ones that could be kept for future use, were smashed and thrown into the *terreiro*'s cesspit. So when I went to visit the couple I had to do so in secret.

The head drummer also left the *terreiro*. His *assentamentos* were dismantled, and the stones called *otá* placed in an earthenware pot in the compound of the *orixá* Tempo. This pot already contained the *otá* of a number of other ex-members of the *terreiro*. The people to whom these *otá* belonged had been turned over to Tempo, whose name means "Time," to deal with.

I could go on to recount the events of my time in Jaraci in greater detail, but that would take me too far beyond the scope of this study, which is intended mainly to characterize the kinds of interaction that take place between people and the various spirits of Candomblé.

I have not said a great deal about the interaction between people and *orixás*. There are several reasons for this. The first is that there were no *orixás* that I got to know in the same intimate way as certain *exus* and *caboclos*. The *orixás* appear only at public ceremonies, where their interaction with the audience is very limited. According to Binon Cossard (1970:184), the *orixás* may speak, to deliver predictions and prophecies, but I have only once witnessed this, and that was from a distance that did not permit me to hear the interchange. I gather that *orixás* speak only after their human vehicles have gained some years of experience in Candomblé.

I should add that I once saw an *orixá* casually chatting with Xilton at the reception after a festival.

The second reason I have not devoted so much attention to the *orixás* is that a number of studies have already dealt with them in considerable detail. The other spirits of Candomblé—*exus*, *caboclos*, and *erês*—have been treated in a few works, but have suffered a comparative neglect. (The two bibliographies by Moura [1982b and 1987b] contain lists of works devoted to the different categories of spirits.)

There is, however, one particular *orixá* who has also tended to be overlooked in the literature, namely Tempo. My own interactions with Tempo were not intimate, but they seemed always to be significant. Accordingly, I have devoted the following, final chapter to this *orixá*.

9. Tempo

It is a curious coincidence that the period of field work on which this account is based began and ended in liturgical seasons associated with the *orixás* of trees.

The phytomorphic deities of Candomblé go by a variety of names (cf. Carneiro 1981:178; Lody 1975:71; Cacciatore 1975:50 and *passim*). In Gege-Nagô *terreiros* the best known is Loko, whose name derives from the Ewe language. Loko is regarded as equivalent to Iroko, whose name derives from Yoruba but is less commonly used, even in those *terreiros* that trace their roots to the Yoruba region.

Some people consider Loko/Iroko to correspond to the Angola *orixá* Tempo; others do not (Cacciatore 1977:235). The reason for this difference of opinion probably has to do with a desire on the part of "pure" Gege-Nagô houses to avoid contamination from Angola influences, since the Angola nation has been branded by some anthropologists as the most "syncretistic" of Candomblé (e.g. Carneiro 1981:178, 192; Bastide 1978:205–6; cf. the discussion in Frigerio 1983:12–16).

But I visited many non-Angola houses that cultivated the tree deity under the name of Tempo. Even when I went to Ilê Axé Opô Afonjá, the most Yoruba-centric of Bahian *terreiros*, the person who showed me around the grounds pointed out a group of enormous trees with pieces of white cloth tied to their trunks and hanging from their branches, and said they were the "trees of Loko or Tempo."

Tempo is the only *orixá* who seems to be more popularly known by a name originating in the Bantu languages than by a Yoruba-derived name. The reason for this distinction probably lies in the allusiveness of the word *tempo* itself. Although the name can be traced etymologically to that of a Bantu deity, Zaratempo (Castro 1971:112), the significance of this link has been obscured by the multiplicity of associations that the second part of the Bantu word has in Portuguese.

Tempo means not only "time" but also "weather," and thus, by extension, "the outdoors." There are also several frequently heard proverbial expressions in which *tempo* occurs, for example:

Tudo com o tempo tem tempo.
"With time there is a time for everything."

Dar tempo ao tempo.
"To give time to time."

Entregar ao tempo, às águas, e a Deus.
"To hand over [a problem] to time, the waters, and God."

All of these proverbs have the sense of allowing things to take their course, of trusting in the unfolding of destiny to bring about just resolutions.

Even the Gege-Nagô *orixá* Loko seems to have been influenced by these associations.

One of the first festivals I attended during this field trip was in honor of Loko, at the oldest Gege house in Bahia, on January 17, 1988. I have mentioned earlier that festivals of the *orixás* take place on or close to the Catholic feast days with which they are associated. The only major holy day around that date is the feast of the Chair of St. Peter at Rome (January 18).

A few days later I attended another festival, this time for what I was told was a particular "brand" of Xangô. The mother-of-saint who received Xangô had on a white costume and cruciform crown similar to those worn by the Gege mother-of-saint who received Loko at the previous festival. The most striking difference was that her Xangô carried an *oxé*, or double-ax, in one hand, and an enormous silver key in the other. Exceptionally, all the *orixás* at both festivals also wore white.

It was not until months later that I came upon some information that allowed me to speculate about the connection of the two festivals with Tempo. As I have said, there are various forms of the tree deity. Sometimes he is regarded as an *orixá* in his own right, and sometimes as a "brand" of another *orixá*. As Loko he is often equated with the white Xangô (especially in Gege-Nagô *terreiros*), and as Tempo with Obaluaiê (especially in Angola *terreiros*). What is significant about his association with the white Xangô is that this *orixá* is represented iconographically as St. Peter. (Some *terreiros* celebrate this *orixá*, as Xangô Airá, on the feast day of Saints Peter and Paul, in June.)

St. Peter, of course, holds the keys to the gate of heaven, and administers justice to the souls of the departed. There are, I think, a number of ways in which this symbolism connects him with the *orixá* of Time. At an abstract level, both St. Peter and Tempo are associated with the justice of destiny, and with the notion of an overview of the total pattern of human lives—an overview that is not available to humans themselves. There is a verse in Dante that is relevant here:

> Oh predestination, how remote is your root from the sight of those who do not see the *whole* first cause! (*Paradise*, xx:130–32).

At a more concrete level, the compound of Tempo frequently stands just inside the front gate of a *terreiro*. (This was true, for example, at Marinalvo's and Biju's.) The reason I was given for this was that Tempo and the *exus* (whose house is also at the front of the *terreiro*) guard the entrance to the world of the *orixás*—the *barracão* and the room of the saints, which are "like heaven."

In addition, at one *terreiro* that I visited in Fazendão the low white wall that surrounded the compound of Tempo was shaped in the form of an enormous keyhole, with the tree of Tempo growing in the circular part, and other shrubs and plants in the shaft. This seemed to be a clear reference to Tempo's role as guardian of an entrance.

It appears, then, that even when Loko and Tempo are treated as separate *orixás*, there is a significant overlap in the symbols with which they are associated.

Celebrations in honor of Tempo himself usually take place on August 10, the feast day of St. Lawrence. Marinalvo held a festival for Tempo on that date, a week before my departure from Brazil. It was the last public Candomblé festival I attended.

Marinalvo's explanation of the connection between Tempo and St. Lawrence had to do with the *ferramenta*, or metal sculpture, that is associated with the *assentamento* of the *orixá*. Often the base of the sculpture is in the form of a miniature brazier covered with a grate. St. Lawrence was martyred by being burned alive on a gridiron, although it is said that, by the grace of God, he was able to overcome the fires of his torment. The link with Tempo, according to Marinalvo, is that all the animals sacrificed to Tempo are broiled. Lody writes that the grate is called the "ear of Tempo" (1975:71). This is perhaps because it is to Tempo that people often turn to request justice.

Not all the *ferramentas* of Tempo that I sketched or made notes on included a brazier; but all are surmounted by a little metal banner. This represents the white flag of Tempo, which flies from the top of a tall bamboo pole in Tempo's compound. Many houses of Candomblé can be recognized from a distance by the fluttering of this flag above trees and rooftops. The use of such a flag is said to be an Angola custom, but it is one that has been incorporated by many non-Angola *terreiros*.

Another frequently occurring element of the *ferramentas* of Tempo is a miniature ladder. The ladder is there, Taís told me, because "Tempo ascends and descends." Taís added that the ladder is "the same as the banner." The equivalence of the two was made explicit in one *ferramenta* I sketched, where the ladder, instead of being placed vertically, was located at the top of a metal rod, and extended from it horizontally, in the manner of a flag. Taís said that people leave notes, on which they have written requests to Tempo, between the rungs of the ladder. If the request is benevolent in its intent, it is placed at the top of the ladder; if it is malevolent, it goes at the bottom.

Requests to Tempo may also be made by means of a *troca de língua*, or "exchange of language," in which ritual experts converse with the spirits. Taís gave me an example:

Ala Tempo, Tempo Zará, Tempo da
Milagongá, Tempo da Muringanga, Tempo
Zirim: assim, Tempo, como você gira prá
frente, eu hei de ver esta pessoa
girando prá 'trás. Ala Tempo!

Ala Tempo, Tempo Zará, Tempo da
Milagongá, Tempo da Muringanga, Tempo
Zirim [these are "brands" of Tempo]: so,
Tempo, as you only turn forward, I have
to see this person turning backward.
Ala Tempo!

Taís added that time itself only goes forward, not backward. But Tempo is capable of reversing the direction of the wheel of fortune for the person against whom such a spell is directed.

Some *ferramentas* of Tempo incorporate various kinds of metal lances, spears, blades, and tools, which Taís said were the "weapons of the slaves [*exus*] of Tempo." These "slaves" belong to Tempo, in the same way that other *exus* belong to their *orixás*, but they are also part of Tempo himself—

his "bad face," as Taís put it. The other *orixás* are separate from their *exus*, and, according to Taís, cannot do evil. Tempo, however, can do both good and evil. Marinalvo's housekeeper Angélica, who is a daughter of Tempo, said to me "Tempo creates and Tempo destroys."

One *ferramenta* I sketched had, above the miniature banner, a kind of horizontal propeller or windmill. This is no doubt connected with the notion of time as cyclic. (Since Tempo's name also means "weather," the windmill is probably associated as well with the movement of the wind, and the changing of weather patterns.) One Tempo song that Taís sang for me expresses this idea of the revolving of time:

O Tempo virou,
Deixa virar.
O Tempo dobrou,
Deixa dobrar.
{Vamos brincar com Tempo
{Até o dia clarear. [bis]

Time [*or* the weather] turned,
Let him turn.
Time bent over,
Let him bend.
{Let us play with Time
{Until day breaks. [twice]

(Carneiro also recorded a song for Tempo that expresses the same idea [1964:154; 1981:177].)

The connection between time and rotation is also clear in the name of one of Tempo's slaves, Exu Gira-Mundo—the *exu* who circles the world, and who is associated with the whirlwind.

There are thus three kinds of movement associated with Tempo. First, he ascends and descends, between the realms of the below and the above. Below are the flames of the brazier and the hell of the *exus*. Above are the white flag and the heaven of the saints. Second, he rotates, reproducing the motion of the world itself, of the seasons, of the heavenly bodies. Third, he bends, as a man bends under the weight of years, and, eventually, he breaks.

Taís sang a song that alludes to this third type of movement. It is associated with a brand of Tempo called Tempo de Afunanga (whom Taís called the "Tempo of Battle").

Na vaquejada eu fui feliz.
*Eu caí do cavalo.
Saravá foi quem quis.

*Eu quebrei o meu pescoço.

*Eu quebrei as minhas pernas.

*Eu quebrei os meus braços.

In the roundup I was happy.
*I fell from my horse.
It was Saravá who wanted this.

*I broke my neck.

*I broke my legs.

*I broke my arms.

(The first and the third lines remain the same in each verse. The second, asterisked, line changes. *Saravá* is usually a greeting in Candomblé. Here, according to Taís, it refers to Oxalá.)

In the dance Tempo performs while this song is sung, he shows the various parts of his body that were broken. As he does so he bends over and becomes increasingly smaller. Finally he has to be covered with a white cloth, so that people do not see what is left of him, because it is a kind of *egum* (spirit of the dead).

One way of interpreting these three kinds of motion of Tempo would be to connect the second two with the first. The turning movement could be seen as a symbol of eternity, and therefore associated with the top of the ladder, to which Tempo ascends; the bending and breaking could be regarded as signifying the ephemeral nature of humankind and of phenomena in general, and therefore associated with the bottom of the ladder, to which Tempo descends.

But there is a problem with this interpretation. I have mentioned earlier that Gira-Mundo, the entity whose name connects him with cyclical movement, is one of Tempo's *exus*. This suggests that there is something diabolical about the idea of eternity. It is absurd because it is inhuman.

Conversely, if one considers the ephemerality of human existence, it is equally absurd because it is not eternal.

Carneiro writes of Tempo as the deity of "clock time" (1981:177), or what we might call "Newtonian time," since it was Newton who said that "absolute, true Mathematical Time, of itself and from its own nature flows equally without regard to anything external" (quoted in Lindbom 1976:71). This idea of rational, uniform time may, perhaps, be one of Tempo's faces. But there is another face that is at least as important. Tempo is also the god of warped, absurd, grotesque, fragmented, irrational time. Tempo is, in fact, a drunkard.

Tempo is the only *orixá* who drinks alcohol—and he drinks heavily. There are several songs that refer to this fact. This is one of them:

> Aê Tempo!
> Tempo está embriagado, [bis]
> Quem foi que lhe embriagou?
>
> Aê Tempo!
> Tempo está embriagado, [bis]
> Não conhece nem pai nem mãe.
>
> Aê Tempo!
> Tempo is drunk, [twice]
> Who was it who got him drunk?
>
> Aê Tempo!
> Tempo is drunk, [twice]
> He does not know his mother and father.

The tree god is also regarded as a madman. Loko, with whom Tempo is often equated, has a name that, like Tempo's, is allusive. *Louco*, in Portuguese, means "mad," "crazy." Taís told me a story intended to explain how the brand of Xangô called Loko became *louco*.

Xangô was involved in a fight with his sister-daughter-spouse Iançã. Iançã threw her sword at Xangô, and it hit a tree of the type called *pé de Loko* (*ficus sp.—Ficus religiosa*, according to Lody [1975:71]). The tree split in two. One half hit Xangô on the head, and he went crazy (*louco*), which is why he is called Loko, and why the tree that struck him bears his name. The other half split open the ground. Xangô disappeared into the crack, and lives there still.

Given his taste for the bottle and his psychotic episodes, it is paradoxical that the tree deity is frequently linked to the Holy Spirit. Several people I spoke to used identical words in making this association. They said, "Tempo is everything," and for this reason is like the Holy Spirit, who is *in* everything. According to Lody there are some *terreiros* in which Tempo is explicitly syncretized with the Holy Spirit (1975:71).

Anthropologists, I think, are in a particularly good position to understand the nature of this paradox.

One of the distinctive characteristics of anthropology as a social science is its goal of "holism." It aims for a complete overview of social life, in which all the different elements are integrated into a coherent synthesis. It attempts, so to speak, to "be in everything," and thus arrogates to itself the perspective of the Holy Spirit.

But there is a difficulty inherent in this endeavor, and it is the same difficulty that makes Tempo a drunkard.

Taís said the reason Tempo can do good or evil to any person is that he has no binding relationships, no family, no home. Having these things, as anthropologists know, entails partiality, partisanship, and a limitation of the universality of one's perspective.

But it is precisely the lack of these things that gives Tempo his taste for the bottle. The question asked at the end of the first verse of the song transcribed above finds its answer in the last line of the second verse. The reason Tempo got drunk is that he has no father and mother. Nor, according to people I spoke to, does he have a wife, siblings, or children. (It is worth noting in passing a contrast with classical mythology, in which Time, in his various forms, has descendants. According to Virgil, for example, "Truth is the daughter of time.")

There is another song that Taís sang me about Tempo's homelessness.

{ Eu avilê
{ Tempo mavila caçanje. [bis]
Tempo não tem casa,
Ele mora na rua.
Aonde Tempo mora?
Orai, meu Deus,
Mora no pé da cruz.

(Taís was not able to give a precise meaning for the African words in the first two lines of the song. The rest translate as follows:)

Tempo has no home,
He lives in the street.
Where does Tempo live?
Pray, my God,
He lives at the foot of the cross.

Here we have yet another twist in the story of this complex *orixá*. The mighty god of time, the all-knowing spirit who is present in every cranny of the universe, the ruler of the whole phenomenal world, discovers that he is the most abject of creatures, a homeless street-dweller, and ends up living at the foot of the image of suffering humanity.

It is perhaps for this reason that some *terreiros* associate Tempo with Francis of Assisi, the saint of the stigmata.

The symbolism associated with Tempo, like the symbolism of Candomblé in general, is too rich, contradictory, and context-dependent for me to feel justified in attempting to systematize it more than this.

The people of Candomblé know about the spirits more through interaction with them in various situations than because they are given to analytic speculation about them. When they do objectify the spirits in oral discourse, they are most likely to do so by means of narratives that weave the spirits into the fabric of the social context in which they and their listeners are participants. Such narratives are rarely attempts to reproduce faithfully an authoritative body of knowledge. Mostly they are creative endeavors whose purpose is to relate to the immediate situation the teller's personal and often contradictory experiences with the spirits, in a way that makes those experiences meaningful to both narrator and listener.

I have tried, at least partially, to adopt a similar procedure in writing about the spirits.

* * *

On the morning of Tempo's festival I walked across the dunes to Marinalvo's for the sacrifice. As I approached I could hear the sound of drums and *agogô*.

The rectangular compound of Tempo is surrounded by a low whitewashed wall with an entrance at the front. On one side of the entrance, painted in faded pink letters, are the words *TEMPO DE ÁMUÍLA*, and on the other, *ORIXÁ DO VENTO* ("*orixá* of the wind"). In the center of the enclosure grows a small tree, of the species known as *arueira*. Strips of white cloth have been tied around its trunk and lower branches. Under the tree the *ferramenta* of Tempo stands on a small pedestal, and is surrounded by earthenware pitchers, pots, and bowls.

When I arrived the preparations for the sacrifice had already been made. Nine candles were burning inside the compound, and offerings had been placed there: plates of *ebô* (boiled white corn) and *acaçá* (cakes of corn meal), and bottles of beer and wine. Popcorn had been scattered over the offerings and the floor.

Although the sacrifice was essentially a private ceremony, it took place in full view of the street, because Tempo's compound is at the front of the yard. Marinalvo had also invited a local politician to join the half dozen members of the *terreiro* who attended.

There were four chickens to be sacrificed. Zita took one of them, opened its beak, and whispered into it a request to be carried to the *orixá*. Then she and Marta held the chickens while Marinalvo slit their throats. He proceeded to sprinkle the blood of each chicken over the offerings, the *ferramenta*, the vessels, and the interior wall of the compound, while we sang the chant "*Menguê, mengá*." (*Menga* is the word used in Angola *terreiros* for "blood.") He plucked out bunches of feathers, stuck them on the streaks of blood, and sprayed all the offerings with beer.

He called the *orixás* of the children-of-saint who were present. In the case of Gilberto, he did this by holding the point of the bloody knife used in the sacrifice to Gilberto's brow.

Then Marinalvo fell to the ground, with his body half inside the entrance to the compound. He writhed violently, knocking against the walls, and growling. His hands were contorted as in an extremity of anguish. Marta and I held him, to prevent any serious damage to the material vehicle into which the *orixá* had descended.

After about three minutes Tempo got up, put his hands behind his back and his nose in the air, and stalked haughtily around the front of the compound. His shirt was streaked with blood. We proceeded to greet him with full prostrations followed by an embrace. He did not speak, and stayed only long enough to receive our homage.

At the public festival that took place that evening, certain conflicts had been resolved. The chief drummer, whose *otá* had gone into the pot in Tempo's compound some time before, had been rehabilitated. I asked Marinalvo's mother what had happened. She said that Iançã, the owner of Marinalvo's head, had instructed him to let the chief drummer return, and to permit the relationship that had caused the difficulty.

There were, of course, other problems to take the place of this one. I slipped away from the festival in the course of the evening to go for a walk with Taís, who received Corquisa. Taís had asked Marinalvo to place an offering to Corquisa among the elements of the morning's ritual. Marinalvo refused. As a result, Corquisa said, she had told Marinalvo that his plans for the festival would not work out. He had intended to take both me and Angélica into seclusion. But this had not happened.

In my case Marinalvo wanted to perform a *catulagem* (clipping of hair). In the case of Angélica, whose owner of the head is Tempo, he proposed to initiate her as a daughter-of-saint.

My own reason for declining the next stage of initiation was that I was leaving Brazil in a week, and had too much to organize to be able to afford the time and the emotional gymnastics. Marinalvo knew this well before the festival.

Angélica, however, had "rebelled" (as one member of the *terreiro* put it) the day before the festival, when all the arrangements had been made, and all the ritual objects purchased. I was to have been her little father.

In other words, life in Jaraci continued as usual.

* * *

A few days later, on my second-last night in Brazil, I walked once again to Jaraci, this time to take my leave.

I said goodbye to Marinalvo and the people at his *terreiro*, who wanted to know exactly where I would be going and when I would be back.

I went to Edivaldo's, where Corquisa was waiting for me. On the table under the window, where we sat, she had placed a vase of yellow wildflowers, a ceramic laughing Buddha, and two glasses. One of the glasses was a present for me. We drank beer, and had the last of our long conversations. At the end of it she said that the length of time she had known me was roughly the same length of time as she had been coming to earth. Now that I was leaving, she would be going away too, to let Sete Saia reign. She allowed me to kiss her hand, embraced me, and left Taís's body.

I said my farewells to the people at Edivaldo's, and Taís and I set out to go to Biju's. On the way we decided to stop for a drink at a new bar that had opened on a hillside in the invasion. The bar had been built by a young man called Felipe, whom I had seen a few times bicycling through Jaraci. I recognized him from a distinctive little crease above the bridge of his nose. The bar had a couple of tables outdoors, and a couple more inside. We were the only customers, and sat indoors because of the stiff breeze that was blowing from the sea. There was a low partition at the back of the bar, behind which Felipe's two children were sleeping. The elder did not look to be more than about two years old.

Taís said Felipe had started young, at the age of thirteen. Felipe said this was a good arrangement, because by the time he was thirty he would be able to retire, and let his children look after him.

There was a tall drum at the back of the bar. I asked Felipe if he was an *ogã*, and he replied that he had been, in a different part of Bahia. He said he was from the same *terreiro* as Marinalvo's ex-boyfriend, Delcir.

The bar had been open only a week, but already it was doing a lively trade. Taís mentioned that a couple of nights earlier there had been several *exus* drinking at the bar, including Taís's own Sete Punhal, who had been making passes at the women present. We laughed at how different Sete Punhal was from Taís.

So the three of us drank on, gossiping about the people and spirits of Jaraci, kidding and philosophizing, finding out from each other how we contended with the human condition.

Taís and I made a move to leave, because we wanted to get to Biju's before it was too late. But Felipe invited us to stay for a complimentary glass of wine. He also took out of its cage a Brazilian cardinal, which he had raised from its chickhood. It ate from our hands, climbed on our bodies, perched on my head, and shat on my sweater.

I have asked myself why it seems important to include this extraneous little scene in my concluding chapter. I think it is because up until that moment I had expected that it would be a relief to be away from the pressures of "the field." But at Felipe's bar I realized that Jaraci was not "the field" in the anthropological sense. It had become my "earth."

Jaracians used the word *terra* ("earth," "land") to refer to a person's native soil.

I recall a party on St. John's day, at Edivaldo's mother's place in Fazendão. Edivaldo's boyfriend—a strong, sensitive young man, who had come from a different part of Bahia, and was subsequently drafted into the airforce—got very drunk and began to weep uncontrollably. When we tried to find out the reason for this display of emotion, he sobbed an explanation: he was so moved that the people of Fernando Pessoa treated him as though he belonged there, as though it was his "earth."

The earth has an important symbolic role in Candomblé. Juana Elbein dos Santos writes that "all the ritual action in the '*terreiro*' is indissolubly linked to the earth" (1977:57). And Marlene de Oliveira Cunha, in her analysis of the "gestural language" of Candomblé, interprets a number of the most important ritual movements as referring to the earth: beating the earth with the feet during the dance; moving with head bowed and body slightly bent during the *roda*, in order to keep the earth in view; touching the earth, then the forehead and the back of the neck, as a gesture of greeting to the ritual space itself and to individual spirits (1986:144).

The axis of the circular dance that takes place during Candomblé rituals is a hole in the ground covered by a tile (or a small arrangement of tiles, usually in the shape of a square or a diamond). This is referred to as the *terreiro*'s "foundation" or *entoto*. The central rite in the founding of a new *terreiro* is the offering of sacrifices to the *entoto*. Later the *entoto* is periodically opened, so that it may be "fed." I was told that Entoto is a brand of the *orixá* Obaluaiê who is connected with the earth.

Felipe, Taís, and I were all relative newcomers to Jaraci. But we all found there an earth in which we managed to grow. This process had not been without its conflicts. But that is part of belonging to an earth.

I realized, at Felipe's bar, that I was glad the people of Jaraci had made me part of their earth; that they had tasted my blood, and that I had tasted theirs.

When Taís and I got to Biju's he already had one visitor, and another arrived shortly after us. Biju soon received his *exua*, Pomba-Gira, and Taís received Sete Saia. We got some wine from Dona Nega's, and a party was under way.

In the course of the drinking Pomba-Gira asked me to accompany her to the house of Exu. She went inside, and I stood at the door . . .

It was the first time I had ever kissed the lips of an *exua*, and this was to lead to a long series of reflections on the interaction between people and spirits.

Epilogue: Egum

A sombra das tuas vestes
Ficou entre nós na Sorte.
Não 'stas morto, entre ciprestes.

....

Neófito, não há morte.

The shadow of your clothing
Remained among us in Fate.
You are not dead, among cypresses.

....

Neophyte, there is no death.

Fernando Pessoa, "Iniciação" (1985:53)

Thus it was that I returned to Bloomington, Indiana, to start "writing up."

It could be said that in so doing I crossed various boundaries—the geographical and political boundaries that separate Brazil from the United States; the cultural boundary that separates life from text; the personal boundary that separates the Jim who was Evaristo in Jaraci from the Evaristo who is Jim in Bloomington.

When I asked Taís why people in the *terreiros* of Jaraci gave me the nickname Evaristo, he said Evaristo was probably a kind of *egum*.

The Jaracians, as usual, were using language to play with boundaries. They made me like themselves—a creature with a foot in two worlds. I was a spirit from the realm of the dead; but there I was, living among them, and playing back at their game.

Here in Bloomington I have continued to play back. By textualizing the Jaracians and giving them pseudonyms, I have made them into beings of another realm; but I have done this so that they may continue to play their game with the people among whom I am presently living—the readers of these pages. No doubt some of these readers will, in turn, play back.

So where is the boundary?

By giving me the name of an *egum*, the Jaracians were playing with the boundary of death.

Jean Baudrillard points out that death is the ultimate boundary, and the one on which all power relations are founded (1976:200–201). He gives an historical explanation for this connection. But let me offer an alternative perspective.

Power is based on objectification, and can be linked to a particular view of death. Participation in social life means being simultaneously subject and object, self and other. If this participation ceases at death, one becomes pure object, pure other.

But in the *terreiros* of Jaraci the dead interact with the living, which means that there is no ultimate boundary, and thus no metaphorical basis for the creation of entities that are pure objects.

The boundary of death does, of course, have a certain provisional reality, even in Jaraci. But by playing with this boundary the Jaracians subvert it, and therewith the possibility of complete objectification. On neither side of the boundary are there pure subjects or pure objects. Power relations, therefore, can never be fixed, but have to be seen in terms of a kind of game in which subjectivity and objectivity, selfhood and otherhood, are tossed back and forth in interlacing patterns that tend to obscure the imaginary line that divides them.

This is not the kind of game that can be understood by means of conventional game theory (cf. Brown 1977:160–71), in which the analyst stands outside the game and identifies the rules, the moves, and the goal. It is rather an interplay of identities that are constantly being tested, circulated, transformed. The only goal of Candomblé's game is to "live the intensity" of the game itself (Sodré 1983:145), so the only way of explaining it is to make one's explanation part of the game. Muniz Sodré has pointed out (drawing an analogy with Gödel's theorem) that it is not possible to create a self-contained formal system out of the rules and moves of this game (1983:94); in fact, to attempt to do so would be to misunderstand the nature of the game.

The view of death that is implicit in this game has an interesting connection with the ideas of Mikhail Bakhtin that I have referred to in an earlier chapter.

Bakhtin writes that "there is no death from the inside; it exists for no one, not for the dying, not for others; it has absolutely no existence" (quoted in Todorov 1984:98).

Tzvetan Todorov takes this passage to mean that "I can die only for others; conversely, for me, only others die" (1984:98). But another interpretation of Bakhtin's remarks is also possible.

In 1918 Bakhtin participated in a public debate in the city of Nevel', which was reported in the local newspaper. The account of Bakhtin's contribution reads, in part, as follows:

> comrade Bakhtin . . . did recognize, and even expressed appreciation of, socialism, but he complained of, and worried about, the fact that socialism had no care for the dead (as if there weren't enough services for the dead!), and that, accordingly, in some future time, the people would not forgive us such neglect. . . . Listening to his words one could form the general impression that this entire buried host, reduced to powder as it is, would shortly arise from its tombs and sweep from the face of the earth all the Communists and the Socialism they promote (quoted in Todorov 1984:4).

If we read these two passages together, it appears that Bakhtin is arguing a case not for the objectification of the dead, but rather for their continuing participation in social life. This would be consonant with the general tenor of his work. Bakhtin's primary concern seems to be to problematize all taken-for-granted notions of boundaries.

* * *

Some *terreiros* have a special place set aside for the souls of the dead. It is called *balé*, and may be a grove of trees (sometimes the trees called Loko), or a room, or a small house. It is usually at the back of the *terreiro*'s grounds. I was told that this is because the *eguns* have to be kept apart from the *exus*. The *eguns* are "cold," while the *exus*, whose house is usually at the front of the *terreiro*, are "hot." Thus in the *terreiro* itself the principles of death and regeneration are separated. But the *eguns* and the *exus* both gravitate to the location where opposites dangerously coincide—the crossroad.

The hut of the *caboclos* may also be in the back part of the *terreiro*'s grounds, because *caboclos* are the spirits of dead Indians, and thus compatible with the *eguns*. Taís also said that the *caboclos* have control over the *eguns*.

In certain contexts people will say that the *exus* and at least some of the *orixás* are also spirits of the dead. This notion may derive from Africa and the worship of divinized ancestors (cf. Santos 1977:102), or from Kardecist cosmology, in which all the entities of the "invisible world" are "disincarnated spirits" (Cavalcanti 1983:35). But in many contexts the *exus* and the *orixás* have taken on a significance that obscures any direct connection with death.

Terreiros of the Angola nation do not commonly have a *balé*. At Marinalvo's, for example, there was just a banana tree in the back yard, at the base of which Marinalvo would light a candle if he had a particular request to make of the *eguns*. The banana tree is connected with the *eguns* because it is said to groan when it is cut. (Bamboo and the cashew plant are also associated with the *eguns*, for the same reason.)

However, I had opportunities to interact with the *eguns* in several other *terreiros* in Fernando Pessoa.

Xilton once told me that "*eguns* do not manifest"—that is, they do not cause trance. However, this is only partly true. The *eguns* did occasionally "manifest" in Jaraci, for example in the context of a type of private ceremony, of Kardecist origins, called a "white table." I saw this happen only once, at the *terreiro* of Edivaldo, when an *egum* materialized in Edivaldo's body.

The proceedings were similar to those of the Kardecist rite of "disobsession" (as described by Cavalcanti 1983:123–31), except that the entity that "manifested" was called an *egum* rather than an "inferior disincarnated spirit," and the entity who controlled it was called a *caboclo* rather than a "superior disincarnated spirit."

In the rituals of Candomblé, as distinct from those with a direct connection to Kardecism, it is less common for the *eguns* to "manifest," and certainly there are no public festivals at which they do so as a group.

In Jaraci the father-of-saint called Oswaldo occasionally received his *egum*, Biscó, at festivals for the *caboclos* or the *exus*. I also met a transvestite mother-of-saint in the city who received an entity called Lesse. This entity, she said, was owner of her head. From what I could make of her complex story, she regarded Lesse as something like the archetype of the *eguns*, in much the same way as people regard Exu as the archetype of the *exus*.

The idea of an archetypal *egum* is one that is encountered in the literature, although according to Santos and Santos (1981:165) this entity, who is the ninth child of the brand of Iançã known as Oiá, is called Egúngún. J. E. dos Santos also provides a different interpretation of the term *lesse*. According to her, *lésè-égún* is the name given to a *terreiro* devoted to the tradition of the *eguns* (1977:103).

The *eguns* do participate as a group in public festivals in some Candomblé *terreiros*, but, although visible, they are not "manifested." They are spirits who perform in costumes that cover them from head to foot, without requiring a human vehicle as their intermediary. People who do not belong to the *egum* sodality (and it may be noted in passing that all initiates in this religious association are men) do not know what is underneath an *egum*'s costume. This secrecy is maintained by the belief that if you touch an *egum*, it burns you.

Until fairly recently the only *terreiros* devoted to the tradition of the *eguns* were in two villages on the island of Itaparica—one in Bela Vista and one in Barro Branco (Omari 1984:41; cf. Santos 1977:119; Santos and Santos 1981; Braga 1984; Ziegler 1977:ch. II). Some *terreiros* on the mainland, such as Ilê Axé Opô Afonjá, have long-standing connections with the *egum terreiros* on the island (Braga 1984:23; Omari 1984:55, n. 56), and mount an annual festival for the *eguns*. I gather that this takes place with the assistance of personnel from the island, and in connection with All Souls' day.

In the past few years, however, at least one initiate from the *egum* houses of Itaparica has established on the mainland a *terreiro* that is also primarily devoted to the *eguns*. It was in the district of Fernando Pessoa called Matungo, and I attended a festival there on the second of July, the "day of the *caboclo*," when this *terreiro* held a festival in honor of the *caboclo egum*, called Baba Iô.

I talked with José, the leader of the *egum* rituals, a couple of times before the festival. His account of the relationship between the entities that are involved in the rituals reminded me of the cosmology of Kardecism. But there were important differences.

In the *egum* tradition there are two types of spirits. First, there are those called *aparacá*, who are recently deceased, and, in the words of José, "do not have light." These are reminiscent of the "inferior disincarnated spirits" of Kardecism, who have not been "educated." These spirits are dangerous, because they are capable of "leaning on" people. Then there are the *babás*, who have received light, and therefore do not lean on people. These are like the "superior disincarnated spirits" of Kardecism, with the significant difference that the process of giving light to an *aparacá* does not consist of allowing it to "manifest" so that it may be instructed, but rather of offering it sacrifices.

Whatever the doctrinal similarities between the *egum* tradition and Kardecism, their rituals are very different. The festival I attended at José's *terreiro* had nothing in common with the "white table" at Edivaldo's.

The *egum* festival began with the despatch of Exu and chants for the *orixás*, none of whom descended. Then there was a break. José and his assistants laid out on the floor of the *barracão* a straw mat, and covered it with a white cloth. They proceeded to bring in bowls, candles, a bottle of palm oil and another of *cachaça*, and six chickens. Seven men with long switches, called *mariô* and made from branches of the oil palm, stationed themselves along the walls.

There are two doors to the *barracão*, both in the left wall. Up to this point the door closest to the front of the *barracão* had been closed, and everyone had come in through the door at the back. Now the public entrance was locked, and no one was permitted to enter or exit (except for a short intermission) before the end of the festival, which was to last until the following morning.

The front door opened, and we heard the noise of a scuffle going on outside. Some of the men with switches lashed at the doorway, others went out, apparently to take part in the fracas, then re-entered.

Before long an *aparacá* made it to the entrance, and peered around it at the audience. All I could see was a white cross on a sheet of dark blue fabric. The *aparacá* retreated, then came back and entered the *barracão*. It danced franticly, lurching around the room and attempting to attack members of the audience. It was restrained by members of the *egum* sodality waving *mariô*.

The costume of the *aparacá* consists of two large square sheets of cloth sewn together on three sides. The result is a virtually two-dimensional square surface—a flat plane that twists and contorts as it lunges about the room.

When the *aparacá* disappeared again, the various offerings that had been placed in the middle of the *barracão* were removed by ritual assistants.

The scuffling outside continued, but now there was also a loud banging on the exterior walls of the *barracão*, and the sound of fireworks being exploded. The men with switches rushed in and out of the front door, as if attempting to defend the *barracão* from an invasion.

In the midst of the hubbub, almost imperceptibly, the first *babá* sidled into the *barracão*. It was the *egum* of the *orixá* Iançã. (Taís once used the word *egũa* for a female *egum*. This may have been a neologism, as I did not hear other people use it.) Iançã rules over the realm of the *eguns*.

The drummers played for her, and she danced briefly, then disappeared again, but re-entered with the *babá* of Ogum. José had previously told me that it was Ogum and Iançã who created the *eguns* (he made the gesture of rubbing the sides of his two index fingers together) and brought them from Africa to Brazil.

Iançã and Ogum danced together, creating a filigree of light and color as the little mirrors they were wearing flashed and the panels of their costumes swirled. Then they seated themselves in the thrones.

There were four thrones at the front of the *barracão*, all with mirrors set into their backs.

In the course of the evening the dances of the *babás* were interspersed with the frenzied performances of the *aparacás*.

There were five more *babás* who entered and danced. One was the *egum* of Xangô. Another, I was told, was the *egum* of "Iançã with Logum." Two others were probably also *eguns* of Iançã. The last to enter was the *caboclo egum*, who wore a feather headdress on top of his masquerade.

All the *babás* were dressed in variants of the same basic costume. I can perhaps most easily convey the impression it created if I say that it struck me as resembling a walking, dancing Punch and Judy show.

The masquerade is suspended from a circular support, which is covered with a rounded cloth top. An inner piece of fabric goes all the way around this support, in the manner of a curtain on a circular curtain rod. Over this hangs an outer piece of fabric that forms a kind of cape, framing the front of the *egum*. The cape is divided into panels, and decorated with mirrors. Where the "face" of the *egum* would be you see only the inner piece of cloth. Above this "face" hangs a fringe of beads. Below it is a kind of apron, also ornamented with mirrors. Short, stumpy arms are built into the costume, and may hold ceremonial objects. The feet are covered with fabric.

From this description it will be evident that the *egum* costume differs from a puppet theatre in a number of ways. For example, the *egum* costume is round, and enclosed at the back, while a puppet show of the Punch and Judy type is a kind of upright box, open at the back. Also the curtain of the puppet theatre parts to reveal a stage on which the puppets act out their routines, whereas the "face" of the *egum*, framed by the cape and the apron, is like a proscenium where the curtain remains closed.

But I doubt that the connection with puppetry, which struck me so forcefully, is purely speculative. One of the earliest forms of puppetry in Brazil is referred to in the literature as "the human stage" (Borba Filho 1966:68–76). Moreover the *eguns*' performance itself included a puppet routine.

The *babá* of "Iançã with Logum" had, attached to one of her arms, a kind of ventriloquist's doll, in the form of what looked to be the head of a deer, painted red, with a round mirror in the middle of its forehead. She used this puppet for a voice-throwing routine, in which the deer's head engaged the audience in a type of litany.

When the stage itself is both actor and puppeteer, it is hard to know what has become of the notion of a proscenium.

Most members of the audience were familiar with the litanies of the *babás*, and responded appropriately. However, some of the *babás* engaged in a dialogue with particular individuals. There were a few members of the audience who understood the language of the *babás*, which is like a rumbling made deep in the throat; but for most it had to be interpreted by a specialist member of the sodality. (It is worth noting in passing that only the male *babás* spoke. The *babá* of "Iançã with Logum" communicated indirectly, via her ventriloquist's doll, in a high-pitched voice.)

These dialogues covered a variety of subjects. In some cases the *babás* had business with particular people. One woman was nominated to a post in the *terreiro*; another was interrogated about why she and her husband had not come to a previous festival. In some cases members of the audience had requests to make of the *babás*. One woman wanted their assistance in finding out who robbed her house. She was told to leave "money on the ground." The *babá* said to her, "If you want something, you have to give something." Many other people, including myself, had to leave money on the ground.

I was, in fact, the first person to be addressed by one of the *eguns*. It was the *babá* of Ogum. He was dressed in a dark blue cape decorated with small oblong mirrors. His apron had a silver star at the center, surrounded by lines of circular mirrors. He carried an unlit candle in his left hand, and a curved silvery rod in his right.

I had to remove my shoes and socks and go forward to the area between the audience and the *babá* to answer his questions, which were interpreted for me.

He asked if I thought he was beautiful.

"Of course," I said.

He asked what I thought he was, whether I thought there was any bone there.

"I don't see any bone," I said.

He asked if I had faith.

"I do, yes," I said.

Then I had to dance.

* * *

I wonder what kind of *egum* is Evaristo.

I imagine him thus: he is dressed like a *babá*, except that the curtain of his face is open, and reveals a stage on which other *eguns* are dancing. All of these *eguns* are wearing the costumes of *babás*, and flashing their mirrors at each other. Each one has a face that is open, to reveal a stage on which other *eguns* are dancing . . . and so on. Evaristo himself is dancing with other *babás* on a stage that is the face of another *egum*, who is dancing on a stage that is the face of another *egum* . . . and so on.

Evaristo dances inside the face of the *egum* called Fernando Pessoa who dances inside the face of the *egum* that is this text who dances inside the face of the *egum* called Bloomington who dances inside the face of . . . ? Perhaps of Oxalá, since Taís once described Oxalá (who, like the *eguns*, is called Babá) as "pure *egum*."

It is hard to describe these *eguns* without making it seem as though they are of different sizes, and contained within each other like Chinese boxes. But the way I imagine them, they adjust to each other's scale, and can move in and out of each other's faces.

There is no one proscenium that frames all the others. What is at one moment the scene may, at the next moment, be an agent, an act, an agency, or a purpose (cf. Burke 1962:xvii).

This metaphor admits of no closure. As I learned from my participation in Candomblé, the boundary between different kinds of reality, whether social, epistemological, or ontological, is not a barrier to interaction.

In Fernando Pessoa the fact that spirits could interact with people at any time and in even the most public locations—I once played snooker with Corquisa at a local bar—meant that most people were aware of the relative nature of the boundary between the world of practical affairs and the games of the gods.

In the *terreiros* themselves this boundary was liable to disappear at any moment. Apparently substantial entities were constantly being removed from the contexts that gave them a fixed identity, and rearranged in patterns that were as fantastic as the clouds of swirling gas that form the heavens, the galaxies, the sun, and the other stars.

Postface

There are many faces in this text apart from those it names. I wish to thank them all for their participation, and also for their help in putting together a life.

The original version of this book was written as a doctoral dissertation in anthropology at Indiana University. I am particularly grateful to the members of my research committee, for their guidance and encouragement over a long period of time, for the inspiration I received from their teaching and writing, and for the innumerable kinds of practical assistance they gave me, including reading and commenting on the draft of this study.

To my dissertation adviser, Bonnie Kendall, I owe special thanks. Without her support and the example provided by her approach to anthropology, I would not have had the courage to believe that ethnography could be written as I have written it. I am fortunate that she and her husband, Charles Bird, were among the first people I met at Indiana University; that they welcomed my interest in becoming a student in the Anthropology Department; and that they helped me to make it to the end of the doctorate.

I am grateful also to Tony Seeger for encouraging my interest in Brazil, for drawing my attention to the richness of its anthropological tradition, and for facilitating my field work there; to Ray DeMallie for his ability to distill an extensive knowledge of the anthropological literature into advice of great subtlety, and for the sensitivity with which he challenged me to clarify my ideas; to Della Cook for bringing a bio-anthropological perspective to my observations on trance and gender, thus demonstrating the continuing relevance to each other of the sub-fields of anthropology; and to Judith Berling, whose ideas about the interaction between religions, and between religion and everyday life, have been a source of inspiration to me since my first semester at Indiana.

To these and all my other teachers at Indiana, as well as to the administrators and clerical staff who smoothed the path, let me say thank you.

I appreciate as well the help I received from a number of other people who read all or part of the draft of this study, and made useful suggestions. These include Michael Jackson, Bonnie Urciuoli, Hédimo Santana, Rick Inman, and the members of the anthropology dissertation support group at Indiana: Trish Clay, Nenny Panourgia, Barb Santos, Kathy Seibold, Maria Villar, and Petronella Wafer. Others who have contributed by discussing with me the ideas I have tried to write about include Mickey Needham, Gail Rosecrance, and Bill Pincheon.

Let me express, too, my deep gratitude for the kindness of the many people who helped me during my two trips to Brazil. Particular thanks are due to my research assistant, Hédimo Rodrigues Santana. It was through him that I was introduced to "Jaraci," and because of my friendship with him that I was treated as an honorary Bahian. He has made a significant contribution to this text by his transcriptions and summaries of numerous field tapes. The story of "Padilha's vow" in Chapter 2 is based directly on one of his transcriptions. He also transcribed for me the "Hymn of Our Lord of Bomfim," used as the epigraph to Part 3, and gave permission for me to quote from his correspondence in Chapter 6, and from his notes on the "festival of the name" in Chapter 8. In addition, he corrected various errors in my own transcriptions of Portuguese.

This study would not, of course, have been possible at all without the help and generosity of the people of Candomblé. I wish to thank in particular Edson Santos Xavier, Waldemir Santiago Júnior, Reginaldo Dias dos Santos, and Amilton Costa; also Antônio-Carlos, Waldemar, Jair, Lídio, Alberto, and Bira (whose last names I never discovered). All made me welcome in the *terreiros* to which they belong. I am grateful as well to the many other people connected with those *terreiros* who gave me the precious gift of their companionship.

On both my trips to Brazil the shock of transition was eased by the kindness of Peter Fry. He acted as my sponsor and adviser when I registered as an intern with the Anthropology Department at the National Museum in Rio de Janeiro; he helped me to make contact with other scholars working with the Afro-Brazilian religions; and he took me to my first festival of Candomblé.

Others in Rio de Janeiro to whom I owe special thanks include Patrícia Birman, who introduced me to the *terreiros* of the Baixada Fluminense; Márcio Goldman and Maria Laura V. de C. Cavalcanti, who gave me copies of their own work on trance religions in Brazil; Elsi Barbosa and her daughter Sónia, with whom I stayed in the Baixada Fluminense; and Eduardo Viveiros de Castro, Caetana Damasceno, Elizabeth Lins, Zélia de

Lóssio e Seiblitz, Yvonne Maggie, Fernandez Portugal, Micênio Santos, and Gilberto Velho, all of whom took time to discuss my project with me.

In Bahia I received a great deal of help, during both my trips, from Luiz Mott, of the Federal University of Bahia. He also provided me with copies of a number of his own publications. I appreciate also the kindness of Vivaldo da Costa Lima, who gave me a copy of his book on kinship in Candomblé; and of Juana Elbein dos Santos and Ronaldo Senna, who contributed their anthropological insights into the Afro-Brazilian religions.

Other people who made me feel at home in Bahia include Raimundo Moreira, Nilton Ferreira, Luiz Carvalho, Bonifácia, Renato, Fernando, Meire, the Gegebetes, and many more.

During the brief trip I made to Pernambuco I was received kindly by Mário Souto Maior of the Fundação Joaquim Nabuco in Recife, and Edwin Barbosa da Silva (Pai Edu) of the Palácio de Iemanjá in Olinda, both of whom provided me with publications relevant to my research.

Three American friends were in Brazil for periods that overlapped with mine, namely Randy Matory, Chris Dunn, and David Brown. They have all helped me in important ways, in one or other or both the Americas.

Acknowledgments are due also to the organizations that provided the financial assistance that made this study possible: the Anthropology Department at Indiana University for a summer research award that supported my first trip to Brazil in 1985, and for the teaching assistantships that supported my two semesters of writing in 1988 and 1989; the Graduate School of Indiana University for a dissertation fellowship, and Sigma Xi, the Scientific Research Society, for a grant in aid of research, both of which supported my field work in Brazil in 1987 and 1988. A postdoctoral fellowship at the Office of Folklife Programs of the Smithsonian Institution in 1989 and 1990 enabled me to prepare the manuscript for publication.

I wish to thank as well Paul Stoller, one of the two General Editors of the Series in Contemporary Ethnography, and Patricia Smith, Acquisitions Editor of the University of Pennsylvania Press, for shepherding this work through the publication process.

There are several people who are in a position to see the periods I spent researching and writing this book in terms of a longer history, and to them I owe a very special debt of gratitude. My parents and other members of my family have been unfailing in their love and support, across distances of many thousands of miles; and Petronella Wafer has been a steadfast friend through many springs and autumns.

This list would not be complete without an expression of appreciation to all the spirits who have opened the ways—in particular to Oxalá and Our Lord of Bomfim; to Oxum and Our Lady of Candlemas; to Ogum and St. Anthony of Padua; to Iançã and St. Barbara; to Corquisa, Sete Saia, and Pomba-Gira; to Tupinambá, Pena Branca, and Sultão das Matas; and to Tempo, Janus, Dionysus, Shiva, Purusha, and Mahakala.

To these, and to any other entities, of whatever realms, who have smiled on this endeavor, my thanks.

Glossary

abebé. 1. Ceremonial fan, as used by Oxum and Iemanjá. 2. Mirror (especially in the case of the *abebé* of Oxum, which she uses as a mirror).

abiã. Person who has taken some preliminary steps towards initiation into Candomblé, but has not undergone the initiation itself.

abicu. Person whose head cannot be shaved during the initiation into Candomblé.

abô. Infusion of herbs and leaves, used in Candomblé as a purifying bath.

aborôs. The male *orixás*.

acaçá. Gelatinous white paste made of fine corn meal, formed into a kind of cake and wrapped in banana leaves.

adjá. Bell, often with two chambers, used in Candomblé rituals.

adjuntó. An individual's third *orixá* (after the owner of the head and the *juntó*).

adoxu. Small cone made of a paste of magical substances, which initiands wear on top of the head to protect the spot through which the *orixá* enters.

agogô. Percussion instrument consisting of two cones of metal attached to a U-shaped bar and struck with a metal rod.

alabê. Head drummer of a *terreiro* of Candomblé.

amaci. Infusion of leaves and herbs used to sanctify ritual objects, animals to be sacrificed, and the head of a person being initiated.

Angola. One of the "nations" of Candomblé, which traces its roots to the region of Africa where Bantu languages are spoken.

aparacá. Spirit of a recently deceased person, which has not been "educated" by receiving sacrifices.

arrepio. "Shiver"—a brief bodily spasm associated with the onset of trance.

Aruanda. 1. Homeland of the *caboclo* spirits, located in the Congo-Angola region of Africa. 2. "Hut" of the *caboclos*, the place where their ritual objects are kept in a *terreiro*.

assentamento. "Seat" of a spirit, that is, the assemblage of ritual objects pertaining to that spirit. (To "seat" a spirit is to set up and dedicate the spirit's ritual objects.)

axé. 1. The ethos of Candomblé. 2. Vital force that animates all things, particularly present in sacred objects or beings. 3. Sacred object.

axogum. Male assistant to the head of a *terreiro*, usually responsible for the sacrifice of animals.

babá. Spirit of a deceased person, when this spirit has been "educated" by receiving sacrifices.

Baiana. 1. Woman from Bahia. 2. Bahian woman who wears traditional dress and sells African food on the streets of Bahia. (In Portuguese the adjective formed from *Bahia* is spelt without an *h*: *baiano/baiana*.)

baixa. Stylized form of verbal abuse.

bakisse. "Room of the saints"—room or small house where the ritual objects of the *orixás* are kept on an altar.

balé. Place set aside for the spirits of the dead within a *terreiro*.

Bantu. Term used to classify together a group of African languages belonging to the Benue-Congo phylum.

barco. (Literally, "boat.") Group of children-of-saint who are initiated at the same time.

barracão. Large room or hall where the public ceremonies of Candomblé take place.

barravento. State of vertigo that signals the onset of trance.

bejes. Spirits of twins, syncretized with Saints Cosmos and Damian, and often regarded as patrons of the *erês*.

berimbau. Musical instrument, of African origin, consisting of a wooden bow that is strung with wire and has a hollow gourd attached to the lower end.

boiadeiro. 1. Cowboy. 2. Member of a class of *caboclos* who are the spirits of cowboys or rural people.

Boiadeiro. Name of a particular *caboclo* spirit who typically dresses as a cowboy.

bolação. The act of "rolling" (see *bolar*).

bolar. "To roll"—to fall into a special state of trance that precedes initiation. (This entails falling to the floor, at a public Candomblé festival, in a position that is considered propitious.)

Bomfim. District of Salvador, named after the Church of Our Lord of Bomfim.

Our Lord of Bomfim. An invocation of Jesus as "Lord of the Good Ending."

Washing of the Church of Bomfim. Annual festival that takes place in

Salvador on the second Thursday of January, involving a procession to the Church of Bomfim and the pouring of water on its steps.

bori. The ceremony of making offerings to the head, which is the first stage of initiation into Candomblé.

brand. See *marca*.

brega. Low-life district characterized by prostitution, crime, and poverty.

cabocla. Female *caboclo*.

caboclo. Entity belonging to a class that includes primarily spirits of Indians and cowboys, but also spirits of royal personages, Brazilian folk heroes, sailors, mermaids, etc.

cachaça. 1. Cheap, uncured rum. 2. Booze.

cainana. Snake-like reptile, denizen of the world of the *caboclos*, and said to have the capacity to fly.

call. To induce a spirit to enter a person's body, thus causing trance.

Candomblé. Brazilian religion of partly African origin, most widely practiced in the city of Salvador, Bahia.

capoeira. Form of martial art that originated with Brazilian slaves and has evolved into a kind of athletic dance.

carnaval. Popular celebration preceding the first day of Lent; "*mardi gras*."

catulagem. "Clipping"—an initiatic process involving the removal of hair from those parts of the head where ritual incisions are made.

child-of-saint. See *son-of-saint*, *daughter-of-saint*.

cleansing of the body. Purification rite intended to remove the negative influence of troublesome spirits.

clipping. See *catulagem*.

come in front of. (Used of spirits.) To cause trance in a person before another spirit who is also trying to do so.

CONTOC. 1. Conference of the Tradition and Culture of the Orixás—Brazilian branch of an international body with representatives from all the nations of Africa and the African diaspora where the religion of the *òrìṣàs* (or their equivalents) is practiced. 2. The international body itself. 3. Meeting of this body.

contra-egum. Armband made of plaited raffia, with the capacity to ward off the negative influence of *eguns*.

cowrie. Type of small shell, used ritually in Africa and Brazil.

throwing the cowries. Divination procedure involving the throwing of cowrie shells and the interpretation of the pattern they form when they fall.

daughter-of-saint. Female junior initiate of Candomblé who experiences trance.

decá. Ceremony or ritual objects that signify the right of a senior initiate of Candomblé to open his or her own *terreiro*.

dijina. (Used in the Angola "nation" of Candomblé.) Name of an initiate's "owner of the head," who is a particular *marca* or "aspect" of an *orixá*.

ebame. Senior initiate of Candomblé, who has been initiated for seven years or more.

ebó. Offering made to a spirit, in particular an offering with a magical purpose.

ebô. Dish of boiled white corn prepared with oil and honey, food of Oxalá.

egum. Spirit of a dead person.

Engenho Velho. Famous *terreiro* of Candomblé in Salvador, also known as Casa Branca.

entoto. Spiritual "foundation" of a *terreiro* of Candomblé, consisting of offerings and sacred objects buried beneath the floor in the middle of the *barracão*, and covered by a tile or arrangement of tiles, or by a center-post.

Entoto. Name of an aspect of Obaluaiê connected with the earth.

equê. False trance.

give equê. To fake being in trance.

equede. Female initiate who does not go into trance, and who acts as ritual assistant and dignitary of a *terreiro*.

erê. Child form of an *orixá*.

erea. Female *erê*.

estrelismo. "Star-ism," the desire to be a star, attention getting behavior.

Ewe. An African language spoken in parts of the People's Republic of Benin (formerly Dahomey), Ghana, and Togo.

exu. Spirit who performs the role of "slave" of an *orixá*, and who is popularly thought of as a devil.

exua. Female *exu*.

exu-mirim. Child form of an *exu*.

farofa. Dish consisting of manioc flour cooked with other ingredients.

father-of-saint. Male religious leader of a *terreiro* of Candomblé.

FEBACAB. Bahian Federation of the Afro-Brazilian Cult—organization that is responsible for mediation between the *terreiros* of Bahia and the government.

fechação. Behavior that is exaggerated and humorous.

federation. Body that represents the Afro-Brazilian religious houses of a particular region in dealings with the government and the wider Brazilian society.

feijão fradinho. Small light-brown bean of the species *Vigna sinensis*, used in dishes offered to Oxum.

ferramenta. (Literally, "tool.") Small metal sculpture that represents the ritual objects associated with a particular *orixá*.

foundation. See *entoto*.

Gantois. Famous *terreiro* of Candomblé in the city of Salvador.

Gege. One of the "nations" of Candomblé, which traces its roots to the region of Africa where Ewe is spoken.

grab. (Used of spirits.) To cause (a person) to go into trance.

gringo. Foreigner.

horse. A spirit's material vehicle, the human body a spirit uses during trance.

iabás. The female *orixás*.

Iançã. Female *orixá* associated with lightning and storms.

iaô. 1. Candomblé initiate who experiences trance. 2. Junior initiate. 3. Any initiate while in seclusion.

ibeje. See *bejes*.

Iemanjá. Female *orixá* associated with the sea.

Ilê Axé Opô Afonjá. Famous *terreiro* of Candomblé in the city of Salvador.

inquice. (Used in the Angola "nation" of Candomblé.) *Orixá*.

invasion. Shanty-town.

Iroko. See *Tempo*.

juntó. An individual's second *orixá* (after the owner of the head).

jurema. Sacred drink of the *caboclos*, made from the plant *jurema* (various species of the genera *Mimosa*, *Acacia*, and *Pithecelobium*).

Kardecism. Spiritist philosophy based on the teachings of the French thinker Allan Kardec (pseudonym of Hippolyte Léon Denizard Rivail, 1804–1869).

Laroiê. Salutation to Exu.

lean. (Used of *eguns*.) To cause (a person) psychic and physical problems.

line of oil. Branch of Afro-Brazilian ritual concerned with black magic.

little father. 1. Senior male initiate of a *terreiro* who acts as deputy to the parent-of-saint. 2. Male sponsor of a person undergoing initiation.

little mother. 1. Senior female initiate of a *terreiro* who acts as deputy to the parent-of-saint. 2. Female sponsor of a person undergoing initiation.

lobaça. Onion.

Logum-edé. *Orixá* who combines the characteristics of Oxosse and Oxum, who are said to be his parents.

Loko. See *Tempo*.

malandro. Con-man, particularly of Rio de Janeiro.

manifest. (Used of spirits.) To appear in corporeal form, by causing trance in a human vehicle.

marca. Type, category, quality, brand (used to refer to the different aspects of any *orixá*, all of which have different names).

mariô. Long pliable stick or switch made from a branch of the oil-palm and used to control the *eguns*.

materialize. (Used of spirits.) To appear in corporeal form by causing trance in a human vehicle.

matter. The material world (as opposed to the world of the spirits), in particular the human inhabitants of that world, considered individually or collectively.

metá-metá. Having two different natures. (Used of spirits, this may mean that they are both male and female, or human and animal, or that they belong to two different spirit realms.)

Mina. Brazilian religion of partly African origin, most widely practiced in the state of Maranhão (also called Tambor de Mina, and having links with the Gege "nation" of Bahia).

mocã. Necklace of plaited raffia, worn by a person undergoing seclusion during rituals of Candomblé.

mother-of-saint. Female religious leader of a *terreiro* of Candomblé.

mulato. Person of mixed race, commonly a person with one Black parent and one white parent. (This term is current in Brazil, though it has fallen into disrepute in English.)

Nagô. One of the "nations" of Candomblé. (The Nagô nation traces its roots to the region of Africa where the Yoruba language is spoken. Yoruba has a number of dialects, such as Ketu [Portuguese Queto], and some of the "nations" of Candomblé trace their roots to the groups speaking these dialects. In this sense Nagô is a "super-nation" that includes other "nations.")

Nanã. Oldest of the female *orixás*, associated with rain and mud.

nation. 1. Any branch or denomination of the Afro-Brazilian religions. 2. A denomination of the Afro-Brazilian religions that traces its roots to a particular language group in Africa.

Obaluaiê. Male *orixá* associated with diseases and their cures, and also with the earth. (Known also as Omolu.)

obligation. Offering presented to a spirit entity.

ogã. Male initiate who does not go into trance, and who acts as ritual assistant and dignitary of a *terreiro* of Candomblé.

Oguiã. See *Oxaguiã*.

Ogum. Male *orixá* associated with warfare.

Omolu. See *Obaluaiê*.

Ordem e Progresso. "Order and Progress"—motto inscribed on the Brazilian flag, and borrowed from Auguste Comte.

orixá. Spirit belonging to the pantheon of West African gods.

Ossãe. *Orixá* associated with leaves and herbs.

otá. Stone that is the principal item among the objects that make up the *assentamento* of an *orixá*, being regarded as the "head" of the *orixá*.

owner of the head. An individual's principal *orixá*.

Oxaguiã. The youthful form of the *orixá* Oxalá.

Oxalá. Male *orixá* often regarded as father of the gods.

Oxalufã. Elderly form of the *orixá* Oxalá.

Oxosse. Male *orixá* associated with hunting.

Oxum. Female *orixá* associated with fresh waters.

Oxumaré. *Orixá* who is both male and female, associated with snakes and the rainbow.

Padilha. One of the best known female *exus*.

paó. Ritual gesture that involves clapping the hands in a rhythm that begins slowly and gradually increases in tempo.

parent-of-saint. See *father-of-saint*, *mother-of-saint*.

passage

give passage. (Used of spirits.) To leave the body of a person in trance in order to make way for another spirit.

pemba. Powder made of substances with magical properties, that comes in the colors of the various *orixás*.

Pomba-Gira. One of the best known female *exus*.

proxemics. (Study of) the way space is used by members of a culture.

Queto. One of the "nations" of Candomblé. (The Queto "nation" traces its roots to the region of Africa where the Ketu dialect of Yoruba is spoken.)

quijuntó. An individual's fourth *orixá*, after the owner of the head, the *juntó*, and the *adjuntó*.

Quimbanda. Brazilian religion that is associated in particular with the *exus* and with black magic.

quitanda. Ceremonial "market" that takes place after the "coming out" rituals of a new initiate.

raise. See *suspend a sacrifice*.

raspagem. "Shaving"—initiatic procedure involving the removal of all hair from the head.

roça. *Terreiro* of Candomblé. (Literally, "cultivated plot" or "small farm.")

roda. Circular dance for the *orixás*, which moves counterclockwise.

roda de samba. Circle formed for dancing *samba*.

roll. See *bolar*.

roncó. Small room where members of a *terreiro* undergo periods of ritual seclusion.

saida. (Abbreviation of) *saida de iaô*; the "coming-out" ceremony of a new initiate, when the latter emerges from seclusion and appears at a public ritual. (Usually there are three *saidas*, during the third of which the initiate calls the name of his or her *orixá*.)

saint. 1. *orixá*. 2. Christian saint.

to receive saint. To go into trance.

samba. Brazilian dance accompanied by songs in a 2/4 rhythm and syncopated drumming.

São Cosme e Damião. Saints Cosmos and Damian, the patron saints of children, popularly regarded as twins.

seat. See *assentamento*.

Sete Facadas. An *exu* said to be brother of Padilha and Pomba-Gira.

shaving. See *raspagem*.

shiver. See *arrepio*.

slave. An *exu* (regarded as "slave" of an *orixá*).

son-of-saint. Male junior initiate of Candomblé who experiences trance.

sotaque. Banter, mocking or provocative utterance.

Spiritism. 1. System of beliefs and practices that involve possession by spirits of the dead, especially when such a system is based on the teachings of Allan Kardec. 2. Kardecism.

suspend.

suspend an ogã or equede. To raise a person to the status of *ogã* or *equede*.

suspend a sacrifice. To take a sacrifice from a ritual space and deposit it outdoors in a place such as a forest, a body of water, or a crossroad.

suspend a spirit. 1. To bring the spirit's human vehicle out of trance. 2. To prevent a spirit from materializing in a person.

Tempo. Male *orixá* associated with sacred trees, the weather, and time. ("Tempo" is the name used for this *orixá* in the Angola "nation" of Candomblé. In the Gege "nation" he is usually called Loko, and in the Queto "nation," Iroko.)

terreiro. "House" or "center" of Candomblé (and some other Afro-Brazilian religions), as place and as institution.

Umbanda. Brazilian religion that incorporates elements of Kardecism, African religions, popular Catholicism, religious practices of the Brazilian Indians, Brazilian folklore, Islam, and eastern religions.

viado. "Faggot." (Scholars suggest that *viado* is derived from *desviado*, "deviant." Hence it is spelt with an *i*, even though it is popularly linked with its homonym *veado*, "deer.")

vunje. (Used in the Angola "nation" of Candomblé.) *Erê*.

white line. Complex of Afro-Brazilian beliefs and practices concerned principally with healing, and regarded as more closely linked to Umbanda than to Candomblé.

work. See *ebó*.

Xangô. 1. Male *orixá* associated with lightning. 2. Brazilian religion, of partly African origin, most widely practiced in the state of Pernambuco.

Yoruba. African language (with various dialects) spoken in parts of Nigeria, the People's Republic of Benin (formerly Dahomey), and Togo.

References

Achenbach, Joel

1988 "Creeping Surrealism: Does Anybody Really Know What's Real Anymore?" *Utne Reader* 30:112–16.

Alvarez, A.

1973 *The Savage God: A Study of Suicide*. New York: Bantam.

Amado, Jorge

1982 *Bahia de Todos os Santos: Guia de Ruas e Mistérios*. 33rd ed. Rio de Janeiro: Record.

Augras, Monique

1983 *O Duplo e a Metamorfose: A Identidade Mítica em Comunidades Nagô*. Petrópolis: Vozes.

Azevedo, Stella

1986 Sincretismo e Branqueamento. Abstract of unpublished paper presented at the Third International Congress of Orisa Tradition and Culture, New York, October 6–10, 1986.

Bakhtin, Mikhail

1981 *The Dialogic Imagination: Four Essays*. M. Holquist, ed., C. Emerson and M. Holquist, trans. Austin: University of Texas Press.

1984 *Rabelais and His World*. H. Iswolsky, trans. Bloomington: Indiana University Press. (Originally published Cambridge, MA: MIT Press, 1968.)

1988 *Marxismo e Filosofia da Linguagem: Problemas Fundamentais do Método Sociológico na Ciência da Linguagem*. 4th ed. M. Lahud, Y. F. Vieira et al., trans. São Paulo: Hucitec. (I have cited the Portuguese edition, because, like the French edition, it attributes the authorship of this work to Bakhtin. The English edition is attributed to V. N. Voloshinov: *Marxism and the Philosophy of Language*. New York: Seminar Press, 1973.)

Bastide, Roger

1978a *The African Religions of Brazil: Toward a Sociology of the Interpenetration of Civilizations*. H. Sebba, trans. Baltimore: Johns Hopkins University Press.

1978b *O Candomblé da Bahia (Rito Nagô)*. M. I. P. de Queiroz, trans. São Paulo: Editora Nacional.

Baudrillard, Jean

1976 *L'échange symbolique et la mort*. Paris: Gallimard.

Berling, Judith

1980 *The Syncretic Religion of Lin Chao-en*. New York: Columbia University Press.

Binon Cossard, Gisèle

1970 Contribution a l'étude des Candomblés au Brésil: Le Candomblé Angola. Doctoral dissertation, Faculty of Letters and Human Sciences, University of Paris.

Birman, Patrícia

1980 Feitiço, Carrego e Olho Grande, os Males do Brasil São: Estudo de um Centro Umbandista numa Favela do Rio de Janeiro. Master's thesis, Postgraduate Program in Social Anthropology of the National Museum of the Federal University of Rio de Janeiro.

1988 Fazer Estilo Criando Gêneros: Estudo sobre a Construção Religiosa da Possessão e da Diferença de Gêneros em Terreiros da Baixada Fluminense. Doctoral thesis, Postgraduate Program in Social Anthropology of the National Museum of the Federal University of Rio de Janeiro.

Bogatyrev, Petr

1983 "The Interconnection of Two Similar Semiotic Systems: The Puppet Theater and the Theater of Living Actors." M. S. Hahn, trans. *Semiotica* 47:47–68.

Borba Filho, Hermilo

1966 *Fisionomia e Espírito do Mamulengo: O Teatro Popular do Nordeste.* São Paulo: Editora Nacional.

Braga, Julio

1984 "Gente de Ponta de Areia: Ancestralidade na Dinâmica da Vida Social de uma Comunidade Afro-Brasileira." *Gente* (Federal University of Bahia) 1:19–36.

1988 *O Jogo de Búzios: Um Estudo de Adivinhação no Candomblé.* São Paulo: Brasiliense.

Brissonnet, Lydie Carmen

1988 The Structuration of Communitas in the Carnaval of Salvador, Bahia (Northeastern Brazil). Ph.D. dissertation, Dept. of Anthropology, Indiana University.

Brown, Diana DeG.

1986 *Umbanda: Religion and Politics in Urban Brazil.* Ann Arbor, MI: UMI Research Press.

Brown, Richard H.

1977 *A Poetic for Sociology: Toward a Logic of Discovery for the Human Sciences.* Cambridge: Cambridge University Press.

Burke, Kenneth

1962 *A Grammar of Motives* and *A Rhetoric of Motives.* Published in one volume, continuously paginated. Cleveland: World.

Cacciatore, Olga Gudolle

1977 *Dicionário de Cultos Afro-Brasileiros: Com a Indicação da Origem das Palavras.* 3rd ed., rev. Rio de Janeiro: Forense-Universitária.

Carneiro, Edison

1964 *Ladinos e Crioulos: Estudos sobre o Negro no Brasil.* Rio de Janeiro: Civilização Brasileira.

1967 *Candomblés da Bahia.* Rio de Janeiro: Tecnoprint.

1981 *Religiões Negras: Notas de Etnografia Religiosa* and *Negros Bantos: Notas de Etnografia Religiosa e de Folclore*. Published in one volume, continuously paginated; 2nd ed. of both works. Rio de Janeiro: Civilização Brasileira.

Carvalho, José Jorge de

1984 Ritual and Music of the Ṣango Cults of Recife, Brazil. Ph.D. thesis, Dept. of Social Anthropology, The Queen's University of Belfast.

Castro, Yêda Antonita Pessôa de

1971 Terminologia e Falar Cotidiano de um Grupo-de-Culto Afro-Brasileiro. Master's thesis, Faculty of Philosophy and Human Sciences, Federal University of Bahia.

1983 "Das Línguas Africanas ao Português Brasileiro." *Afro-Ásia* 14:81–106.

Cavalcanti, Maria Laura Viveiros de Castro

1983 *O Mundo Invisível: Cosmologia, Sistema Ritual e Noção de Pessoa no Espiritismo*. Rio de Janeiro: Zahar.

Comaroff, Jean

1985 *Body of Power, Spirit of Resistance: The Culture and History of a South African People*. Chicago: University of Chicago Press.

Costa, P. Valdeli Carvalho da

1980 "Alguns Marcos na Evolução Histórica e Situação Atual de Exu na Umbanda do Rio de Janeiro." *Afro-Ásia* 13:87–105.

Couto, Hildo H. do

1986 *O Que é Português Brasileiro*. São Paulo: Brasiliense.

Cunha, Marlene de Oliveira

1986 Em Busca de um Espaço: A Linguagem Gestual no Candomblé de Angola. Master's thesis, Dept. of Social Sciences, University of São Paulo.

Dantas, Beatriz Góis

1982 "Repensando a Pureza Nagô." *Religião e Sociedade* 8:15–20.

Douglas, Mary

1973 *Natural Symbols: Explorations in Cosmology*. New York: Random House (Vintage).

Durand, Gilbert

1969 *Les structures anthropologiques de l'imaginaire: Introduction à l'archétypologie générale*. Poitiers: Bordas.

Eilberg-Schwartz, Howard

1988 "Witches of the West: Neo-Paganism and Goddess Worship as Enlightenment Religions." In *Neo-Paganism: A Feminist Search for Religious Alternatives*. Mary Ellen Brown, ed., pp. 93–120. Women's Studies Program, Indiana University, Occasional Series No. 3.

Ekunfeo, Obalorun Temujim

1986 The Sacred as Root of the Secular: Divination Verses as a Source of "Popular" Tales in the African Diaspora. Unpublished paper presented at the Third International Congress of Orisa Tradition and Culture, New York, October 6–10, 1986.

Fabian, Johannes

1983 *Time and the Other: How Anthropology Makes its Object*. New York: Columbia University Press.

Ferreira, Almiro Miguel

1984 "Candomblé-de-Caboclo." In *Encontro de Nações-de-Candomblé: Anais do Encontro Realizado em Salvador, 1981*, pp. 59–67. Salvador, Bahia: Ianamá/CEAO.

Ferreira, Aurélio Buarque de Holanda, et al.

1975 *Novo Dicionário da Língua Portuguesa*. Rio de Janeiro: Nova Fronteira.

Feyerabend, Paul

1978 *Against Method: Outline of an Anarchistic Theory of Knowledge*. London: Verso.

1985 *Science in a Free Society*. London: Verso.

Fichte, Hubert

1976 *Xango: Die afroamerikanischen Religionen—Bahia, Haiti, Trinidad*. Frankfurt a/M: Fischer.

Foucault, Michel

1977 *Language, Counter-Memory, Practice: Selected Essays and Interviews*. D. F. Bouchard, ed., D. F. Bouchard and S. Simon, trans. Ithaca, NY: Cornell University Press.

Frigerio, Alejandro

1983 The Search for Africa: Proustian Nostalgia in Afro-Brazilian Studies. M.A. thesis, Dept. of Anthropology, University of California, Los Angeles.

Fry, Peter

1976 *Spirits of Protest: Spirit-Mediums and the Articulation of Consensus among the Zezuru of Southern Rhodesia (Zimbabwe)*. Cambridge: Cambridge University Press.

1982 *Para Inglês Ver: Identidade e Política na Cultura Brasileira*. Rio de Janeiro: Zahar.

Gates, Henry Louis, Jr.

1988 *The Signifying Monkey: A Theory of African-American Literary Criticism*. New York: Oxford University Press.

Geertz, Clifford

1973 *The Interpretation of Cultures: Selected Essays*. New York: Basic Books.

1983 *Local Knowledge: Further Essays in Interpretive Anthropology*. New York: Basic Books.

Goffman, Erving

1959 *The Presentation of Self in Everyday Life*. Garden City, NY: Doubleday (Anchor).

Hofstadter, Douglas

1980 *Gödel, Escher, Bach: An Eternal Golden Braid*. New York: Random House (Vintage).

Holquist, Michael

1981 Introduction to Bakhtin 1981, pp. xv–xxxiv.

Irvine, Judith

1982 "The Creation of Identity in Spirit Mediumship and Possession." In *Semantic Anthropology*, David Parkin, ed., pp. 241–60. London: Academic Press (ASA Monograph No. 22).

Jackson, Michael
1989 *Paths Toward a Clearing: Radical Empiricism and Ethnographic Inquiry.* Bloomington: Indiana University Press.

Kendall, Martha B.
1982 "Getting to Know You." In *Semantic Anthropology*, David Parkin, ed., pp. 197–209. London: Academic Press (ASA Monograph No. 22).

Lakoff, George, and Mark Johnson
1980 *Metaphors We Live By*. Chicago: University of Chicago Press.

Landes, Ruth
1947 *The City of Women*. New York: Macmillan.

Lapassade, Georges, and Marco Aurélio Luz
1972 *O Segredo da Macumba*. Rio de Janeiro: Paz e Terra.

Latour, Bruno, and Steve Woolgar
1979 *Laboratory Life: The Social Construction of Scientific Facts*. Beverly Hills, CA: Sage.

Lépine, Claude
1982 "Análise Formal do Panteão Nàgó." In Moura 1982a, pp. 13–70.

Lima, Vivaldo da Costa
1977 *A Família-de-Santo nos Candomblés Jeje-Nagôs da Bahia: Um Estudo de Relações Intra-Grupais*. Thesis published as a book by the Postgraduate Program in the Human Sciences of the Federal University of Bahia, Salvador.

Lindbom, Tage
1976 *L'ivraie et le bon grain, ou le royaume de l'homme à l'heure des échéances.* Milan: Archè.

Lody, Raul Giovanni da Motta
1975 *Ao Som do Adjá*. Salvador, Bahia: Departamento de Cultura da SMEC, Prefeitura Municipal de Salvador.

Lukes, Steven
1985 Conclusion. In *The Category of the Person: Anthropology, Philosophy, History*. Michael Carrithers, Steven Collins and Steven Lukes, eds., pp. 282–301. Cambridge: Cambridge University Press.

Maffesoli, Michel
1984 *A Conquista do Presente*. M. C. de S. Cavalcante, trans. Rio de Janeiro: Rocco. (Original: *La conquête du présent*. Paris, 1979.)
1985a *La connaissance ordinaire: Précis de sociologie compréhensive*. Paris: Librairie des Méridiens.
1985b *A Sombra de Dionísio: Contribuição a uma Sociologia da Orgia*. A. R. Trinta, trans. Rio de Janeiro: Graal. (Original: *L'ombre de Dionysos: Contribution à une sociologie de l'orgie*. Paris: 1982.)
1987 *O Tempo das Tribos: O Declínio do Individualismo nas Sociedades de Massa*. M. de L. Menezes, trans. Rio de Janeiro: Forense-Universitária. (Original: *Le temps des tribus: Le déclin de l'individualisme dans les sociétés de masse*. Paris:1988.)

Maia, Vasconcelos
1985 *ABC do Candomblé*. 3rd ed. São Paulo: Edições GRD.

Matory, J. Lorand

1988 "Homens Montados: Homossexualidade e Simbolismo da Possessão nas Religiões Afro-Brasileiras." J. J. Reis, trans. In *Escravidão e Invenção da Liberdade: Estudos sobre o Negro no Brasil*. João José Reis, ed., pp. 215–31. São Paulo: Brasiliense.

Megenney, William W.

1978 *A Bahian Heritage: An Ethnolinguistic Study of African Influences on Bahian Portuguese*. Chapel Hill: North Carolina Studies in the Romance Languages and Literatures.

Mott, Luiz R. B.

1988 "Acotundá: Raizes Setecentistas do Sincretismo Religioso Afro-Brasileiro." In Mott, *Escravidão, Homossexualidade e Demonologia*, pp. 87–117. São Paulo: Ícone.

Motta, Roberto

1987 "Religiões Populares do Recife como Resposta à Ecologia Tropical da Cidade." In *Anais do Seminário de Tropicologia. Conferências, Comentários e Debates do Seminario de Tropicologia da Fundação Joaquim Nabuco, no Ano de 1977*, R. Motta, org., pp. 78–91. Recife: Massangana/Fundação Joaquim Nabuco.

Moura, Carlos Eugênio Marcondes de

1981 (Org.) *Olóòrisa: Escritos sobre a Religião dos Orixás*. São Paulo: Ágora.

1982a (Org.) *Bandeira de Alairá: Outros Escritos sobre a Religião dos Orixás*. São Paulo: Nobel.

1982b "Candomblé, Xangô, Tambor-de-Mina, Batuque, Pará e Babassuê: Bibliografia Prévia." In Moura 1982a, pp. 123–91.

1987a (Org.) *Candomblé: Desvendando Identidades. (Novos Escritos sobre a Religião dos Orixás.)* São Paulo: EMW Editores.

1987b "Orixás, Voduns, Inquices, Caboclos, Encantados e Loas: Bibliografia Complementar." In Moura 1987a, pp. 149–68.

Omari, Mikelle Smith

1984 *From the Inside to the Outside: The Art and Ritual of Bahian Candomblé*. Los Angeles: Museum of Cultural History, UCLA, Monograph Series, No. 24.

Perlongher, Nestor

1987 *O Negócio do Michê: Prostituição Viril em São Paulo*. São Paulo: Brasiliense.

Pessoa, Fernando

1985 *Os Melhores Poemas de Fernando Pessoa*. 3rd ed. Selected by T. R. Lopes. São Paulo: Global.

Peters, Larry

1981 *Ecstasy and Healing in Nepal: An Ethnopsychiatric Study of Tamang Shamanism*. Malibu, CA: Undena.

Pomorska, Krystyna

1984 Foreword to Bakhtin 1984, pp. vii–xii.

Rabelais, François

1936 *Gargantua and Pantagruel: The Five Books*. J. LeClercq, trans. New York: The Limited Editions Club. (In five volumes.)

Ribeiro, Carmem

1983 "Religiosidade do Índio Brasileiro no Candomblé da Bahia: Influências Africana e Européia." *Afro-Ásia* 14:60–80.

Ribeiro, José

1985 *O Jogo de Búzios, e as Cerimônias Esotéricas dos Cultos Afro-Brasileiros*. 4th ed. Rio de Janeiro: Polo Mágico.

Ribeiro, René

1952 *Cultos Afrobrasileiros do Recife: Um Estudo de Ajustamento Social*. Bulletin of the Instituto Joaquim Nabuco, Recife. Special issue.

Roett, Riordan

1984 *Brazil: Politics in a Patrimonial Society*. 3rd ed. New York: Praeger.

Sangirardi Jr.

1983 *O Índio e as Plantas Alucinógenas: Tribos das 3 Américas e Civilizações Pre-Colombianas*. Rio de Janeiro: Alhambra.

Santos, Juana Elbein dos

1977 *Os Nàgô e a Morte: Pàdè, Àsèsè e o Culto Égun na Bahia*. 2nd ed. Petrópolis: Vozes.

Santos, Juana Elbein dos, and Deoscoredes M. dos Santos

1981 "O Culto dos Ancestrais na Bahia: O Culto dos Égun." In Moura 1981, pp. 153–88.

Santos, Micênio Carlos Lopes dos

1984 "Caboclo: Da África ou do Xingu?" Micromonograph No. 144 of the series *Folclore*, published by the Centro de Estudos Folclóricos, Fundação Joaquim Nabuco, Recife.

Scopel, Paulo José

1983 *Orações e Santos Populares*. 11th ed. Porto Alegre: Escola Superior de Teologia São Lourenço de Brindes.

Segato, Rita Laura

1984 A Folk Theory of Personality Types: Gods and their Symbolic Representation by Members of the Ṣango Cult in Recife, Brazil. Ph.D. thesis, Dept. of Social Anthropology, The Queen's University of Belfast.

Silva, Joselina Maria Magalhães

1986 Estereótipo e Preconceito com Relação à Religião do Orixá nas Escolas Brasileiras. Unpublished paper presented at the Third International Congress of Orisa Tradition and Culture, New York, October 6–10, 1986.

Silverstein, Michael

1977 "Cultural Prerequisites to Grammatical Analysis." In *Linguistics and Anthropology*, M. Saville-Troike, ed., pp. 139–51. Washington, DC: Georgetown University Press.

Sodré, Muniz

1983 *A Verdade Seduzida: Por um Conceito da Cultura no Brasil*. Rio de Janeiro: Codecri.

Stoller, Paul

1989 *The Taste of Ethnographic Things: The Senses in Anthropology*. Philadelphia: University of Pennsylvania Press.

Stoller, Paul, and Cheryl Olkes

1987 *In Sorcery's Shadow: A Memoir of Apprenticeship among the Songhay of Niger*. Chicago: University of Chicago Press.

Taussig, Michael

1986 *Shamanism, Colonialism, and the Wild Man: A Study in Terror and Healing*. Chicago: University of Chicago Press.

Teixeira, Maria Lina Leão

1986 Transas de um Povo de Santo: Um Estudo sobre Identidades Sexuais. Master's thesis, Dept. of Social Sciences, Institute of Philosophy and Social Sciences, Federal University of Rio de Janeiro.

Todorov, Tzvetan

1984 *Mikhail Bakhtin: The Dialogical Principle*. W. Godzich, trans. Minneapolis: University of Minnesota Press.

Trindade, Liana

1985 *Exu: Poder e Perigo*. São Paulo: Ícone.

Trindade-Serra, Ordep José

1979 "Pureza e Confusão: As Fontes do Limbo." *Anuário Antropológico* 79: 148–67. (Rio de Janeiro: Tempo Brasileiro.)

Turner, Victor

1969 *The Ritual Process: Structure and Anti-Structure*. Chicago: Aldine.

Velho, Yvonne Maggie Alves

1977 *Guerra de Orixá: Um Estudo de Ritual e Conflito*. 2nd ed. Rio de Janeiro: Zahar.

Verger, Pierre

1981 "Bori, Primeira Cerimônia de Iniciação ao Culto dos Òrìṣà Nàgô na Bahia, Brasil." In Moura 1981, pp. 33–55.

Williams, Paul V. A.

1979 *Primitive Religion and Healing: A Study of Folk Medicine in North-East Brazil*. Cambridge: D. S. Brewer, and Rowman and Littlefield, for the Folklore Society.

Ziegler, Jean

1977 *Os Vivos e a Morte: Uma Sociologia da Morte no Ocidente e na Diáspora Africana no Brasil, e seus Mecanismos Culturais*. A. Weissenberg, trans. Rio de Janeiro: Zahar.

Index

Abiã, 36, 88
Abicu, 139
Aborôs, 86
Acaçá, 28–29, 121, 175
Adjuntó, 16
Adoxu, 137
Africa, 9, 62, 183; deities of, 4–5, 16, 56, 69; languages of, 5, 13, 67, 74, 124–25; religions of, 56, 85
Afro-Brazilian religions, 4–5, 13, 23, 57, 58, 94–95, 98, 147
Agent, 103–4
Agogô, 136
Alabê, 130–31
Alencar, José de, 83
All Souls' day, 184
Almiro, 113, 115, 116
Amaci, 149–50
Amado, Jorge, 8, 9
Angélica, 112, 115, 170, 176
Angola (Africa), 69, 70, 83
Angola nation, 5–6, 70, 122–23, 125, 166, 167, 169, 183
Anne, Saint, 126
Anthony of Padua, Saint, 25–26
Anthropology, 57, 117, 173
Aparacá, 185–86
Archipiado, 10, 23, 24–25, 26, 37, 38–39, 88, 100, 164; and Corquisa, 27, 30, 38, 40; and *erês*, 133; at festival at Marinalvo's, 108–9, 110, 111–12, 113, 114–16; and *ogã* initiation, 122, 143, 144, 145, 149, 151, 152–53, 154, 155, 156, 157, 158–59, 160–62, 163; and trance, 90–91, 92, 93–98, 99, 116–17
Aristocrats, 62
Arrancatoco, 28
Arrepio ("shiver"), 111
Aruanda, 63, 71, 83
Assembly of God, 5
Assentamento. *See* "Seat"
Australia, 53
Axé, 18–20, 21, 28
Axogum, 130
Azevedo, Stella, 56, 57

Babás, 185, 186, 187–88
Bahia, city of. *See* Salvador
Bahia, state of, 7, 20, 23; festivals in, 10, 53, 54–55; religion in, 5, 45, 58
Baixa, 35–36
Baixada Fluminense, 100
Bakhtin, Mikhail, 55, 58, 59–62, 63, 105, 162, 182
Bakisse ("room of the saints"), 112; *assentamentos* of, 122, 123, 130, 132; seclusion in, 121, 132, 144–45
Balé, 183
Bantu language, 5, 125, 166
Barbara, Saint, 130
Barracão, 26, 53, 72, 132, 185; of Edivaldo, 41; of Marinalvo, 88; Tempo and, 168; of Xilton, 9–10
Barravento, 114; of Archipiado, 92, 93, 96, 97, 111; *samba de*, 80–81
Bastos, Carlos, 8
Baudrillard, Jean, 181
Beads, 126; washing of, 112, 113, 115
Beer, 27
Berger, Peter, 94
Berimbau, 75
Biju, 29, 42, 43, 106, 176; as father-of-saint, 31, 140, 164, 178; *terreiro* of, 25, 26, 168
Birman, Patrícia, 100, 146–47
Biscó (*egum*), 43, 184
"Black magic," 57, 58
Blacks, 56
Blood: and *axé*, 19, 21; in initiation rituals, 42, 151, 153, 175; in *jurema*, 79; in Padilha's vow, 11, 12, 21
Boca de Fogo (*exu*), 114
Boca da Mata (*caboclo*), 65

Body symbolism, 62; "grotesque body," 59–60, 61, 62, 63–64
Boiadeiro (*caboclo*), 55, 69, 71, 89, 142–43
Boiadeiros, 55
Bomfim. *See* Our Lord of Bomfim
Bori, 131
Boundaries, 59, 61, 104, 181, 182, 188–89
Braga, Julio, 114
Brasília, 28
Brazil, 4, 8, 33, 181; flag of, 9, 53, 54, 93; independence, 53–54; language in, 64, 124; race in, 6; religion in, 5, 9, 25, 28, 55–56, 57, 94–95. *See also* Afro-Brazilian religions
Brazilian Anthropology Association, 111
Brega, 33, 46, 124; in Padilha's vow, 11, 12, 17, 20, 21, 27
Brown, Diana, 94, 95
Bumpkins, 64, 68
Burke, Kenneth, 102, 103

Caboclos, 23, 26, 27, 46–47, 85, 87, 116, 128–29, 142; behavior of, 91, 92, 99, 102; and *eguns*, 183; festivals of, 44–45, 46, 53, 54–55, 58, 59, 64, 68–82, 88–92, 98–100, 112, 116–17, 129, 184; mythology of, 83–84; and sexuality, 63–64, 106, 127; speech of, 48–49, 65–68; types of, 55; in "villages," 108
Cachaça, 9, 27, 30, 34
Cainana snakes, 71–72, 83
Caipó (*caboclo*), 68
"Call," 46, 80–81
Candomblé, 9, 10, 37, 98, 109, 116, 117, 182, 188–89; *axé*, 18–20, 21; and Catholicism, 13–14, 15, 25, 58, 126–27, 167; cosmology of, 13–14, 85, 183, 184–85; *exus* in, 4, 5, 9, 13–16; festivals of, 18, 30–31, 45, 55–56, 58; initiation in, 16–17, 122; language in, 64, 65, 67, 74, 100–101, 124–25; mythology of, 83, 84, 85–87; nations of, 5–6, 71; parents-of-saint in, 6, 140; re-Africanization, 56–58, 62; rituals, 15–16, 62–63, 177–78, 184–85; spirits of, 14, 18, 29–30, 33, 44, 100–101, 165, 166, 174; symbolism in, 123, 174, 177–78; trance in, 34, 90–91, 102, 103, 106. *See also* Festivals; Initiation; *Terreiros*; Trance
Capa Preta, 31, 32
Carnaval, 8, 10, 23, 24, 34–35
Carneiro, Edison, 172
"Carnival principle," 55–56, 57–58, 59, 63, 84, 162
Castro, Yêda Antonita Pessôa de, 124–25
Catholicism, 13, 15, 56, 57; feast days, 167; saints, 8, 10, 15, 25, 56, 58, 126, 130
Catulagem ("clipping"), 131, 132, 176
Causality, 104, 105
Celso, 136, 142, 143–44, 156, 157, 158, 159
Chair of St. Peter, feast of, 167
Children-of-saint, 13, 17, 31, 89, 112, 122–23, 131, 132, 147
Christianity, 5, 85, 126–27; mythology of, 14, 15. *See also* Catholicism
Christmas, 53
Church of Our Lord of Bomfim. *See* Our Lord of Bomfim
Class, of *exuas*, 32, 33
"Cleansing of the body" (purification ritual), 28–29, 114, 141, 143
"Come in front of," 32, 40, 128
Coming-out ceremony (*saida de iaô*), 97, 112, 123, 125, 136–37, 142, 156
Communitas, 54
Comte, Auguste, 54
Congo, 69, 70, 83
CONTOC (Conference of the Tradition and Culture of the Orixás), 4–6, 56
Contra-eguns, 121, 130
Corquisa (*exua*), 19, 25, 26–30, 31, 32–34, 44, 46, 101–2, 176, 189; festival to "seat," 38, 39, 40; songs of, 27, 29, 65; "work" rite, 47–48
Cosmology, 13–14, 85, 183, 184–85
Cosmos and Damian, Saints, 125, 126
Cossard, Gisèle Binon, 165
Couto, Hilda H. do, 65
Cowries, throwing of, 10, 16, 110–11, 113–14, 128, 164. *See also* Divination
Cravo (*erê*), 132–33
Crossroads, 28, 128–29, 160, 183
Cumeeira, 142
Cunha, Marlene de Oliveira, 178
Cuts, 111, 145–46

Dancing, 26, 46, 63, 78, 89, 91–92, 178
Dante Alighieri, 168
Daughter-of-saint. *See* Children-of-saint
Death, 16, 63, 181, 182–83
De Barros, Carlos, 10
Decá, 16–17
Delcir, 24, 112, 115, 177
Devil (Lucifer, Satan), 1, 4, 13, 14, 15, 65

Dialogue, 59
Dias, Gonçalves, 83
Dinho (*ogã*), 29, 43
Dionysus, 104
"Diurnal regime," 104–5, 106, 107
Divination: using cowries, 10, 16, 110–11, 113–14, 128, 164; using onion (*lobaça*), 42, 48
Dona Clara, 123, 139
Dona Laura, 132, 133, 139, 144, 149–51, 152, 153, 155, 156, 157, 160
Dona Nega, 3, 34, 178
Douglas, Mary, 62
Dudu, 130–31
Durand, Gilbert, 63, 64, 104–5, 106, 128

Ebame, 28
Ebó. *See* "Works"
Ebô (boiled white corn), 121, 124, 175
Edivaldo, 42, 65; as father-of-saint, 26, 29, 140; spirits of, 36, 37, 183, 185; *terreiro* of, 28, 31, 32, 41, 43, 176
Egúngún (*egum*), 184
Eguns, 43, 102, 171, 183–88; "cleansing of the body" and, 114, 143; Evaristo, 181, 188. *See also Contra-eguns*
Embarabô, 28, 32
Engenho Velho da Federação, 58, 125
Entoto, 142, 178
Equê (false trance), 34, 77, 101, 103
Equedes, 16, 89, 91, 102, 131–32, 136, 146, 163
Erês, 23, 63, 125, 132–33; in initiation, 112, 122, 124, 125–26, 135–36; and *orixás*, 124, 127–28, 129; and sexuality, 133–35; speech of, 67
Espirito Santo, 7
Estrelismo, 8, 21, 35
Eṣu, 14
"Euphemization," 63–64
Evaristo, 181, 188
Evil, 14, 15, 170
Ewe language, 5, 166
Exu, 9, 14, 123, 124, 184; despatch of, 136, 156, 185; house of, 9, 16; offerings to, 6–7, 9, 16, 45; and sexuality, 7, 17
Exuas, 3, 12–13, 26, 28, 31, 32, 36–37, 178
Exu-mirim, 124
Exus, 4, 9, 11, 13–17, 31, 46–47, 85, 101–2, 108, 128–29; behavior of, 23, 27, 63; festivals for, 38, 39, 42–45, 46, 184; offerings to, 15, 42, 89; *orixás* and, 14, 16, 22, 86, 128, 168, 169–70; "seat" of, 3, 5, 16, 28, 36–37, 183; and sexuality, 7, 17–18, 28, 33, 127; speech of, 44, 68

Fantasy, 63, 105
Father-of-saint. *See* Parents-of-saint
Fazendão, 138–39, 168
FEBACAB (Bahian Federation of the Afro-Brazilian Cult), 139, 140
Fechação, 35
Federations, 4
Feijão fradinho, 47, 48
Filipe, 176–77, 178
Fernando Pessoa, 23, 25, 37, 62, 109, 139, 140, 177, 188, 189
Ferramentas, 130, 168–69, 170, 175
Festivals, 10, 56, 159; of the *coboclos*, 44–45, 46, 53, 54–55, 58, 59, 64, 68–82, 88–92, 98–100, 112, 116–17, 129, 184; of the *eguns*, 184–85; of the *exus*, 38, 39, 42–45, 46, 184; of the *orixás*, 44–45, 58, 69, 72–73, 88, 97, 108–9, 111, 167; of Tempo, 168, 174–76
"Flowers of the Old One," 163
Forest, 128–29
Foucault, Michel, 105
Francis of Assisi, Saint, 174
Frigerio, Alejandro, 58

Game theory, 182
Gantois, 58
Gege-Nagô, 166, 167
Gege nation, 5–6
Gelson, 88, 89, 91, 93, 97, 100, 112, 116–17
Gender: *caboclos* and, 67, 106; *metámetá*, 86–87; roles, 136, 146–48; of spirits, 17
Gilberto, 131, 175
Giletão, 141
Gira-Mundo (*exu*), 170, 171
"Give saint," 100
Goffman, Erving, 161
Goméia, Joãozinho da, 114
"Grotesque body," 59–60, 61, 62, 63–64

Heaven, 14
Hell, 12, 13, 14, 17, 20–21, 27, 28, 29
Heteroglossia, 60–61
Hofstadter, Douglas, 107
Holquist, Michael, 61
Holy Spirit, 173
Hotei, 10

"Hymn to Our Lord of Bomfim." *See* Our Lord of Bomfim

Iabás, 123
Iançã (*orixá*), 31, 115, 126, 127, 128, 175; *assentamentos* of, 113, 130, 131; relations with other spirits, 158, 172, 186
"Iançã with Logum," 186, 187
Iaô (daughter-of-saint), 36–37
Iemanjá (*orixá*), 84, 114, 123, 126, 127, 131
Ilê Axé Opô Afonjá, 56, 58, 166, 184
Incest, 84
Inconfidência Mineira, 54
Indians, 46, 54, 55, 83; spirits of, 55, 63, 67, 183
Initiation, 4, 15, 16–17, 147–48; of children-of-saint, 111, 112, 123; coming-out ceremony, 97, 112, 123, 125, 136–37, 142, 156; cuts, 111, 145–46; *quitanda* ("market"), 163; seclusion, 112, 121–24, 129, 136; shaving and clipping, 131–32
International Congresses of Orisa Tradition and Culture, 4
"Invasion," 24, 109, 139, 141
Iroko, 166
Itaparica, 10, 184

Jaraci, 30, 37, 83, 109, 139, 163–64, 176, 177, 178; festivals in, 45, 108; religion in, 23, 39, 110, 136; *terreiros* in, 24, 25, 31–32, 109, 140, 181
Jardim de Alá, 10
Joana, 131, 139
João VI (king of Portugal), 53–54
Joãozinho, 10, 23, 116, 123, 125, 126, 128, 129, 140, 145, 155; at festival at Marinalvo's, 108–9, 110; spirits of, 131, 132, 133, 137–38; stories of, 11, 13, 17, 22
John, Saint, feast of, 53
Jorge, 88, 90, 93, 94, 97
José, 184–85, 186
Julemeiro (*exu*), 31
Juntó, 16
Jurema, 75–76, 79–80, 83, 91

Kardec, Allan (Hippolyte Léon Denizard Rivail), 5
Kardecism, 5, 16, 85, 183, 184–85
Kértesz, Mário, 111

Lacerda Elevator, 17
Laje Grande (*caboclo*), 115
Language, 22, 44, 59–61; African, 5, 13, 67, 74, 124–25; of Candomblé, 64, 65, 67, 74, 100–101, 124–25; Portuguese, 5, 13, 15, 44, 55, 64–68, 124–25
Lapassade, Georges, 58
Lasca-fogo, 28
Latour, Bruno, 108
Lawrence, Saint, 168
Lesse (*egum*), 184
"Liminal spaces," 128–29
"Line of oil," 16
Lody, Raul Giovanni da Motta, 132, 168, 173
Logum-edé (*orixá*), 87
Loko, 166, 167, 168, 172, 183
Lucifer. *See* Devil
Luisa, 131
Luiz, 25, 42, 43, 140
Lukes, Steven, 103
Luz, Marco Aurélio, 58

Machiavelli, Niccolò, 108
Macumba, 13
Maffesoli, Michel, 104, 105, 108
Magic, 47; "black magic," 57, 58
"Make saint," 31
Malandro, 44
Mané, 138–39, 159
Manioc flour, 6, 16
Manuel (Sete Facadas), 13, 21
Maranhão, 5–6
Marcas, 9, 122–23
Márcio, 88, 94, 97–98
Maria Eugênia, 43
Marinalvo: *coboclo* festival of, 64, 68; divination, 110–11, 112, 113, 114–16; as father-of-saint, 24, 37, 38, 108–11, 116, 122, 123, 138–39, 141, 142, 157, 164; festival for Tempo, 168, 174, 175, 176; initiation festival, 136–37, 143, 144, 145, 146, 149, 150, 151–53, 155, 156, 158, 160–62, 163; spirits of, 83, 114–15, 116, 133, 135; *terreiro* of, 23, 31, 125, 130, 131, 136, 139–40, 148, 168, 183
Mariô, 185
Marriage, 20, 149
Marta, 131, 156, 157, 160, 175
Matter, 14, 18, 28, 46–47, 62. *See also* Spirit-matter continuum
Megenney, William W., 69
Men, 17–18, 35

Menininha of Gantois, 132
Metalanguage, 57
Metá-metá, 86, 87, 129
Middle Ages, 55, 56, 63
Miguel, 10
Mina nation, 5–6
Minas Gerais, 95
Mirrors, 9, 22, 128
"Money on the ground," 42–43
Moré tribe, 81
Morgan, Lewis Henry, 83–84
Mother-of-saint. *See* Parents-of-saint
Motta, Roberto, 57
Movimento Negro Unificado, 56
Mutalambô (*caboclo*), 89
Mythology, 173; *caboclo*, 83–84; of Candomblé, 83, 84, 85–87; Christian, 14, 15

Nagô nation, 5–6
Nanã (*orixá*), 84, 123, 126, 127
Nascimento, Abdias do, 98
Nations, 5–6, 71
Neuza, 110, 112, 138, 139, 140–41, 152
Newton, Sir Isaac, 172
Nóbrega, Fr. Manuel da, 17
"Nocturnal regime," 104–5, 106, 107
Novelization, 61

Obaluaiê (*orixá*), 31, 33, 113, 126–27, 131, 137, 157, 167, 178; "flowers of," 163. *See also* Omolu
"Obligations," 88
Offerings, 88, 121, 123, 128; to the *caboclos*, 64; to the *exus*, 15, 42, 89; to the *orixás*, 62, 150, 163
Ogãs, 16, 35, 102, 114, 146–47, 163; at festivals, 43–44, 89; initiation, 23, 24, 131–32, 136, 147, 152, 155, 157; suspension of, 90, 91
Oguiã (*orixá*), 127
Ogum (*orixá*), 25, 127, 128, 131, 137, 157, 158, 159, 186, 187–88
Oiá (*egum of*), 184
Oil, 16
Olga of Alaketu, 55
Olinda, 25
Omolu (*orixá*), 113, 114, 126. *See also* Obaluaiê
Onion, throwing of, 42, 48
Ordem e progresso, 54, 93
Òrìṣàs, 9
Orixás, 55, 56, 82, 85, 89, 112, 154, 183, 185; *assentamentos* of, 16, 122, 125, 126, 130–31, 132, 142, 168; behavior of, 8, 33, 62–63; "belonging to," 16, 17, 31, 48, 113, 114, 116; brands (*marcas*) of, 9, 122–23, 167; entry ("receiving") of, 4–5, 100, 101, 111, 117, 137, 175; *erês* of, 63, 124, 125, 129; and *exus*, 14, 16, 22, 86, 128, 168, 169–70; festivals of, 44–45, 58, 69, 72–73, 88, 97, 108–9, 111, 167; genealogy of, 126–28; punishment by, 135; and sexuality, 18, 84, 86, 87; speech of, 62, 165; Tempo, 166, 167–68, 172; and waters, 128–29
Ossãe (*orixá*), 85–86, 87, 129
Oswaldo, 43, 140, 184
Otá, 19, 130
Our Lord of Bomfim, 9, 126; Church of, 7, 9, 10, 119, 162; Hymn to, 9, 119
Oxalá (*orixá*), 86, 115, 119, 171; *assentamentos* of, 126, 131; *erês* of, 124; as father of the gods, 9, 72–73, 84, 89, 114, 126–27; food of, 47, 48, 114, 121; offerings to, 150, 163; as "pure *egum*," 188; waters of, 109, 123, 128
Oxalufã (*orixá*), 114, 127
Oxé, 167
Oxosse (*orixá*), 31, 85–86, 115, 124, 127, 128, 130, 142
Oxum (*orixá*), 12, 48, 86, 115, 117; *assentamentos* of, 130, 131; *ereas* of, 124; food of, 47; genealogy of, 126, 127, 128; mirror of, 9, 22, 128; and Salvador (Bahia), 9; waters of, 123
Oxumaré (*orixá*), 31, 86, 87, 126, 129, 157, 158, 159

Pachorô, 124
Padilha (*exua*), 13, 43, 115; vow of, 11–14, 18, 20–21, 27, 84
Parents-of-saint, 6, 7, 20, 24, 57, 123; and children-of-saint, 17, 31, 38, 84, 130, 131–32, 163; divination, 10, 31, 110–11, 114, 116; and festivals, 71, 72; gender of, 146–48; registration of, 139; and spirits, 91, 102; "works," 16
Paul, Saint, 167
Paulo, 112
Pedro I (emperor of Brazil), 53–54
Pelourinho, 9, 25
Pemba, 79, 89, 137

Pena Branca (*caboclo*), 89, 90, 91–92, 99–100
Perlongher, Nestor, 124
Pernambuco, 5–6
Pessoa, Fernando, 23, 179
Peter, Saint, 167–68
Peters, Larry, 94
Places, 14. *See also* "Liminal spaces"
Pomba-Gira (*exua*), 3, 4, 22, 25, 26, 43, 178; in story of Padilha's vow, 11, 12–13, 14, 20–21
Pomorska, Krystyna, 60
Portuguese, 5, 13, 15, 44, 55, 64–68, 124–25
Praça Castro Alves, 23
Prostitutes, 34, 124
Protestantism, 15, 29
Puppetry, 186–87
Purification ritual. *See* "Cleansing of the body"
Putti, 8

Queto nation, 5–6
Quijuntó, 16
Quimbanda, 58
Quitanda, 163

Rabelais, François, 1, 55, 56
Racism, 6
Raio do Sol (*caboclo*), 89
Raspagem ("shaving"), 131, 132
Re-Africanization, 56–58, 62
"Receive saint," 16, 81, 100, 101. *See also* Trance
Recife, 147
Rei das Cobras (*caboclo*), 89, 91, 96, 97
Ribeiro, José, 114
Ribeiro, René, 147
Rio de Janeiro, 6, 13, 58, 100
Rita, 47, 48
Ritual objects, 9, 19, 32, 42, 130
Rituals, 15–16, 62–63, 177–78, 184–85
Roads, 15. *See also* Crossroads
Roça, 163–64
Roda, 89, 178
Roett, Riordan, 54
"Rolling" (*bolação*), 31, 90–91
Roncó ("retreat room"), 112
Rory, 6, 7
Rosilene, 131, 140

Sacrifices, 42, 46, 68, 131, 151, 175, 185
Saida. *See* Coming-out ceremony
Saints, Catholic, 8, 10, 15, 25, 56, 58, 126, 130. *See also* individual saints
Salvador (Bahia), 5, 8–9, 17, 23, 34, 54, 100, 109, 100–11
Samba, 46, 73–74, 76, 78, 80, 82–83, 92
Sangirardi Jr., 79
Santos, Juana Elbein dos, 177–78, 184
São Cristóvão, 6
São Paulo, 124
Satan. *See* Devil
"Seat" (*assentamento*), 19; of *erês*, 125; of *exus*, 3, 16, 28, 36–37, 183; of *orixás*, 16, 122, 125, 126, 130–31, 132, 142, 168
"Seating": of *caboclos*, 68; of *erês*, 125; of *exus*, 5, 32, 39, 45; of *orixás*, 16
Sebastião, 122, 130, 131, 133, 136, 142, 143, 145, 153, 156, 157, 162, 163
Sérgio, 98, 100, 112
Sete Espadas (*caboclo*), 89, 95–96
Sete Facadas (*exu*), 11–12, 13, 84
Sete Punhal (*exu*), 26, 31, 42, 43, 177
Sete Saia (*exua*), 3, 25, 26, 31, 32, 33–34, 35, 39–41, 42, 43, 44, 65, 176, 178
Sete Serras (*caboclo*), 89
Seu Antônio, 140
Sexuality, 20, 110, 141, 148–49; *caboclos* and, 63–64; *erês* and, 133–35; *exus* and, 7, 17–18, 28, 33, 127; incest, 84; *metá-metá*, 86, 87, 129; *orixás* and, 18, 84, 86, 87
Socialization, 62
Social science, 94, 103, 105, 106, 162
Sociolects, 64–65
Sodré, Muniz, 182
Songs, 86, 125; *caboclo* festival, 68–82, 83; of *erês*, 133–34; of *exus*, 40–41, 46, 65; to Tempo, 170–71, 172, 173
Son-of-saint. *See* Children-of-saint
"Sorcery," 16, 22, 28
Sotaques ("banter"), 74–77, 124
Spiritism, 5, 13
Spirit-matter continuum, 85, 106, 107, 128
Spirits, 14, 18, 29–30, 33, 44, 100–101, 165, 166, 174
Sultão das Matas (*caboclo*), 83, 84, 89, 114–15
Suspension, 90, 91
Symbolism, 123, 174, 177–78
Syncretism, 56, 57

Taís, 24, 30–32, 35, 36–37, 41, 55, 63–64, 65, 85–86, 106, 164, 177, 178; and *caboclo* festi-

val, 68, 69–70, 72, 73, 75, 76, 78, 79, 80, 83; and Corquisa, 26, 27, 29, 31, 33–34, 38, 39, 40, 176; and *eguns*, 181, 183, 186, 188; at festival at Marinalvo's, 111, 112; spirits of, 26, 31, 42, 44, 45, 46, 49, 101–2; and Tempo, 169–71, 173
Tanuri Junçara, 125
Taussig, Michael, 51
Tempo, 126–27, 129, 165, 166, 167–68
Terreiros, 4–5, 17, 19–20, 57, 128, 131–32; *barracão*, 9–10, 53; compound of Tempo, 168; and *eguns*, 183, 184; festivals at, 45, 53, 58, 72, 125; of Gelson, 88; house of Exu, 9, 16; registration of, 140; "seat" of *orixás*, 16; sexual relations in, 84; as social institutions, 24, 31–32, 38, 94–95, 109, 124, 146, 164, 189; of Xilton, 9–10
Tiradentes, 54
Todorov, Tzvetan, 182
Toninho, 43, 65
Tranca-Rua (*exu*), 13, 25
Trance, 4–5, 16, 90–91, 103–4, 106, 124, 146, 147; of Archipiado, 92, 93–94, 95, 96; *barravento*, 80–81, 92, 93; *equê* (false trance), 34, 77, 101, 103; of Taís, 31; terms used for, 100, 101–2
Transgression, 103
Transvestites, 34–35
Trovezeiro (*caboclo*), 81, 89, 90, 91, 92, 93
Tupã, 83, 84
Tupãs, 84
Tupi language, 55, 124
Tupim, 83
Tupinambá (*caboclo*), 26, 37, 43, 47, 48–49, 73
Tupiniquim (*caboclo*), 89
Turner, Victor, 54

Umbanda nation, 5–6, 85, 98, 100, 140

Veloso, Caetano, 119
Viados, 34–35, 141
"Villages," 108
Virgil, 173
Virginity, 20, 32–33

War, 15, 25, 77, 128
"Washing the beads," 112, 113, 115
Water, 36, 128–29; of Oxalá, 109, 123, 128
Weaponry, 128
Weather, 126, 166, 170
"White line," 16
"White table," 183, 185
Women, 4, 17, 18, 20, 35, 136
Woolgar, Steve, 108
"Works" (*ebó*), 15–16, 47–49

Xangô (*orixá*), 62, 127, 128, 131, 167, 172, 186
Xangô nation, 5–6
Xaxará, 33
Xilton, 6–7, 9–10, 16, 17, 111, 125, 165, 183
Xuxa, 33

Yoruba language, 5, 9, 14, 62, 124–25, 166

Zaratempo, 166
Zé-Pelintra (*exu*), 43
Zezé, 29
Zita, 131, 136, 141, 144–45, 149, 151, 152, 163, 175

University of Pennsylvania Press
CONTEMPORARY ETHNOGRAPHY SERIES
Dan Rose and Paul Stoller, General Editors

John D. Dorst. *The Written Suburb: An American Site, An Ethnographic Dilemma*. 1989

Douglas E. Foley. *Learning Capitalist Culture: Deep in the Heart of Tejas*. 1990

Kirin Narayan. *Storytellers, Saints, and Scoundrels: Folk Narrative in Hindu Religious Teaching*. 1989

Dan Rose. *Patterns of American Culture: Ethnography and Estrangement*. 1989

Paul Stoller. *The Taste of Ethnographic Things: The Senses in Anthropology*. 1989

Jim Wafer. *The Taste of Blood: Spirit Possession in Brazilian Candomblé*. 1991

This book has been set in Linotron Galliard. Galliard was designed for Mergenthaler in 1978 by Matthew Carter. Galliard retains many of the features of a sixteenth century typeface cut by Robert Granjon but has some modifications which gives it a more contemporary look.

Printed on acid-free paper.